Quotes, Ruminations & Contemplations

Volume II

A random selection of quotes and commentary from Corey Wayne's articles and video coaching newsletters on pickup, dating, relationships, success mindsets, self-reliance, personal responsibility, philosophy, purpose, negotiation, health, inspiration, high achievement, goal setting, time management, career, entrepreneurship, wealth creation and sales.

Written and Narrated by

Corey Wayne

*All rights reserved.
This book or any portion thereof
may not be reproduced or used in any manner whatsoever
without the express written permission of the publisher.*

© 2022 by Corey Wayne

ISBN# 978-1-4583-8398-3

The Corey Wayne Companies, Inc.

HONOR

This book is dedicated to the American soldier. No matter whether the cause is popular or not, I am in awe of the fact that when their country calls them, they go, and they go willingly. They take our place on the battlefield, risking everything they have, because it is part of who they are. They are all my heroes, and I owe all of my success, happiness, and opportunities to past, present, and future generations of their kind. May God keep them safe and speed the day to us when their sacrifice is no longer required, because humanity has learned that the real enemy is hatred itself, and the way to real happiness is unconditional love. Until that day comes, I take great pride and comfort in knowing they will continue to stand up and show us what real honor and integrity is. I dedicate my life to helping bring humanity closer together and always giving my gifts to the world in hopes that I may honor all of their collective sacrifices, so they are not in vain.

ACKNOWLEDGEMENTS

I would like to thank my mother who taught me to be so determined and never give up, no matter what. I would also like to thank Tony Robbins for being such a great leader and mentor in my life. I'd like to thank my dad for teaching me the difference between right and wrong. I am grateful for the close relationship we have today. I love you very much.

To my Aunt Char and Uncle Richie, I love you both. I would also like my brother Chris to know how proud I am to have you as my brother. All you have gone through to achieve your dreams is inspiring to me. I love you very much.

To my awesome team who keeps my business running, growing, balanced, prosperous, stable and successful, thanks for being awesome in everything you do to go above and beyond what is asked of you. I couldn't do it without you.

I would also like to express my gratitude to you, the reader. You are embarking on a continuing journey that will change the world. By becoming the best version of yourself that you are on the inside and reaching your full potential, you unconsciously give permission to all others around you to do the same. This will continue to impact society for generations to come and start reducing the amount of people in society who are living lives of quiet desperation, mediocrity, and less than they are capable of living.

Instead of a world where most people are simply existing and trying to get through the workweek, they will be replaced by a world where, collectively, people are making it a better place, because they have come alive on the inside by being in total alignment with their true purpose and calling. Just imagine how much more awesome, prosperous, happy, safe and exciting the world will be when high achievers and visionaries like Steve Jobs, Elon Musk, Jeff Bezos, Larry Page, Sergey Brin, et al. are abundant and commonplace, instead of unicorns and exceptions to the rule.

Table of Contents

Introduction 1

STANDING OUT 3

Overcoming Job & Relationship Loss 3
The Gift Of Hard Times 6
Fear Inhibits Us From Moving On 9
The Weak, Dithering & Hesitating Beta Male 12
Failure To Launch 14
Starting Over 17
You Deserve The Very Best 19
Money & The Choices It Brings 22
34 Principles Of High Achievement 24
Fear & Acceptance Of Moving On 27
Getting Your Center Back 30
Getting Better At Dating & Seduction 32
I Think She's Cheating On Me 35
Changing Everything About Your Life 37
Finding Self Worth Again 40

MAKING A GOOD IMPRESSION 43

Effortless Sex, Dating, Love & Relationships 43
Pickup & Date Questions That Build Attraction 45
Never Brag About Yourself 47
Counter-Intuitive Dating Magic 50
When Brutal Honesty Is & Isn't Appropriate 54
What Is My Purpose? 56

The Freedom Of Self-Love 59
Dating, Sexual Confidence & Being Present 61
She Wants To Feel Independent 64
Dating: Terrible Texting Turnoffs 66
Acting Like A Horny Virgin Teenager 69
You Deserve To Be Loved Unconditionally 72
She Wanted Closure, But I Got Her Back 74
Why Women Feel Empowered Chasing Men 76
Masculine Vacillation 79

SELF IMPROVEMENT 81

Dating: Master The Progression 81
Pulse Nightclub Terror Attack In Orlando 83
12 Principles Of Successful Relationships 86
Living Together Changes Everything 88
I'm Not Worth Your Time? 90
Why We Settle For Less 92
Does Age Matter To Women? 94
Starting To Attract Women 96
Life Imbalances Lower Attraction 98
Get Ex Back: Eliminating Your Competition 101
Having Awesome Dates 103
I Need To Get My Life Back In Order 105
Online Dating: A Woman's Perspective 107
Hacking The Girl Code 110
Leaving Behind Those Who Disrespect You 113

STANDING UP FOR YOURSELF 115

Banishing Your Inner Wussy 115
The Power Of Learning To Say "No" 117
I'm Sorry, But You've Changed! 120
She Canceled Last Minute 122
Patience & Inaction Ruined My Life 124
Why She Tries To Change Your Plans 126
Have Some Self Respect! 129
WTF? She Expects Me To Pay Her Bills? 131
Is It Time To Move On? 134
Why You Shouldn't Take Her Back 137
How Much Contact Is Too Much? 139
Dating Delusions 141
Why Did She Blow Me Off? 143
Love Is Giving, Not Possessing 146
In Fear Of Losing, I Lost 148

THE POWER OF CONFIDENCE 152

The Power Of Words 152
Are We Good For Each Other? 154
Be Proud Of You! 157
What's Really Important To You? 159
Confidence & Authenticity Vs. Manipulation 161
Getting Her To Friend-Zone Your Competition 163
Are Men Intimidated By Successful Women? 167
Realizing My Own Self-Worth 169
Acting Neurotic Ruins Attraction & Respect 171
She's Jerking Me Around 173

No Defeat Is Final 175
We Project What's Inside Of Us 177
Pickup: The Non-Approach Approach 179
I Never Do This! 182
True Friends Want The Best For You 184

OVERCOMING STRUGGLE 188

Letting Go Of The Past 188
I Manipulated Her Into Marrying Me? 190
Crazy Women You Should Avoid 192
Contemplating Life: 1 In The Chamber 194
Men Only Care About Sex! 198
Pickup & Approaching By The Numbers 201
Be Happy For Your Ex 204
Heartbreaks, Rebounds & Moving On 207
The Best Way To Get Her Number 210
Life Equals Pain 213
Why Does Life Suck So Bad Sometimes? 215
Insecurities, Regrets & What-If's 218
Wanting Reality To Be Different 221
She Lost Attraction & Needs Space 224
Becoming The Right Man 226

BEING A DOER 228

No Longer A Wussy 228
The Boomerang Date 230
You Stink Of Fear 232
Building Confidence Is A Process 235

Paralysis Of Analysis 239
Try To Get A Little Better Each Day 242
I've Found My People & Passion! 244
Life Keeps Kicking My Ass 250
Becoming An Awesome Catch 253
Accepting Your Present Situation 257
The Illusion Of Action 260
Why Tom Brady & Bill Belichick Win 263
Avoiding Failure To Ensure Success 265
Making Excuses Vs. Taking Action 267
Own Your Purpose, Own Yourself 269

ENERGY & APPEAL 271

Her Curiosity & Interest Soared 271
The Moment You Start Losing Her 274
Epic Virgin Date: Redemption 278
Submissiveness Is Feminine, Not Masculine 280
Staying On Purpose 282
Masculine & Feminine Energy 284
Unbalanced Sexual Polarity 286
Making Women Want You 288
The Courtship Is Initiated By Men 290
The Damage Over-Pursuing Does 293
Dating: Over-Eagerness & Over-Thinking 295
James Bond: Men Lead. Women Follow. 297
Changes, Happiness & Feeling Good 299
Sexual Polarity & Rekindling Romance 301

Sexuality Polarity 303

PURSUING YOUR CALLING 305

The 45-Year-Old Virgin 305

Why We Settle 308

Not Looking For A Relationship 311

I Turned My Life Around Completely! 314

Maintaining Mystery & Interest 317

Crotch On Fire! 319

Thinking About Making Big Life Changes? 321

I'm Sure She's Seeing Another Dude 323

I Am At Peace With Who I Am 326

A Man Does What He Must 328

Hopeless Messed Up Life 332

Success Attracting Women 335

Beaten Down By Life 337

Discovering Your Purpose, Passion & Mission 340

Problems Are A Sign Of Life 343

FURTHERING SUCCESS 346

The Happiest I Have Ever Been 346

Self Perceptions 349

The Science Of Achievement Fundamentals 352

Men Are Not Soft 354

A Better Playbook For Success 356

Stay Together Or Breakup? 359

Young Lust, Love Or Delusion? 362

At A Crossroads In My Career 366

The Attraction Of Indifference	369
New Year's Resolutions	372
Trusting Intuition & Inner Voice	374
The Freedom Of Having Options	377
Dating: It's All In The Numbers	379
Think, Walk, Talk & Act Like An Alpha	381
Creating A Social Life Of Abundance	383

REACHING HIGHER ... 387

Ending Unhappy Relationships	387
Trying Too Hard Vs. Not Trying At All	390
You Are So Different	392
Avoiding Relationship Pitfalls & Mistakes	394
Never Put Others On A Pedestal	397
Relationships: Casual To Committed	400
Why She Didn't Want To See You Again	402
Dating Fantasy Vs. Dating Reality	405
Date Outside Of Your Comfort Zone	408
Is She Just Shy, or Not Interested?	413
Attraction, Pursuing & Interest	415
Should I Break The No Contact Rule?	418
Weaknesses Are Revealed After Heartbreak	420
When Your Family... Sucks!	423
Dating Unhappy People	426

EMBRACING THE UNCOMFORTABLE ... 429

Quick Ways To Improve Attraction Skills	429
Am I Being Used?	431

I'm Afraid To Get Rejected 435

No Longer A Sad Case 437

Teaching Old Dogs New Tricks 439

How To Build The Life You Deserve 443

Life, Work & Relationship Balance 446

Are You Good For Me? 449

Effortless Seduction 452

The Subtle Nuances Of Attraction & Seduction 454

I've Always Been Intimidated By Women 458

Attraction Turnaround 460

Sexual Frustration 462

Time Is On My Side 465

I Thought She Was "The One" 467

BEING CAUTIOUS 469

What Women Want 469

Never Treat Dates Like Girlfriends 471

Their Shortcomings Aren't Your Fault 473

Men: When Your Game Is Tight… 476

Betrayed By The Perfect Woman 479

Relationships That Will Never Work 481

Dating Single Moms 484

I Dated A Narcissist 487

Understanding Why I Got Dumped 491

Impossible & Toxic Relationships 494

She Has A Boyfriend 497

Should I Wait Around? 499

Rejection, Inner Peace & Confidence 502

Once A Cheater, Always A Cheater! 505

Facebook Posts & Your Relationship 508

MAKING RELATIONSHIPS EASY 510

The Game Of Love Vs. Manipulation 510

Needing Someone Else To Feel Validated 512

Finding Myself Again 514

I Love The Pace We Have 516

Am I Fighting A Losing Battle? 518

Problems Are Signs Of Life 520

Complacency Ruins Relationships 522

Healing Our Inner Child 524

Breakups As A Weapon 527

Is She Bored, Disinterested Or Turned Off? 529

Don't Neglect Your Woman 533

You Don't Bring Me Flowers Anymore 535

Kissing, Touching & Sexual Advances 538

I Wasn't Behaving Like A Man 541

Pushing For A Commitment 543

NON-ATTACHMENT 545

Move Forward Together Or Walk Away? 545

Crazy Needy Jealous Love 547

Masculine Men Keep Women Feminine 550

Dating: Texting, Calling & Messaging 553

The Promise Of More Later 556

Trying To Force Things 559

xv

My Girlfriend Might Move Away 561

Love Is Giving, Not Holding Back 564

Never Chase After Being Dumped 566

I Made A Mistake, I Want You Back 569

She Wants To Be Friends First 572

The Clueless Creepy Stalker 575

Dating Your Employee 578

Attachments Create Suffering 581

I've Finally Started Living Again 584

BEING INDEPENDENT 587

Wounds Become Your Strengths 587

People Who Change Our Lives 589

Mindsets, Monogamy, Marriage & MGTOW 593

What A Jerk I Was! 595

He Got His Man Card Back 597

Work Affairs 599

I Have Tremendous Anxiety 603

Success, Ambition & Attraction 606

How To Live & Be A Man 609

How To Meet More High Quality Women 611

Attracting The Right Woman 614

She's Slowly Ceasing Contact 617

Self-Improvement & Sexual Attraction 619

Haters Gonna Hate 621

Never Feel Sorry For Yourself 623

STAYING HEALTHY & HAPPY 625

She Discarded Me Like Trash! 625

Do You Miss Me? 628

The Right Headspace 631

Time, Space & Love 634

Gaining Clarity & Closure 636

How To Make Corey's Green Juice 639

Staying Centered, Peaceful & Certain 642

Sometimes It's Not Meant To Be 645

Coaching Services 648
Closing Credits 649

Introduction

For many years, my readers, listeners and viewers have been asking me to write a book of quotes that is a compilation of the self-help quotes I have written for my website articles and video coaching newsletters. I didn't want to just do a book of quotes and me reading them for the audio book. So, what I've tried to do is create a useful blend of me reading the quotes like I do on camera at the beginning of my video coaching newsletters and add freestyle ruminations and contemplations in a stream of consciousness style format that my viewers and listeners have told me they really love about my delivery and style.

This book is a random selection of quotes and commentary from my articles and video coaching newsletters on pickup, dating, relationships, success mindsets, self-reliance, personal responsibility, philosophy, purpose, negotiation, health, inspiration, high achievement, goal setting, time management, career, entrepreneurship, wealth creation and sales.

My intent with this book is to create a useful learning and inspirational tool that you can listen to or read in the gym, car, home, office or leisure activity to help you implement and master the self-reliance concepts taught in my first book, *How To Be A 3% Man, Winning The Heart Of The Woman Of Your Dreams*, and my second book, *Mastering Yourself, How To Align Your Life With Your True Calling And Reach Your Full Potential*. I hope that you find it useful, insightful, enlightening and inspiring and come back to it over and over to read and/or listen to it 10-15 times like all of my most successful students do to get the best results.

Great success comes from being a great student and applying what you learn on a daily basis in order to try and get a little better each and every day. Most importantly, try to find a way to have fun while you are working to create the life and lifestyle you've always dreamed of.

I have also included the original article titles from each quote, so you can use a search engine to find and read the original articles and watch any related videos. My assistants have also added a QR code for each article to make navigation from the print and digital versions to my website, UnderstandingRelationships.com, quick and easy.

STANDING OUT

Overcoming Job & Relationship Loss

"Everyone gets tested in life. It's through our trials, tribulations, and challenges that we are forced to become more than we are today. The only constant in life is change. You may lose your job overnight. Your lover may leave you when you thought your relationship was solid. Someone close to you may die unexpectedly. Changes in the market or business climate may destroy your successful and lucrative business seemingly overnight. It's easy and natural to feel like you want to give up and quit when calamity happens. The reality is that everyone you love and everything you build in life will eventually die and dissolve. If you're still here, then it means your journey is not over, and you still have more to do. More successes to be had. More achievements and goals to be accomplished. When life seems hopeless, you can either let your circumstances paralyze and define you, or you can choose to take action towards what you want to create. If you choose to persist, recover, and move forward, then you have accepted the challenge to become better, stronger, and more adaptable to life. Therefore, anything is possible for you. Nothing is impossible for a person who refuses to give up." ~ Coach Corey Wayne

This is definitely something I have struggled with my whole life, and quite frankly, it's a mental battle every day. Because I'm always striving to achieve audacious and extremely ridiculous goals in the eyes of most average people. And the reality is, success is long in coming. And even though I teach this stuff and I live this stuff and I have for many decades, every day is a battle—whether it's taking the time to work out, to do cardio, to eat healthy, to spend time with friends and family, to take time for myself, to take time to help others, to take time on growing something inside my business, or trying to change and adapt to market conditions. Especially this past year with everything that's happened with Covid, and all of the lockdowns, and all of the people that I know who have had their lives and businesses totally destroyed.

And then you see these clowns that are supposed to be our leaders doing nothing to help people. They talk about how they're going to help people, and then they point the finger and blame each other for the fact that they're not helping anyone. And the reality is, you have to look at this and just remember that nobody is coming to save you; you have to do it yourself. If you want to get from where you are right now to where you want to be in the future, it is up to you. One hundred percent of your efforts and your actions are going to determine where you end up in the future.

It's totally up to you. Nobody can do it for you. Because as soon as you start depending on other people or circumstances outside of yourself changing to fix your life, or fix your problem, or solve your problem, or help you overcome a challenge, you then have absolved yourself from any personal responsibility for making the changes and taking the actions that are required to go from where you are to where you want to be. If you totally depend upon yourself and blame yourself for your failures as well as your successes, then everything that is in your life is your personal responsibility.

LINK: https://understandingrelationships.com/overcoming-job-relationship-loss/16961

The Gift Of Hard Times

"One of our six human needs is certainty. We need to know that we have a roof over our heads, can pay our bills, get what we want in life, etc. However, when we don't have certainty about our future, we often will compromise our values and goals and settle for something that is less than ideal in order to gain some sense of certainty and comfort. Sometimes in life, you have to do things you hate for a period of time until you can create the conditions that enable you to do what you love. Just like a minimum-wage entry-level job should only be a temporary steppingstone in a long career, instead of a permanent destination, you should never stop working on your side hustle when you are forced to temporarily do something you hate until you can do what you love. Otherwise, settling for mediocrity will become a way of life and permanent condition, instead of a temporary stop on your long life journey." ~ Coach Corey Wayne

Success is a process, and if you're unhappy in your career or you started a business on the side, it's going to take time to get from where you are to where you want to be. It's going to cost way more money and way more time than you've estimated that it's going to take. That's reality. Anytime I've put time frames on businesses or careers or things I wanted to accomplish—especially when you don't know how you're going to accomplish everything, which is typical when you start out on your journey—it's like, you figure things out along the way. It's like, nine times out of ten I usually don't end up hitting those deadlines.

Eventually, I achieve them, but it always takes way longer and way more capital than I expected.

The important thing is, no matter what's going on in your life—whether you're working for yourself, or you're working for somebody else, and your employment or your business situation is less than ideal—you have to spend the time. You have to put the time in trying to grow your business, trying to grow your side hustle. If you're trying to change jobs, you've got to set aside extra time so you can put your resume together, so you can go do job interviews, so you can make phone calls to prospective employers.

That's why it's always so important to know what you want, why you want it. And then always be looking at your life and measuring the results that you're getting, because if you're not getting the results you want, you need to be taking some kind of corrective action. Mediocre people, when they recognize that their job sucks, all they do is complain about it; they don't do anything about it, typically. Same thing with the relationship that they're in that sucks and is mediocre—they complain about it, but they don't do anything, because they associate too much pain from moving on and being single, to find something else, or putting the resume together, or calling other prospective employers. They come up with excuses— "I'll do that next week," "I'll do that next month," "I'll start that the first of the year," whatever it happens to be.

If you want to become self-reliant and you want to reach your full potential in every area of your life that's important to you, when you recognize that some part of your life is unsatisfactory, you've got to figure out what's unsatisfactory. You've got to figure out what you want instead, and then you've got to implement a massive plan of action to start moving from where you are to where you want to be. That's what high achievers do. Mediocre people just tend to ponder, space out, and avoid doing things they know they need to do—and that's why they never reach their full potential and never accomplish anything close to what a high-achieving person does.

LINK: https://understandingrelationships.com/the-gift-of-hard-times/33006

Fear Inhibits Us From Moving On

"Many people stay in relationships long after it is time for them to end. However, when they become fearful that they will never find anyone better or that they will never find anyone else, they will either stay and continue being miserable, or try to go back to their exes, because it's easier and more comfortable than moving on. Staying in a relationship longer than you should or going back to a familiar ex does not serve you or the other person and will only delay both of you getting more suitable lovers in the long run. In order for a new relationship and a better match to manifest in your life, you must first create a space for someone new to fill." ~ Coach Corey Wayne

Tony Robbins says that "The quality of your life is in direct proportion to the amount of uncertainty that you can consistently live with." No matter what you're doing—whether it's a new career, a new business, a new job, a new city, a new relationship, ending an old relationship—we don't have crystal balls, and we can't predict the future, and we don't know what's going to happen in the future. And you have to get good at being uncertain about your future and being comfortable with it, because if you can be comfortable being uncomfortable, then you can focus on the work that you need to do today and each and every day going forward to move your life towards the things that you want to achieve, accomplish, and experience.

And even though it's scary and you don't know when you're going to meet somebody new if you ended an old relationship, you've got to think back to, why did you end the relationship? And what's your emotionally compelling reason for ending that relationship? And what's your emotionally compelling vision of what you want to create in the future? What kind of a person do you want to attract in the future? What kind of qualities and characteristics do they have? Because that's why you left in the first place—because you weren't satisfied. And if you weren't satisfied then and then you go back to that person, you're going to go back to being unsatisfied just because you allowed yourself to become overwhelmed by your irrational fears about what may or may not happen in the future.

And that's why, when you get obsessed and busy, immersed in doing what you need to do today and right now to move your life forward, you live in the present moment, and you're not worried about what may or may not happen in the future, because you're focused on taking action and being busy being productive. If you're busy being productive, you don't have the time or the emotional space and energy to imagine and worry about what may or may not happen in the future. The reality is the only moment that exists is the present moment. The future's not here yet, and you can't go back in time and fix what happened in the past, so focus on what you need to do right now.

LINK: https://understandingrelationships.com/fear-inhibits-us-from-moving-on/21504

The Weak, Dithering & Hesitating Beta Male

"Masculine energy is all about purpose, drive, mission, succeeding, accomplishing, achieving goals, breaking through barriers, etc. It's also direct, decisive, and fearless. Women like men who go for what they want in spite of their fears and the potential for failure. A woman will always have more respect for you—even when she rejects you—when you fearlessly go for a kiss on a date, or you quickly get to the point and try to set a date when you meet her for the first time. The process to be successful in any endeavor in life requires you to not be deterred by failure or rejection, but instead look at it as a process of getting through the 'No's in order to get to the 'Yes's." ~ Coach Corey Wayne

Men who are successful in getting the things that they want in life, they're direct, decisive, they get right to the point. They don't dither, they don't hesitate. They don't try to fly under the radar and hide their attraction; they blurt it out and go for what they want when they feel the impulse. They act upon their desires without any fear or regret or remorse. They show up and they extend their invitations to women they have interest in, and they're okay with whether or not she says yes or no. To them, the important thing is that they show up as men and go for what they want.

Men who are weak, who are unsure of themselves, will dither and hesitate, try to fly under the radar and act like a friend when their interest is really romantic, and they never seem to get to the point when it comes to asking for a date, nailing down definite plans; they leave things up in the air and hope that the woman will guide them and tell them what to do. Women don't want to teach men how to be men—they want men to know it and understand it before they meet them—and they're repulsed with guys who dither, who hesitate, who act weird, who act creepy, and hold back.

LINK: https://understandingrelationships.com/the-weak-dithering-hesitating-beta-male/18011

Failure To Launch

"Most people live lives of quiet desperation inside their self-constructed prison boxes of their identities. Human beings tend to avoid rejection, failure, and not feeling good at all costs. One of the key ingredients to personal peak performance and your ability to achieve your goals and dreams is to become okay with failure, rejection, and setbacks. Otherwise, if you let your fears hold you back and hijack your life, one day, you'll wake up and not like your life or the person you have become. If you spend your life trying to avoid failure, rejection, and setbacks, you'll only end up living a mediocre life that is less than what you are capable of living." ~ Coach Corey Wayne

Everything you want—all of your dreams, all of those nice cars you want to drive, that beautiful house that you want to live in, that great teammate and partner you want as a girlfriend, or wife, or to just casually date—it requires stepping outside your comfort zone and expanding and growing beyond your current level of competence and abilities. Most people avoid this at all costs; they avoid things that are difficult or don't bring them immediate pleasure or results. And, therefore, when it comes to going for the things that they really want in life, all they have is excuses and reasons and a story that tells them why they "can't," or they're "not capable," or they're simply "not ready" to start pursuing the things they want.

And being 50 years old now, I've got lots of people who have come and gone in my life. Like, one of my old business partners always wanted to make it big in the music business, and he was right on the verge of it back when he was in his late 30s, early 40s, but because he was starting a family, he gave all of that up because his wife basically sandbagged his success. But it always fucking tortured him his whole life. He never really went for it, even though he played with some really amazing, well-known acts. And after we got out of real estate, he kind of half-ass got back into it and never really went for it because of the story that he was telling himself and his fears.

And I know through other people that I've talked to about those last few months of his, one of the things he said is, "You've got to finish." He just didn't finish some of the things that he really wanted to do with his life, and I look at that as a tragedy. We used to have these conversations, and he was like, "Yeah, I need to do this. I need to do that," "I've got to sell these jet skis first," "I've got to get my house fixed," "I've got to sell this other house," "I've got to get my insurance straightened out," "I've got to straighten things out with the IRS."

It was always a list of excuses and a list of stories because, deep down, he was afraid that he wasn't good enough and, therefore, he wasn't willing to put in the time to really become good at it. He came up with a lot of excuses because of the pain and rejection that he had had when he was younger, when he just gave up on it because things weren't moving fast enough. Even though he had all of this evidence around him and all of these big-named people he was playing with, he just walked away from it, because his wife was constantly chirping in his ear and he didn't stand up to her.

He was just tortured about it the whole rest of his life, and it wasn't until those last few months that he was alive and on his deathbed that he recognized that, you know, he just didn't go for it. And he regretted it. You don't want to be on your deathbed thinking about all the things you didn't do or the things you didn't go for. At least if you go for the stuff that you want and you fail, you get better, you learn from it. But if you're not taking action, if there's this really attractive girl you've always wanted to ask out you never do it, you're always going to be wondering, "What if?" But if you go for it and you ask her out and she rejects you, at least you can cross her off that list.

LINK: https://understandingrelationships.com/failure-to-launch/14729

Starting Over

"Sometimes in life, everything that you hold dear and that is important to you completely dissolves and falls apart. Even though difficult times can be very hard to get through, everything that happens in your life is happening for a reason. There are no accidents, and there are no victims. Before you can create an even better version of yourself, the old version must die. Every person and circumstance is coming into your life so you can fulfill your destiny. The key is to focus on moving towards what you love and desire by relentlessly taking action, noticing what's working and what's not working, adjusting your approach along the way, and finding a way to enjoy the journey to creating the masterpiece that is your ideal life." ~ Coach Corey Wayne

If you look at life as not having any accidents, and there being no victims, and the buck stops with you, then no matter what happens in your life—even when it's often things that are completely out of control—high achievers, the way they think is that "Well, maybe it was my thoughts. Maybe it was the tone of my voice. Maybe it was my actions." Whatever happens, good or bad, we drew it to ourselves through our thoughts, words, deeds, and actions. Because anytime you start to blame other people for your circumstances—whether it's the government, or the person you're in a relationship with, or somebody that didn't do what they said they were going to do—at the end of the day, the buck stops with you.

Nobody is coming to save you; you have to do that yourself. Your life, your success, your failure, your goals, your dreams are your responsibility, and the only way they're going to happen and you're going to achieve them is by you taking 100% ownership for everyone and everything and every circumstance that shows up in your life. Because as soon as you blame other people for your problems, you become powerless to do anything to change them, because if it's not your fault, then it's also not your fault to fix it or do anything to better yourself or your life.

LINK: https://understandingrelationships.com/starting-over/14328

You Deserve The Very Best

"Most people in life tend to settle for the first person who comes along, and they also tend to major in minor things in life. Getting to a place where you have a great career or successful business, an outstanding relationship, are financially secure, and you have the freedom to spend your life in your own way is a long process that can take many years or even decades to accomplish. You deserve to have everything you want in life, and you deserve the very best, but not everything you want comes all at once. It's a slow process that requires failure, learning from your mistakes, experiencing pain, rejection, and sorrow along the way. Since human beings tend to do more to avoid pain than to gain pleasure, most people are simply unwilling or too fearful to pay the price in time and effort to get what they want. Sure, you can find someone to have a relationship with and find an average, good paying job, but in order to create a truly spectacular life, it requires an inner patience and strong internal constitution that most people simply do not have or refuse to believe in, because their self-doubt is greater than their desires. When you are surrounded by people who settle for mediocrity in every area of their lives, they try to get you to do the same so they feel better about themselves and their choices. Staying committed to what you want requires that you have really strong and emotionally compelling reasons for why you want what you want. Otherwise, you'll simply give up and follow the rest of the herd instead of being a leader and creating a spectacular life for yourself." ~ Coach Corey Wayne

You should know, if you are listening to this or reading this book, then you're way ahead of 97% of everybody else on the planet. Most people simply won't do what it takes to make themselves and their lives better; they won't take the time to grow their reserve of knowledge, and they won't take the time to develop their gifts, skills, and talents so they can become better.

This is why perseverance and persevering when it seems hopeless is going to set you apart from all of the average, mediocre people over time, especially when you look at it over the course of a decade. Because if you take an average person who has given up on themselves at the beginning of a decade and another person who is also average, but the difference is they believe that somehow, someday, some way things are going to turn out in their favor and they take relentless, consistent action, they learn from their mistakes, they measure their results when their approach isn't working, they change it. In other words, they're slow to change their mind about what they want, but they're quick to change their approach and how they go about it. When you look at or you compare the two of them and their results over the course of a decade, that's why two average people, but one of them who's determined and persistent will go way further in ten years than a mediocre person that does nothing.

LINK: https://understandingrelationships.com/you-deserve-the-very-best/16433

Money & The Choices It Brings

"Sometimes in life, you have to create companies, peer groups, associations, clubs, relationships, etc. where there was nothing before when you have a hard time finding people who understand and support you in your own social and family circle. Being a leader and visionary in your own life sometimes requires you to shed your preconceived notions about who you are, so you can become what you might be. The quickest way to silence your critics is to accomplish what they say you can't." ~ Coach Corey Wayne

There's an old saying in sports that goes, "Winning solves a lot of problems." It is so true. The best medicine for haters is to persist and eventually succeed anyway. The reality is, when you're striving to achieve your greatest, grandest goals and dreams, everybody else, deep down, innately knows that they should be doing the same in their own lives. And when you are doing that in your life and they're not, it's a reflection to them—and it's a painful reflection to them—of how mediocre they're being in life. That's why you often get attacked, even by people who are in your inner circle or, oftentimes, your own family.

That's why it's critical to your long-term success to have positive, optimistic people around you who always have a positive, encouraging word and tell you that you can do it when you're having a rough day and might not necessarily be believing in your full potential at that particular time. Because life is not all sunshine and roses; you're going to have lots of days where it's going to seem like nothing goes your way. And the best way to get through those days is to put your head down and start taking action and lose yourself in the process of taking action. Because what happens is, when you come out on the other side, at the end of the day, you feel great and productive because you got a lot done.

LINK: https://understandingrelationships.com/money-the-choices-it-brings/13782

34 Principles Of High Achievement

"Successful people think and act differently than people who live lives of quiet desperation and mediocrity. Our brains are naturally wired to cause us to move away from fear, danger, and uncertainty for survival. However, succeeding and reaching your full potential is a process that requires you to take action in spite of your fears and doubts. Overcoming challenges, pushing past your own perceived limitations and fears, is an unavoidable necessity and prerequisite to accomplishing your grandest goals and dreams. Managing your focus, mindset, staying in the present moment, and taking consistent perpetual action over many decades is a discipline every successful person must master. If you don't master your emotional self-control, you will be mastered and dominated by your fears and never reach your full potential." ~ Coach Corey Wayne

I was at dinner last night, having dinner and drinks with an old friend of mine. He's married and he's got a couple of young kids, and he was just glad to get out of the house and just have an evening away from his wife and his kids and just hang out, have some beers, talk about the old days when we were younger, have some laughs, talk about guns, talk about girls, women we used to date, old relationships, old business partners that we had and people we were involved with. And it was really cool to hang out and catch up. And one of the things he said because he's also, you know, a real high achiever and has done really well for himself, was, he looked at me and he's like, "You're not normal, dude." He says that "I'm not normal either."

And it's true; high achievers are just different than most people. We think differently. And if you're listening to this or you're reading this, then you probably understand what I'm talking about; that you're usually the person in your family or your peer group that is several years ahead of everybody else and what they see and what they believe. In other words, you're doing things that people might find disconcerting, or unsettling, or intimidating, or maybe some people are even jealous of it, but a few years down the road what happens is everybody looks at you and sees that you were kind of a visionary and everything that you were saying and doing tends to come to pass.

When you look at Steve Jobs and what people who knew him said about him was that he had a "reality distortion field"—meaning he could see things as he wanted them to be and operated and acted in a way that showed that he assumed it was just simply a matter of time before his hopes, his dreams, and his visions came to pass, oftentimes to the point where it drove other people around him nuts and made them feel like he was being unreasonable—but he always pushed people beyond what their comfort zone was and what they thought their own limitations were so they could achieve truly great things.

LINK: https://understandingrelationships.com/34-principles-of-high-achievement/27622

Fear & Acceptance Of Moving On

"Life is a continuous process of re-creating our lives, movement, change, personal growth, taking risks, overcoming fears, and stepping outside of our comfort zone so we can reach our full potential. The reality of life is it is always changing and never stays the same. People come into and out of our lives to give us experiences and to help us grow. Resisting change leads to instability, unhappiness, disease, and chaos. Embracing change and going with the flow is necessary and essential to your happiness, health, and enjoying life. You can't stop an earthquake any more than you can change the weather, but you can adapt to the changes they bring. The more you can adapt to, look forward to, and embrace change, the more successful you will become at maintaining your happiness, growth, balance, and inner peace." ~ Coach Corey Wayne

The truth about life is the only constant is going to be change. Nothing is going to stay the same; that includes your body, that includes your friendships, that includes your family, that includes your relationships, that includes all the people that, when you're young, you look up to them. One of the hard things that I personally have come to recognize as I've gotten older is, when I was really young, all those older people that I looked up to that made me feel safe in the world and gave my life in the world meaning and balance to me, almost all of them have since passed on and died. And that's a harsh reality about life.

Life really is like a tragedy because you realize that everybody that you love, everything you build, on a long enough timeline, it's all going to turn to dust and not really matter. All those things that you're worried about today, in the future, it's really not going to matter. We're all living in bodies that are going to die, but how many of us really, truly embrace what we are and try to become all that we can be?

Time is going to pass no matter what we do. It makes sense to spend our lives trying to influence and become better people, developing our talents, our gifts, our skills, and growing our reserve of knowledge, and on a constant basis, negotiating on our behalf to earn more income, earn better job opportunities, better business opportunities, and better friendships. You always should be striving to become better in every area of your life that is important to you. Because, just like in nature, when something stops growing and contributing, it dies and is eliminated.

The more you can add value to the world, the more alive you're going to feel, the more your life is going to feel purpose-oriented, and the more you're going to have and experience joy in your life because you bring so much joy and happiness to other people. The best way to happiness is trying to live your life in a way that brings other people happiness through your acts of service or through some kind of useful product that you create.

LINK: https://understandingrelationships.com/fear-acceptance-of-moving-on/25116

Getting Your Center Back

"In order to move on from a breakup or a dissolution of life circumstances that no longer serve you, you must first accept the reality of your life as it is right now, in the present moment. Once you have accepted what is in your life, you can let go of any attachment you may have to the way things were or the people who are no longer in your life. When you no longer have any attachments to your past, then it is easy to look towards the future with positive expectations of new people and better circumstances coming into your life. By having positive expectations and being open to what you want to create in the future, you now will create the necessary space for the right people and circumstances to effortlessly manifest in your life." ~ Coach Corey Wayne

I heard when I was younger that once you accept your past and your flaws, nobody else can use them against you. In other words, once you have peace with yourself and within yourself about who you are, where you come from, and what's happened to you in the past, nothing anybody says or does is going to make you feel bad about that. That's part of what being centered is all about: being centered in your masculine core, (or feminine core, if you're a woman), living your truth, loving your truth, living your life the way you want, and be damned the consequences and the opinions of other people; they're simply irrelevant. Remember, other people's opinion of you is none of your business.

The most important relationship that you have is the relationship that you have with yourself. And as long as you're doing what you do because it's what you feel like you should do on the inside, then everybody else's opinion really should not matter. If you're satisfied and you're content with your life, and then other people come along to try to make you feel bad for your life choices or how you are living, just remember, they're projecting what's inside of them onto you because they're not happy. And if you're happy living your life the way you're living it, the real reason that they're challenging you is because deep down on the inside they don't believe in themselves and they doubt themselves. And that's why they attack you. Because if they attack you and you're not deterred, then that means that you're a good example to follow, because you're centered in your core.

LINK: https://understandingrelationships.com/getting-your-center-back/18324

Getting Better At Dating & Seduction

"Life is a continuous process of interacting with other people who have shown up in your life on purpose to help you smooth out your rough edges, turn your weaknesses into strengths, and to facilitate experiences enabling you to reach your full potential in the journey of your life. You can either look at life as though everything that happens is a miracle or as if nothing is a miracle. When you view life and everything that happens to you as a miracle with a purpose, then you can see the universe conspiring to help you achieve your most emotionally compelling goals, and things tend to flow even more effortlessly. If you perceive life just happens to you at random, without any purpose at all, then life will always be a struggle and your choices will unknowingly bring you even more struggles. Life can be beautiful, or it can be a total bitch; it's simply a matter of the meanings you give to the circumstances of your life. Choose wisely." ~ Coach Corey Wayne

As I talked about in my second book, *Mastering Yourself*, what I try to do is really detail out all of the different people that I've interacted with over the course of my life that I learned something from. Because the most effective way to teach is through storytelling. And that's what all of my books are about, is telling stories where I can share a piece of wisdom, and then I can share the experience of how I either acquired that wisdom or I learned the lesson the hard way.

When I was younger and I didn't know any better, I had a lot of people in my life whose goals and values weren't really aligned with my own. And as I became older and gained wisdom, I acquired new people who helped me achieve my goals and my dreams. And some of those people that were once really important to me when I was younger, they just kind of faded away. Because, like Wayne Dyer used to say, "It's never crowded along the extra mile." When you're choosing to do really great, exceptional things with your life and reach your full potential, as the years and the decades roll by, you're going to start to recognize that there's very few people on that path and on that journey. Very few people go for and reach their full potential in life. It's a tragedy, but you can also look at it as a testament to yourself and your mental ability and your intestinal fortitude that you kept moving forward; you kept learning even when you had setbacks, when things didn't go well, and when life was a challenge.

That's what it takes to be truly exceptional—to persist without exception when everybody around you is giving up. As the years roll by, you're going to realize that, if you're like me, you'll probably be able to count on one hand the number of people that are in your inner circle who always believe in you, who always tell you that you can do it. They're going to be really essential, because you are going to have times and days and weeks and months, cumulatively, where you aren't going to feel so hot, you're not going to feel so smart, you're not going to feel like you have all the answers. And when you have people in your inner circle that can pat you on the back, pick you up off the ground, give you a hand to lift you up, and help dust you off, those kinds of relationships stand the test of time, and those kinds of people are the kind of people that really help you reach your full potential.

LINK: https://understandingrelationships.com/getting-better-at-dating-seduction/25762

I Think She's Cheating On Me

"When we fear an undesirable outcome and solely focus on trying to avoid what we fear, we consciously and unconsciously take actions and say things from the perspective of acting as if what we fear is already a reality. In order to conquer your fears and learn to live at peace and at choice, you must learn to act as if what you desire is already a reality and act accordingly. It is only by facing your fears and letting go of your attachments to your fears and undesirable outcomes that you can transcend the illusion of 'F.E.A.R.' False Evidence Appearing Real." ~ Coach Corey Wayne

It's very helpful to think from the end: to visualize the way you want things to be, to visualize the way they could be, and to imagine the positive, empowering emotions that you will experience when things are the way you want them to be. This can also be helpful if you're dating a girl you really like, but you find yourself being overwhelmed by emotions. Thinking from the end, "How would I be acting if I knew she was mine? How would I be acting if she had just told me for the tenth time over the last three days how much she loves me? How content would I feel? What kind of peace would I feel in my body? What would my body language be? What would my physiology be? How would the tone of my life be? What would I be saying and thinking? Would I be having an extra spring in my step? Would I be talking with extra enthusiasm to people that I'm talking to?"

Think from the end. Imagine how it would be if everything you wanted was already in your life today. Would you be stressed out, or would you be feeling ease, and delight, and peaceful, and relaxed? Because if you can put yourself in a state emotionally that resonates with the way you want things to be, your actions are going to tend to be way more efficient and way more in harmony with bringing about more peace, more ease, and delight in your life.

LINK: https://understandingrelationships.com/i-think-shes-cheating-on-me/14022

Changing Everything About Your Life

"Life is change; the only constant that you can depend upon is that nothing is going to stay the same forever. What you love doing today for a living might become boring, dull, and monotonous in the future. The more you are willing to follow your heart and explore opportunities as they present themselves, the more life will seem to flow and progress naturally and effortlessly. The less you are willing to follow your heart, the more unpleasant, difficult, and challenging life will be. We are spiritual beings having a human experience, not a bunch of mindless meat bags who exist by accident or chance. Everything in life happens for a spiritual reason. If you don't believe that, then life and things that happen to you will never seem to make any sense or have any real purpose." ~ Coach Corey Wayne

Being a successful, well-rounded human being means embracing the truth that life is change and it's constantly changing for us, not so much happening to us. I don't believe in luck; I believe that we make our own luck. And by taking action and moving towards the things that we want, we stack the odds in our favor that something that supposedly other people consider luck will come around, and in reality, that luck is just preparation meeting opportunity. If you're focused on growing your reserve of knowledge—developing your gifts, your skills, your talents, trying to improve a little bit each and every day—when opportunities present themselves in your life, you'll be ready for them, and when they happen, you will be able to take advantage of it.

This reminds me of something when I was in the construction industry. I loved what I was doing. I was a project engineer, and I was very good at it. I was very well organized. I remember one of the vice presidents of the company came over a couple weeks before he was about ready to leave the company and go work for a developer and be the main guy there. He just wanted to come over and spend time with me, and I remember the words he said to me. He said, "Corey, you're the most organized person I've ever seen." He'd worked at some of the best, largest construction companies in the industry, and I took that as a very great compliment.

I just loved what I was doing, and I was detail oriented. I wanted things to run well. I wanted my superintendent on the job to have everything that he needed, so he could build the building in the field. Any coordination or any logistics, all that stuff was done and worked out ahead of time, and so everything was like a nice, beautiful ballet on that particular job. And other people noticed. I remember after working for that particular company for about a year, year and a half, I guess it was, I started getting phone calls from recruiters offering me to come work for other companies. And what they had all said was, "I heard about you," and I was like, "Well, who told you?" And he said, "Well, we've got a lot of contacts in the industry."

If you're really good and you're really exceptional at what you do, other people are going to notice. And what will happen is, over time those recruiters will find out about you and they will track you down and be offering you other jobs, and employment, and career opportunities. And so, I look at something like that and say, that wasn't luck that that guy called me. That was the result of me kicking ass and doing a great, exceptional job, doing a better job at what I did than anybody else in the company. And people notice exceptional people.

Just like we recognize Tom Brady, the great football player. He is exceptional. He goes way above and beyond, more than anybody else in the football world is going to do between work, and training, and studying, and learning, and working out his body, and eating healthy. Everything is set up in his life to help facilitate him being exceptional, and everybody in the world notices that. So, go out and become exceptional at something you love, and you enjoy, and that you're passionate about. And even if you're not that excited about what you're doing, make sure you do an exceptional job. That should be the standard for how you operate in life, is always doing a great job.

LINK: https://understandingrelationships.com/changing-everything-about-your-life/32184

Finding Self Worth Again

"Success is a process, not a destination. Success is the result of applying the fundamentals of the science of high achievement in a consistent and focused manner and using failure as simply part of the learning and growing process to get better. With enough time, repetition, persistence, and learning from your mistakes, you can overcome any setback or challenge and succeed like never before. Winners take action despite the risks and potential for failure, while losers make excuses and do nothing to move their lives forward. Every day we decide to either take the required action to move our lives forward or do nothing by wasting time and avoiding life. Your life is the result of the actions you take or the actions you avoid taking. Choose wisely." ~ Coach Corey Wayne

Every day you get up, you have a choice. You have a clean slate. You can either be productive and take action to move your life forward, or you can make excuses and do nothing and keep yourself stuck in place. Most of the people around us are not living up to their full potential, and therefore, they're never going to reach and experience the glory of what it's like to reach your full potential.

Getting up every day and having exciting, compelling goals and dreams that you want to accomplish and achieve will give meaning to your life. If you get up every day and are just trying to get through the day and the workweek to get to the weekend to have some peace, you're like most of the low achieving people that never really get anywhere in life.

What's interesting is a few years back I was talking to a friend of mine who's a cardiologist, and we were discussing what people do or are willing to do when they come to him after they've had a heart attack or a stroke. Because I wanted to know how many of them were open to diet, exercise changes, and lifestyle changes, versus which ones have the attitude of, "Just give me the pill, Doc," and get out of the office. And what's interesting is, he said about 75% of the people that are 55 and younger will take the dietary advice—they'll make changes, they'll start exercising, they have a will to live. And what's really shocking is 75% of the people that are 55 and older are just like, "Fuck it. Give me the pill," and they don't care.

And so, I look at that as a coach, and to me, for whatever reason, 55 seems to kind of be the age where most people have just given up and won't do anything to help themselves. Because as soon as you lose hope, what's the point of going to the gym? What's the point of picking up that phone and calling somebody that you care about and letting them know how much you love and care about them? What's the point of eating a healthy meal, or going to the gym, or starting a business, or going for the things you want if you've already given up? People that have given up already have one foot in the grave. At the end of the day, we all have a limited amount of time on this earth, and how we choose to spend it determines what we get to experience in life. Choose wisely.

LINK: https://understandingrelationships.com/finding-self-worth-again/38027

MAKING A GOOD IMPRESSION

Effortless Sex, Dating, Love & Relationships

"It is your birthright to be loved by someone you love and adore and to have a life full of effortless sex, dating, love, and relationships. The only thing that really gets in the way of having what you want romantically in life is the story that you tell yourself of why you can't have it. If you don't think you are deserving of what you want in any area of your life you will act and speak in ways that are congruent with that limiting and inaccurate belief. Start to think from the end regarding having what you want in life. In other words, how would you act, speak, and behave differently if you had more potential lovers, friends, jobs, money, and opportunities than you could handle? You would be more discerning, picky, and would accept only the very best and never settle. Why? Because you don't have to. You must become the type of person you want to attract and act as if the life you really want is already a foregone conclusion at some point in the future. Therefore, you would simply live your life by taking the necessary actions moment by moment without any worry about things working out in the future. You would know it is simply a matter of time, efficient and effective focus, refinement of your approach along the way, and repetition to eventually creating your dream life." ~ Coach Corey Wayne

You have to act in a way that communicates that you deserve what you want. People who deserve what they want, expect to get what they want, and, eventually, experience getting what they want have a relaxed, peaceful, balanced amount of certainty in their lives. Everything may look like it's in doubt in the future, but still, eventually, they see on a long enough timeline if they keep applying themselves that, eventually, they're going to get from where they are to where they want to be in life.

LINK: https://understandingrelationships.com/effortless-sex-dating-love-relationships/17092

Pickup & Date Questions That Build Attraction

"Most people don't really have that much exciting stuff going on in their lives. When people go out, they are usually looking to escape from their boring lives. The best way to create rapport and attraction with members of the opposite sex is to talk about positive and uplifting topics that elicit good feelings. This will cause them to see you as unique, fun, different, and exciting to be around. If they're smiling, feeling good, and laughing with you, it will create sexual attraction." ~ Coach Corey Wayne

Taking a sincere interest in other people, being curious, asking them the kinds of questions that they would enjoy answering is a great way to take all of the pressure off of yourself when you're worried about "What am I going to do?", "What am I going to talk to her about?", or "What am I going to talk to this employer about in the interview?" If you're asking questions and being sincerely, authentically interested in what the other person has to say and they can feel that, they will typically open up to you and share what they're thinking and feeling.

The more you can get people to open up and talk about themselves, their hopes, their dreams, the things they're excited about, their passions, the easier it's going to be for you to create rapport with other people, and most importantly, get people to like you, trust you, want to do business with you, want to be your friend, want to date you, want to buy your product or service, etc.

LINK: https://understandingrelationships.com/pickup-date-questions-that-build-attraction/13871

Never Brag About Yourself

"Successful men who have a healthy self-esteem are happy to talk about their accomplishments and successes when asked. Men who are insecure, who have self-esteem issues, or who are needy, desperate, or unsuccessful feel that they lack something on the inside that would make them desirable to other people. Therefore, in order to be liked by others or women they are attracted to, they try to make up for what they feel they lack on the inside by bragging about themselves or their accomplishments, talking about how much money they have, talking about material things that they own, or talking about things that they can offer the other person. They also tend to be terrible listeners because they are so focused on gaining the love or approval of others that they feel they must dominate all conversations by talking about themselves constantly. Women who initially liked them quickly get turned off and lose interest. Taking a sincere interest in other people, asking questions, and being a good listener will always win you friends, enable you to influence others, and attract women." ~ Coach Corey Wayne

The best way to create rapport with other people is to take a sincere, authentic interest in them. Ask them the kind of questions that they would enjoy answering. Ask them about their passions, their interests, their hobbies, things they love and enjoy, what they love to do for fun, and things of that nature, and be a good listener. Because when you are a good listener and you ask questions of the other person, you're behaving just like somebody who is really close to them would behave.

Think about when you run into an old friend in the grocery store or out somewhere. What do you typically say? "Hey, what have you been up to?", "What's so-and-so up to?", "How's the wife?", "How're the kids?", "How's that job?", "How's life going overall?" In other words, if you know somebody and you care about them, you're going to want to know how they're doing and what they're up to, and this takes all the pressure off of yourself.

It doesn't matter whether you're on a date, or in a job interview, or in a negotiation, the more you take the time—even if it's just five, ten, fifteen minutes—to ask the other person and take a sincere, authentic interest in them, they will be happy to tell you about themselves. And as they're telling you about themselves, they start to view you as somebody who is like a friend—somebody that they're already close to. This creates rapport. And after five, ten, fifteen minutes of them talking, just by the natural law of reciprocity, they feel like they should want to find out more about you, and then they start asking you questions about yourself. And if somebody starts to feel, because they're talking about themselves to you and you're actually listening and then asking them questions—if they start to feel like you actually care about them—they start to like you, and if they like you, they start to trust you.

And one of the things that are absolutely essential in sales—whether you're selling yourself to a member of the opposite sex on a date, or you're selling yourself to a prospective employer or customer—is you have to get people to like you and you have to get them to trust you.

Because if people don't like you and they don't trust you, they are not going to buy what you're selling.

LINK: https://understandingrelationships.com/never-brag-about-yourself/17261

Counter-Intuitive Dating Magic

"Much like kids test their parents to see what they can get away with and push the boundaries, adults do this with each other in all aspects of life and human interactions. Salespeople test your willingness to part with your money and accept terms that are more favorable to them. Lovers and potential lovers test each other to see what the other person is made of. Setting healthy boundaries is part of any good personal and professional relationship. Being willing to enforce those boundaries by walking away and never looking back if you are not treated the way you want and deserve is sometimes necessary to communicate that you mean what you say and are not bluffing. People will love and respect you more and give you what you want if you mean what you say. If you allow others to walk all over you and treat you like a doormat, they will eventually see you as being worthless and unworthy of respect. You don't get what you deserve in life, only what you negotiate. Negotiating from a position of strength is always necessary to ensure that you get what you want in life and are treated how you want to be treated." ~ Coach Corey Wayne

I was doing a phone session yesterday with a client of mine, and one of the things he's trying to overcome is being too much of a nice guy and a pushover. His girlfriend basically had two or three things that she really had a problem with him on, and part of the problem is that he wouldn't stand up for himself and he wouldn't stand up to other people, and this obviously caused her to doubt his masculine core.

And one of the other issues that he was having with his girlfriend is she would ask him to do something, and he would say yes, he's going to do it, and then he wouldn't follow through with it. And so, obviously, his short-term memory is not very good, so what we discussed was to make a to-do list. And so, whether it's his girlfriend or somebody else, he's got to put things on his to-do list. Because after talking to him, I could tell he's a little bit of a disorganized scatterbrain. And, you know, if you constantly tell your girlfriend or your wife that you're going to do something and then you don't do it, and you keep making the same mistakes, eventually, at some point, she's going to give up on you. His girlfriend has been getting to the point where she's about ready to give up on him because they've been together three years, I believe, at this point. And so, what we discussed is to make a to-do list and work off of that and let her know what he's doing, instead of just Kentucky guaranteeing her that "Oh, yeah I'm going to fix it," "I'm going to do this," "I'm going to do that."

And one other thing is, he's a pretty smart guy, and he doesn't like stupid people, and he tends to get irritated when somebody is saying something stupid or doing something stupid. Because he's a pretty smart guy, and he tends to get a little abrasive, and verbally abusive, and condescending when somebody is saying something or believing in something that he believes is stupid. And so, he does this with his girlfriend, he does with his friends; he gets kind of condescending and arrogant. And so, what we discussed was for him to talk to his girlfriend and engage her help. Tell her, just say, "I tend to be a bit of an arrogant dickhead at times, which obviously you know, and so when you notice or you catch me being a condescending asshole to you or somebody else, I want you to call me out on it right away. Tell me right away, saying 'Hey, you're kind of being a dick to me right now, and this is what we talked about.'" Because it has to be brutally honest, so he can catch himself in the moment and recognize that he's doing something that's causing him to look unattractive to his girlfriend, and it's pissing his friends or family members off who he does that to.

So, by asking everybody that's close to him and telling them about this issue of his that he's trying to correct, he's engaging them to help him help himself. Therefore, his girlfriend will be able to see that he's actually doing something about it, instead of just going, "Oh, I'm going to change. I'm going to change. I'm going to change." If you tell a woman something like that for many months or years and then you don't change, eventually, at some point, she's going to start to think you're totally full of shit; and that's basically where his girlfriend has gotten to. So, if he comes up with this new approach, asks her to help him, and gets her to call him out in a brutally honest way, then he can catch himself, and self-regulate, and not be such a jerk to people.

LINK: https://understandingrelationships.com/counter-intuitive-dating-magic/31515

When Brutal Honesty Is & Isn't Appropriate

"People will not always remember what you said, but they will always remember how you made them feel. A true friend is someone to whom you can speak aloud and without being judged, being wrong for your opinions, and with whom you can give and receive loving, blunt, and brutal honesty. Acquaintances or people who you do not know very well will often not handle brutal honesty or truth without getting butthurt, pissed off, or offended by you. Therefore, save your brutal honesty for your true friends and family who really know, love, and understand you, and only give advice to people who ask for your honest opinion. Unsolicited advice from strangers or acquaintances is rarely welcome, sought, appreciated, understood, or valued. The average person is simply not ready, willing, able, or capable of being woken up from their ignorance. Some people simply can't handle the truth. Carefully choose your battles." ~ Coach Corey Wayne

Great friends, great lovers, great family members are people that will always give you honest and brutally honest feedback when it's warranted. They're not going to let you suffer or flail around, and they don't say things to hurt you or to piss you off; they're saying things that they know that you probably wouldn't listen to anybody else other than them. And that's the value of having great people in your life, is they give you honest, brutal feedback, even when you might not be looking for it, or think that you did anything wrong, or that you should change how you're showing up.

The other thing you've got to remember about brutal honesty and telling it like it is, is that the reality is there's a lot of really low IQ people in the world, and it's an incredible waste of your time to try to argue with somebody who's just fucking stupid. There's no nice way to say it. We see this all the time online—people going back and forth on social media posts. And what's interesting about social media: it's the first time in history that low IQ people are able to easily interact with high IQ people. And so, if you've had the same experience where you realize that you're just talking to a moron online, or sometimes in person, it's just better to save your breath and not try to convince somebody who's just stupid. Because some people you just can't reach. Bless them, wish them well, move on with your life.

LINK: https://understandingrelationships.com/when-brutal-honesty-is-isnt-appropriate/17216

What Is My Purpose?

"Our work life is where we spend most of our time. Studies have shown that the overwhelming majority of people are stuck in dead-end jobs or careers that simply do not uplift, motivate, or inspire them to greatness or to reach their full potential. If you do not like what you do for a living, you will never be able to force yourself to put in the time and effort to become great at it. Follow your heart, curiosity, passion, and intuition when searching for a career to pursue or a business to start. Great wealth comes as a byproduct of providing a useful service people are happy to pay for. The more inspired, enthusiastic, and passionate you are about the service or product that you provide for people who need, value, and want it, the more you will enjoy, relish, and appreciate your life." ~ Coach Corey Wayne

What's interesting about the fact that most people are stuck in mediocre jobs, or jobs that do not inspire them, and jobs they don't have a passion for is, if you're able to sit down and figure out the things you love doing most and enjoy in life, and then seek to pursue a job, or a career, or even a business, (if you're an entrepreneur), you're going to be way more ahead of the competition; more than 97% of the people that you're competing against. And what's interesting from an employer perspective—as somebody that's hired and fired literally hundreds of people over the course of his career—is that all employers, all managers love having self-motivated, low maintenance employees. And those kinds of people that are self-motivated and low maintenance are very positive, very optimistic, they're self-starters, they go above and beyond what's asked and required of them. And then, when they run out of things to do, or they feel like they've hit the glass ceiling, so to speak, they're always looking for the next challenge. And so, they continually make the people that they work for look good to their superiors.

And when you're interviewing or you're just simply selling a product, people can sense the enthusiasm. And so, if you're interviewing for a job where there's literally hundreds of applicants, almost all of those people that you're competing against for the job are going to have a mediocre level of enthusiasm. More than likely, they're not very good at the interview process, and so when you sit down and you apply the things that I talk about in my second book, *Mastering Yourself*, on how to handle yourself in a job interview, it's going to be obvious that you're the best person for the job. Because people that have a lot of enthusiasm work because that particular work feels like playing to them; they love it, they enjoy it, they have a passion for it. So, find some kind of a job, some kind of a purpose, some kind of a business to start that's exciting and compelling to you, some kind of product, some kind of service that you're in love with, and you will easily set yourself apart from the people you're competing against. It won't be a contest at all; you'll be able to completely dominate in your field.

LINK: https://understandingrelationships.com/what-is-my-purpose/16647

The Freedom Of Self-Love

"One of the smartest decisions you can make in life is to learn to love and accept yourself as you are and where you are, and to no longer look to or expect someone or something outside of yourself will make you happy. When you make your happiness dependent upon the actions of others matching your unreasonable expectations or upon your life circumstances being a certain way, you set yourself up for unnecessary suffering and disappointment. The superior approach is to love as your gift to others instead of loving and expecting something in return. Love is about giving. You should also focus on creating a life and lifestyle that is emotionally compelling, which gives meaning to your life and existence. When you love your life, yourself, and you give others the freedom to love or leave you, then you create the space and freedom for the right people to show up and stay because they want to, not because you need them to." ~ Coach Corey Wayne

You've got to learn to be patient with yourself, and your life, and your progress. If you're busy taking action on a daily, consistent basis, trying to get better, trying to refine your approach, trying to look for the edge, trying to find a way to be more efficient so your actions bring you quicker and better results overall, what this is going to do, it's going to put you in a place where you feel more confident and more courageous, because you got so busy taking action that you are able to completely live in and embrace the present moment. And the present moment is really where all life is lived, anyway.

Anytime you're fearful or you're worried about the future, or the past, or what may or may not work out for you, get busy taking action trying to get better, and lose yourself in the process of taking action to make your greatest goals and dreams a reality. And before you know it, time will zip by, and you'll be very productive. And then, when you're at home at night and you're about to put your head on your pillow to go to sleep, you're going to feel peaceful, relaxed, and content because you're going to feel like you had a very productive day, where you got a lot of things done. And you'll be excited about what you're going to do tomorrow to be potentially even more productive, because it builds upon itself the more you do this, day in and day out, with a relentless pursuit of excellence and trying to get better.

LINK: https://understandingrelationships.com/the-freedom-of-self-love/25960

Dating, Sexual Confidence & Being Present

"In life, it's always best to focus your intentions on staying in and living in the present moment. After all, the only moment that exists is right now. When we get into our heads and start thinking about the future and what may or may not happen, we engage in a mental mind fuck that causes us to say and do things out of fear, instead of letting things happen and simply enjoying them for the gifts that they are. When we get into our heads and worry about the future and what could go wrong, we actually create a vibration that makes what we fear happen. This can lead to dates that were going well going sideways, creeping the other person out, inability to perform sexually, and unnecessary rejection." ~ Coach Corey Wayne

This is especially helpful for guys that are on a date, guys that are always worrying, "What do I say to a girl to get her to like me?", "How do I keep entertaining her?", "What if I run out of things to talk about?" The idea is creating rapport with women and other people in general really comes from a sincere, authentic interest in wanting to get to know the other person, who they are, what their dreams are, what they're passionate about, the things that they love, the things that they enjoy, getting the other person to talk about things they enjoy doing or enjoy studying, or whatever it happens to be. Because if you care about somebody, you want to know what's going on with them, including the boring day-to-day minutia, whatever it happens to be. You're never going to be in a situation where you're constantly making the other person laugh and they're making you laugh. If you do that, you can do it for a while, it's sustainable, but at some point, that's just simply not normal behavior. You're not going to be cracking jokes all day long and all night long when you're on a date.

Humor, and fun, and playfulness comes and goes in waves just like Mother Nature does. So, if you're ever worried about what you're going to say, focus on getting the other person to talk and tell you things about themselves that you're interested in knowing. Because it's in getting to know the other person that you get enough information that you can make an intelligent, informed decision on whether or not you actually like listening to them. You should want to be with somebody who you enjoy the sound of their voice, and you enjoy what they have to say. But if you're too worried about trying to talk and fill up the space in between your talking with words, you're never going to get to that place, because you always feel like you're having to perform. You're not a circus performer; you're a human being. So, take a sincere, authentic interest in the other person and just ask them questions—the kind of questions that they would enjoy answering and that you would enjoy hearing about.

LINK: https://understandingrelationships.com/dating-sexual-confidence-being-present/14545

She Wants To Feel Independent

"When people feel out of control or that their life circumstances are too random and unpredictable for their liking, they tend to try to control themselves, other people, and their environment as much as possible. The need to feel free is an innate human quality that must be honored. If you fail to honor the free will and right of self-determination of your friends, coworkers, lovers, family, etc., they will all naturally want to remove themselves from your presence to regain their freedom." ~ Coach Corey Wayne

People who don't feel like they have any control over life, or the circumstances of their life, are driven by a state of fear, because their life success strategies suck. They don't know the science of high achievement fundamentals. And so, the way that they go about gaining certainty in their lives and feeling like they can relatively count on a certain set of things happening or a certain group of people being in their life, they typically will try to force things. Because, deep down, they're worried that nobody wants to be with them; this is their fear.

And so, when time and space happens in between those interactions with other people that they want to love them, and they start to feel that they are not loved, they try to force interactions. They call too much, they text too much, and what this does is it causes the other person or people to feel like they're losing their freedom. All human beings resent having their freedom infringed upon, having their rights infringed upon.

We naturally are all repulsed by this and tend to move away from people, (and governments, for that matter), that try to control and regulate every aspect of our lives. When it comes to your intimate and your personal relationships, if you're trying to control and regulate all of the behavior of the women you're dating, they're not going to stick around for very long.

LINK: https://understandingrelationships.com/she-wants-to-feel-independent/13665

Dating: Terrible Texting Turnoffs

"It's a pleasant surprise, compliment to you, gift, and an honor when a woman you are dating reaches out to you first. You should always be charming and playful and assume she is thinking about you and wants to see you. Therefore, your outcome should be to set the next date to get together. The more a guy talks and texts with a woman he just started dating, instead of simply making dates when she reaches out to him first, the higher the likelihood is that he will talk her right out of liking him by saying or texting something stupid—or worse, become her therapist and get stuck in friend zone. The more you talk and text digitally, the less time you will spend with her in-person having fun, getting to know each other, hooking up, and growing her attraction for you." ~ Coach Corey Wayne

Just reading this quote reminds me of how I was in my early 20s. You know, back then, this is before we would text. Mobile phones back then were like the size of fucking brick, so it wasn't just something you had in your pocket or your backpack with you. We would have things like pagers and, obviously, a home phone. And when I would get phone numbers back when I was in my early 20s, I would spend several weeks talking to these girls several times a week. They'd be calling me and really into me. I didn't realize it at the time, but they were calling me all the time, and I would just sit there and talk on the phone for a few hours, and then once we kind of ran out of things to talk about, the conversation would end. And then, as two or three weeks rolled by, I could feel that she seemed to be calling less and seemed to be expressing less enthusiasm on the phone. And then, when I would finally get around to asking her out, I would hear, "Well, Corey, I just kind of think of you as a friend."

So, literally, they started out really liking me, and because I never got around to setting a date and getting together in person—because I thought I was being nice and respectful and letting them get to know me before we actually went on a date, because I didn't want them to think I was trying to get into their pants or anything—that by the time I finally got around to making a move, they recognized that I didn't have game, and didn't have any confidence, and didn't know what the hell I was doing. And then, I'd be stuck in friend zone.

The reality is, if a girl likes you, get her out on a date. If you meet digitally over the internet, you shouldn't have to talk more than 30 days before one of you is ready to hop on a plane and go see the other one. And the reality is, if you're talking to a girl that you met over the internet and you're talking for 30 days and she's unwilling to make plans to come see you or have you come see her, then you're just fucking wasting your time. I've seen plenty of cases over the years with guys I'm doing phone sessions with who get in situations with these women that are grifters, and they start sending them money, and yet, even when they go visit that part of the world, these women are never available to get together with them in person. But, you know, "Hey, please keep sending me the money." They'll give them jobs working for their company, and all kinds of other things, because they're trying to fix this girl and think, "Hey, she'll like me more if I do all these nice things for her." The reality is, there are parasites out there; there are women out there that just don't pull their weight. And there's lots of gullible, desperate, needy guys who don't know any better, and you don't want to be those dudes that fall into that particular trap.

Just like people in sales, if you're calling around to different car dealerships asking about cars, they're going to try to get you to come into the dealership to take a look at it, to take it out for a test drive. Because if you're unwilling to come into the car dealership, then you're just a tire kicker and you're not really a serious buyer. And the same thing happens when it comes to dating. If you're just chitchatting with a girl but she won't ever meet you in person, she more than likely enjoys the attention and validation, but she's not really romantically interested in you. Don't fucking let people like this waste your time. Just move on. Tell them to get in touch if they ever want to get together, and never call or text for any reason after that.

LINK: https://understandingrelationships.com/dating-terrible-texting-turnoffs/32003

Acting Like A Horny Virgin Teenager

"In order for a man to seduce a woman successfully, he must make her feel safe and comfortable and that she is very special to him. Women want to avoid being labeled a slut, being used for sex, getting a disease, and being alone with a man who doesn't immediately stop his sexual advances when she says 'No,' 'Stop,' or 'Slow down.' Men who are impatient, insecure, controlling, who get angry and frustrated, disrespectful, or who treat women like a piece of meat to be used and then tossed aside are going to immediately set off a woman's internal safety and comfort alarm. Once that alarm sounds inside of a woman, her legs will close, and she will start withdrawing from him. Once a man starts acting like a horny virgin teenager, the chances of him recovering and having sex with her are almost zero." ~ Coach Corey Wayne

I get lots of emails and I see this often in my phone sessions with clients. One of the strategies for seduction that I teach in my book, *How To Be A 3% Man,* is "Two steps forward, one step back." This helps you come off as non-attached. In other words, you're thinking from the end. In your mind, sex is going to happen eventually, whether it's your second or third date, or your first date, (or, if you're ultra-religious, it's happening on your wedding night). The bottom line is that you're okay with having it or not having it.

Sometimes, when you're rushing things, or you're moving too fast for a woman, it's going to exceed her level of safety and comfort, and she's going to want you to slow down or ask you to stop. Guys in these situations make the mistake of thinking they should stop forever and never try again, or try on the next date. All it really should mean is that you just need to slow down your advances; you're moving too fast. The idea—the perfect sweet spot, so to speak, when it comes to seduction—is you want to go a little slower than she wants to go. Because when you can do that properly, what you'll notice is the women kiss you more passionately, they tend to chew on your lips, chew on your tongue, bite you, pull you in closer, squeeze you harder, squeeze you tighter, wrap their legs around you tighter, moan more. These are the kinds of things that you're going to notice when you're going just a little bit slower and she is.

If you could tell a woman is not really into your touching her, slow it down. Take your time to caress her body and be with her. And if she's resisting you caressing her body, ask her some questions, get her to talk, get her to open up as you gently and lightly caress her. Then, what happens is, she continues to talk, and you continue to listen, looking into her eyes, giving her the vibration that you're listening, you're 100% present, and you care what she has to say—and that's what causes her to start feeling more sexual anticipation and arousal to you. It's an art, it's not an exact science, and you have to notice what a woman is doing, thinking, and feeling.

If you're ready to bump uglies and you can tell she's not really even liking touching you or kissing you, it means you're moving too fast. It means you need to slow things down a little bit—probably 2 to 3 times slower than you want to go. But, in the long run, when she gets really turned on, she becomes really wet, really aggressive, and it's a lot easier for her to climax, just because you're taking your time.

LINK: https://understandingrelationships.com/acting-like-a-horny-virgin-teenager/18450

You Deserve To Be Loved Unconditionally

"Why real love is worth the wait: real, true love is easy and effortless with no holding back. It's total unconditional love, acceptance, and support of each other. The wrong person will hold back, create unnecessary drama, and cause you to question your idea of who you are. If you can be happy with you, exactly where you are right now in life, you will allow another to come into your life and love you as you are, where you are. If you love and accept yourself unconditionally, you will love and accept another unconditionally. Total self-acceptance leads to unconditional love and acceptance of the one you love, with all of their warts, shortcomings, flaws, and faults." ~ Corey Wayne

A great attitude that guys should have when it comes to dating is to be cocky, charming, humorous, and humble. And when I say humble, I mean not taking yourself too seriously—being willing to admit your mistakes and laugh at yourself. Laugh at the fact that you made mistakes, and not look at it as something to be insecure about or to be ashamed of, but something to kind of laugh about because you acted ridiculous at one point in your life. Because we've all done this. When you communicate that you're humble, and you're humorous about it, and you don't take yourself too seriously, you come off as being approachable and a real human being that has problems, just like everybody else. Nobody is perfect. Cut yourself some slack.

If you're in a pressured situation, one of the best ways to handle it is to always have a funny, humorous comeback to diffuse the situation. Especially when your girl gets irritated or angry with you and you know her behavior's a little out of line, you can use humor, and tease her, and be playful in a way that lets her know that her behavior is kind of inappropriate, and she should be easygoing and laugh at herself a little bit more instead of being a mean jackass.

LINK: https://understandingrelationships.com/you-deserve-to-be-loved-unconditionally/13618

She Wanted Closure, But I Got Her Back

"Love is supposed to be playful and fun, not serious and full of drama. Humor, charm, love of life, playful banter, and making your lover or potential lover smile and laugh is the most effective tool you can use to diffuse a tense situation, dissolve anger and hurt, and cause someone to become loving, sweet, affectionate, horny, and desire you again when they have become cold and distant. Skillfully using humor and being playful is an essential characteristic of any great seducer, lover, and man who is universally loved by women and other people. Remaining calm, loving, playful, and sweet despite the best attempts of others to agitate, irritate, and diminish you enables you to talk anyone into anything, make allies of enemies, and soften even the hardest heart. It's impossible for someone to remain pissed and angry at you when they're laughing." ~ Coach Corey Wayne

Learning to master the skill of when to be playful and fun and to humorous comebacks but also when to be a good listener is essential, especially in your intimate relationships. And a big part of what I see when I do phone sessions with men that are struggling in this area is that they're kind of behaving like a guy that's got a fucking stick up their ass; they're too serious all the time, they take things too personally, they get upset, and instead of being playful and fun and joking around, they're kind of stiff all the time and they're not a lot of fun. And women bluff to test a guy's strength; they mess with him on purpose to try to intimidate him. If a guy doesn't have a fun, playful comeback and doesn't recognize that she's just bluffing and messing with him... Because that's part of what flirtation is in dating and courtship and interacting with women. It's being fun, being playful, making her smile, and if you can get a woman to laugh, it's impossible for her to stay mad or pissed off at you for very long.

Now, it doesn't mean that every single sentence that comes out of your mouth or hers warrants a joke or a smartass comment. Like I talk about in my first book, *3% Man*—typically, you want to be 10% kind of the naughty, playboy kind of guy, and 90% you want to be charming James Bond. But any time you're pressured, it's always good to come back with humor or playfulness to make light of the situation, so you can keep the vibe fun and playful. Because love is playful and fun; it's not serious, and pissed off, and angry, and irritable all the time.

LINK: https://understandingrelationships.com/she-wanted-closure-but-i-got-her-back/17301

Why Women Feel Empowered Chasing Men

"It's true that men should pursue and initiate dates that can eventually lead to intimacy and a relationship, but there is a fine line between pushing too hard for sex and a relationship and not pursing enough to make the woman feel wanted. A man should focus on creating opportunities to hang out and have fun together, because this is what causes a woman to associate good feelings with being with him, which is a necessary prerequisite to her feeling safe and comfortable enough to open up to receive him mentally, emotionally, spiritually, and physically." ~ Coach Corey Wayne

What I teach in my book, *How To Be A 3% Man,* is that it is true that a man is supposed to pursue, but, typically, this really only needs to happen in the first few weeks of the courtship. And the reason that this is, is because as they continue to spend time together—and the reality is, most women sleep with a guy by the second or third date—after two or three weeks of dating and then they start having sex, if a guy is just simply calling once a week and making one date on average every week, week and a half, what happens is, because there's so much time in between them seeing each other and several days usually go by without them talking, the woman starts to think that he's not that into her. She starts to wonder what's really going on.

At times, she also starts to worry that she may be losing him potentially to another woman, or maybe he's lost interest in her. And what typically happens is they will call, or text, or reach out in some way just to say they were thinking about them or force some kind of interaction to kind of find out where they stand with the guy, so to speak. And the guy should just assume that if they just had a date two or three days ago but hadn't talked, and then now she's texting him about some random thing, (like, she saw a movie last night and one of the characters reminded her of him), he should assume that if she's reaching out and texting, she probably wants to see him, so he should use that as an opportunity to set a date.

As the weeks go by, and you get in the third, fourth, and fifth week, what happens is the woman is usually calling and texting two to three times a week, and then the guy can simply use that as an opportunity to set the next date. And that's how he keeps from over pursuing her and goes at her pace. As she becomes more attracted and more interested, she calls more, she texts more, she causes more social interactions between the two of them, and the guy can simply use that as opportunities to facilitate getting together. If a woman is always chasing you, you never have to worry about getting dumped.

LINK: https://understandingrelationships.com/why-women-feel-empowered-chasing-men/35345

Masculine Vacillation

"It is incredibly unattractive to women when a man is incapable of making a decision, is unsure of himself, he dithers and hesitates, and does not understand how to be the leader in his relationship. Some men are natural-born leaders, and leadership comes easily and naturally for them. Men who are not good leaders can be taught to lead only if they are open to it and determined to become better. However, men tend to be very egocentric. Therefore, asking for help or admitting that they are clueless is often unthinkable, but preferable to seeking help or changing their approach because this would mean admitting failure. When faced with admitting failure or a lack of ability, most men will choose to continue failing. This is why stopping and asking for help or directions is something most men will refuse to do at all costs, even though most women consider it to be common sense to do so." ~ Coach Corey Wayne

This is the kind of behavior that a man displays when he's unsure of himself. He constantly abdicates his leadership role to the woman. Instead of coming up with a great place to go eat, making the reservations, taking care of any babysitting arrangements ahead of time, and telling her what kind of clothes she should wear for the occasion, men that don't know any better often will say, "Gee, honey. What do you want to do tonight?" And she'll say, "I don't know. What do you want to do?" And what she really wants is the guy to make a fucking decision, come up with something fun to do, and invite her to join him, where she can either accept the invitation or maybe suggest something that's even a better idea to do.

The point being, it's up to the man to be direct, decisive, get to the point, and make something happen—whether that's getting a phone number, making a date, making dinner reservations, taking care of the babysitter, booking the flights, booking the hotel, whatever it happens to be. Be the leader and invite her to join you on your fun bus. Women don't like manginas or guys who sit around waiting for a woman to tell them what to do. They don't want to be your mommy; they want to follow your lead.

LINK: https://understandingrelationships.com/masculine-vacillation/19991

SELF IMPROVEMENT

Dating: Master The Progression

"Like Sun Tzu said, 'Every battle is won before it is fought.' Succeeding and winning any competition, in life, in your career, at business, or in love is determined by what you do and how you prepare ahead of time. Becoming great at anything requires countless practice repetitions to develop and hone your skills. Most people have the desire to win, but few people possess the will, determination, dedication, and discipline to prepare to win. In life, you're either preparing to and expecting to win or making excuses that guarantee losing." ~ Coach Corey Wayne

I can't remember who it is, but there was a success quote that basically said something like, "Success is preparation meeting opportunity." And the things I talk about in both my books—*3% Man* and *Mastering Yourself*—are essential fundamentals. The science of high achievement fundamentals is how you're able to set yourself apart from everybody else in the world, spending your time in an efficient way, improving your skills, your gifts, your talents, and growing your reserve of knowledge. It's simply a way of life; getting up every day trying to get a little better than you were yesterday. And when you focus on this simple goal, just trying to get a little better each and every day—a little happier, a little more grateful, looking for more reasons to be grateful in your life, becoming a better employee, becoming a better entrepreneur, becoming a better husband, better boyfriend, better guy to date, better friend, better human being, whatever it happens to be—is the result of a relentless pursuit at self-improvement and bettering yourself.

LINK: https://understandingrelationships.com/dating-master-the-progression/24754

Pulse Nightclub Terror Attack In Orlando

"Human beings have six basic fundamental needs they are always trying to meet through their thoughts, words, and deeds. The first need is a desire for Certainty. This means you are "certain" you have a roof over your head, a job, money, know where your next meal is coming from, etc. The second need is Variety. In other words, we like to have a variety of different experiences and people in life, instead of every day being exactly the same. The third need is Love and Connection. This is simply bonding with, connecting to, and loving other people. The fourth need is Significance. This means you are important, you matter, and your life has meaning. The fifth need is Growth. This is growing as a person, expanding your knowledge, skills, etc. The sixth need is Contribution. This is doing things for other people. By focusing on helping and contributing to the welfare of others, you actually meet all of the six other human needs in the process." ~ Coach Corey Wayne

Understanding the six human needs can be really helpful, because it helps us understand why we do what we do. Obviously, the need for certainty is one of the biggest needs, and especially when it comes to relationships, we want certainty on whether or not the person still likes us. And because we are driven to seek out certainty and to have certainty, when we're in a place and we're fearful and we're worried that things won't work out in our favor, we try to do things to force ourselves to get to a place of certainty or inner peace, if you will. But also, what's interesting about guys is one of our six human needs also is variety. We like variety, and the longer a guy is in a relationship, he oftentimes has that natural desire to have freedom, which is why the running joke has kind of always been, when it comes to relationships, (at least it used to be, in the old ways), guys were the last ones to want to agree to a commitment. It's like, you want to be in a relationship, but by the same token, you also have that strong desire for freedom.

So, as a man, you're trying to figure out what's the right way to balance that, especially those two—certainty and variety. And one that's very important to us as human beings is our need for growth, and that also includes spiritual growth. We have to feel like we're growing as human beings and we're improving. And if we're not focused on fulfilling all six of these human needs, we're always going to feel like something is missing. And by focusing on the sixth human need, which is contribution, just like the quote says, we're able to actually fulfill all the rest of the needs. And so, if you're struggling in your life or you're just having a difficult day, focus on your need for contribution. What can you do to be an active service to other people? And then, focus on that and take action to make that happen. It'll make you feel a lot better, especially if you're having a rotten day.

LINK: https://understandingrelationships.com/pulse-nightclub-terror-attack-in-orlando/26253

12 Principles Of Successful Relationships

"People who have high standards for themselves and who crave success are repulsed by the thought of settling for a life that is less than what they are capable of living. Successful people want the best that life has to offer in their personal lives, careers, businesses, health and lifestyles. When you give life your best effort, it gives you peace of mind to accept any and all outcomes without second-guessing yourself. People who are too timid and fearful to give their very best are forced to live a life of mediocrity and feeling like the grass is greener on the other side. The greatest tragedy in life is to get to the end of your life and realize you never have truly lived and made the effort to see what you are truly capable of." ~ Corey Wayne

What's the point of living life if you're really not going to go for the things that you want and see what you're really capable of? The purpose of life is to have fun and to enjoy it, and a friend of mine who is retired Special Forces, he's got such a great outlook on life after his four combat tours and seeing all of the death and destruction that he saw overseas. He's one of the happiest people that I know. He's always smiling, he's always looking for a reason to laugh and to giggle, and to enjoy himself, and it's just a blessing to be around him. I want to be a better man myself when I'm around him, because he's squared away, he takes care of his body. Everybody that knows him and meets him absolutely loves him. And his whole philosophy in life, he's got two things he focuses on: number one, he wants to have fun, and number two, he wants to learn something. And that's all he does; every day when he gets up, he wants to have fun and wants to learn something

LINK: https://understandingrelationships.com/12-principles-of-successful-relationships/25870

Living Together Changes Everything

"You cannot give away what you do not have for yourself. If you feel you are still lacking and do not have enough to fill up your own cup, that makes it almost impossible to give to another to fill up their cup or the cup of self-esteem of your children and those who depend upon you." ~ Corey Wayne

Well, just like the quote says, you really have to get to a place where you love yourself, you value yourself, you love your life, the people that are in it and the circumstances that are in it, and most importantly, as a man, that you love your purpose and your mission in life. It might not necessarily mean that you love your current job; it might just simply mean that your current job is a steppingstone and a means to an end to eventually doing something that's way more fun, exciting, and compelling. And sometimes you just have to do things you hate in order to eventually do things that you love.

Once you get to a place where you're happy, you feel whole, you feel complete, you feel like you love your life, you actually love being alone—you can have a blast, you could sit by yourself in your house all weekend long, watch movies, do errands, work in your toolshed, work on your car, work in your backyard, whatever it happens to be—when you can get to a place where you really love having fun by yourself, that's when you're in a great place to attract a woman who makes a great complement to your life. It's just like the quote says: you can't give away what you don't already have for yourself. So, do whatever it takes to get yourself into a place where your life is happy, whole, complete, content, and you have enough of everything. Then, you're going to feel no longer like you have to hold back when you're in your relationships, because now you're in an abundance mentality.

LINK: https://understandingrelationships.com/living-together-changes-everything/13626

I'm Not Worth Your Time?

"Breakups are hard to deal with because when we date someone for an extended period of time, our identity becomes associated with being with our ex. Post-breakup, it can often feel like we don't know who we are anymore, because the other person defines so much of our life, our routines, and how we spend our time. It's healthy and necessary after a breakup to be alone and single for a period of time, when another person does not define you, so you can get back to who you were before you met your ex. This enables us to go inward and work on ourselves so, we can become a better version of who we are. When you become a better-quality person because you've worked on yourself, you will increase your value and improve the quality of lovers you are able to attract. However, people who don't focus on getting better tend to attract the same kind of people and relationships over and over." ~ Coach Corey Wayne

I've read studies where it said or it was concluded that the average person takes about a year and a half to get over a breakup with somebody that they spent a couple of years in an intense relationship with. And what that means is a year and a half to get to the point where you're no longer getting up every day and thinking about them, and feeling remorse, or feeling sad, or feeling depressed, or feeling lonely, or being bothered by what happened in the past.

As the old saying goes, "Time heals all wounds," and when it comes to breakups, you're just going to have to take the time to be alone, to get over it, to get back on the horse and start dating, even when you don't feel like it, just so you can go out and take your mind off of things. Because what I've personally found, the easiest, quickest way to get over a breakup is meeting somebody that's hotter, more fun, and easier to be around. It's just like, if you're having a bad day and a smoke show walks by you, you're just enamored by her beauty, and you completely forget about all of your problems or the fact that your last relationship didn't work out. And if you practice and you're ready for those opportunities, even though you might be having a crummy day, you get filled with so much joy on the inside that you think to yourself, "I've got to at least go talk to that girl. Worst case, I don't want to be thinking about her for the next two or three days, kicking myself in the ass, thinking, 'Damn, I should've gone up and talked to that girl. She was fucking amazing, and she looked right at me and smiled.'"

LINK: https://understandingrelationships.com/im-not-worth-your-time/24939

Why We Settle For Less

"Most people settle for a life that is less than what they are capable of living. They settle for mediocre jobs, lifestyles, lovers, friends, etc., because they are driven by their fears and tend to do more to avoid pain and failure than they are willing to risk in achieving the happiness and pleasure they really want and deserve. Everyone has a finite number of days in their lives to create and experience their dreams. Someday, we will all run out of time. No matter what you do or do not do, you will end up somewhere in the future. Doesn't it make sense to move towards a future you want and take the risks to get there, instead of trying to avoid failure or what scares you, since time is going to pass anyway? In life, you're either taking action to shape your destiny, or you're a passenger along for the ride who will someday end up at an unhappy destination." ~ Coach Corey Wayne

The reason why most people don't have what they want in life is because of the story that they tell themselves about why they can't have it. If you don't think you're smart enough, you don't have enough time, you don't have the ability, you don't have the skills, the wisdom, the knowledge, the education, the background, the support group, whatever it happens to be—if that's your belief about yourself, if that's the story that you tell yourself in your mind—it's going to be absolutely impossible to move towards the things you want and enjoy, because your story makes it impossible to move towards that.

LINK: https://understandingrelationships.com/why-we-settle-for-less/24158

Does Age Matter To Women?

"In life, your self-perception will tend to be how others perceive you also. If you perceive yourself as too old, too inexperienced, undesirable, not smart enough, not good enough, not good looking enough, lacking something, etc., members of the opposite sex will tend to perceive you that way also. Why? Human beings tend to act in accordance with their beliefs about themselves, whether those beliefs are accurate or not. The best way to banish limiting beliefs and perceptions about yourself is to take action in spite of your fears consistently to manifest what you really want over time. Eventually, there will be overwhelming evidence in your life of what you wanted but once feared you could not have or become. It's easy to be confident and certain when your dreams are a reality, so sometimes you'll have to take action based upon faith and desire only, and trust that things will work out for you someday." ~ Coach Corey Wayne

You've got to get to a place in life where you like what you see in the mirror every day, and even better, you love what you see in the mirror every day. You talk nice to yourself. In other words, you have nice, kind self-talk. If your self-talk was a good friend that always had a positive word of encouragement and always had some optimism even when you felt down, how would you talk to yourself? This is extremely important. And even when you don't feel like it, by having good self-talk and then busying yourself taking action—the kind of action that is productive, that's essential to achieving your goals—what happens is 10, 15, 20 minutes in when you're taking action, you forget about the fact that you were unhappy, you were upset, you really didn't feel like taking any action, and you just lose yourself in the process of taking action. If you don't feel happy, if you don't feel enthusiastic, if you're having a rough day, the best thing you can do is put your head down and take action doing things that are absolutely essential, things that are on your to-do list that correspond to your most important goals. If you focus on those and lose yourself in the process of doing that, time will fly by, and then when you go home at night before you go to bed, you're going to have peace and contentment, because you did everything that you could possibly do to move your life forward.

LINK: https://understandingrelationships.com/does-age-matter-to-women/14403

Starting To Attract Women

"It's never too late to become the person you were meant to be. Even if you are not very happy, fulfilled, or successful with members of the opposite sex, you can instantly become more attractive and happy by focusing on and pursuing a mission and purpose in life that excites you. Being unhappy and lonely is unattractive and repulses potential lovers. Being happy and single is very attractive and makes everyone notice you more. Even if your goals and dreams are still decades away from becoming a reality, having an emotionally compelling vision and mission for your life will instantly make you more desirable, attractive, interesting, and approachable, so you can start enjoying your life right now, instead of putting your life and happiness on hold while you wait for the perfect moment, which usually will never come." ~ Coach Corey Wayne

If you're not happy with yourself, and your life, and what you do for fun, what you do for a living, and you're not excited about your future, and you're not enjoying being single and enjoying your life, it's going to be very hard to convince other people, especially women, to be excited about spending time with you. That's why you want to get to a place where your life is filled up with people, events, activities, and some kind of life's work that is exciting and emotionally compelling to you.

If you're happy and you're fun to be around, you're going to be fun to date as well. If you're miserable, and you're not happy, and you're hoping that another person will make up for this and make you happy, they might make you happy for a while, but once the infatuation wears off and the honeymoon period is over, eventually, you realize that you're still the same unhappy person that you were before you met them. Do the work on yourself first; that is the most important thing. Find a way to get up every day, to improve yourself, to get better, to learn something, and most importantly, have fun while you're doing it.

LINK: https://understandingrelationships.com/starting-to-attract-women/21964

Life Imbalances Lower Attraction

"Men tend to withdraw, stay single, and/or avoid relationships or commitments when they are having personal, financial, health, career, or business problems and imbalances. In order for a man to feel comfortable in a relationship, open to having one, and allowing a woman into his heart, he must feel like his life is in order, balanced, financially secure, and like he is succeeding at accomplishing his life's mission and purpose. When a man feels like a failure or that success is a moving or elusive target, he may avoid dating, relationships, or any interactions with women that can lead to sex or romance. When men take care of their life, work, health, finances, and areas of their lives that are important to them, their relationships tend to become more stable, loving, balanced, long-term and fulfilling. Sometimes it's better to get your life in order and have more short-term relationships while you do this and have longer-term relationships once your life is in order and balanced. It's healthy and essential to get to know and enjoy yourself when you are not defined by another person." ~ Coach Corey Wayne

I was on a phone session with a young guy yesterday—I think he was 20 years old, and so he still wasn't 21 and old enough to drink—and we went through a scenario with a woman that he had met earlier in the year and made out with at a party. They Snapchatted back and forth for a few days, or a week or so, and then she basically just kind of stopped replying and he never actually got to go out on a date with her. And then, a few months later during the coronavirus lockdowns, he reached back out to her and started messaging back and forth a couple times and asked her to meet up. And then, she told him that she was kind of seeing another guy. And because he really hadn't been practicing what the book teaches—he'd only been through the book once or twice in the past 8 or 10 months that he's been following me—he really hadn't learned the material, and he hadn't done much practicing to get any better.

But recently, he had been on several dating apps, and actually, the night before we talked, he actually went on a first date and hooked up with this girl on the first date. He was still thinking about the one that didn't progress very far that he met earlier in the year. And I explained to him the reason being was, obviously, rejection breeds obsession, and it's also because he hasn't found anybody that he liked more than this particular woman. And I pointed out the fact that he just simply needed to do more interacting with other women, and he also needed to work on his peer group, because all of his friends tend to be shy and insecure around women the same way. And so, what I explained to him without him realizing it is that when he goes out with his friends, he's hanging out with a bunch of guys that give off that same insecure vibe. And it makes it hard for him to interact with women, because he's got guys that are unwilling to read my book and learn the stuff in there and practice it so they can get better.

What I did was I instructed him to start spending more time with guys that are on the same path—guys that are trying to get better and that have the balls to go out and take risks. And where he was at in his life, he wasn't necessarily looking for a relationship; he just wanted to get good at meeting, dating, and picking up women, and seducing them successfully. Because he's so young and he doesn't have a lot of life experience, he really doesn't know what he wants. Therefore, he's got to spend time interacting with, dating, and taking several women through the seduction process so he can figure out what he likes, what he doesn't like, what's important to him, and what doesn't really matter.

He's also in college and he doesn't really have his life in order or stable, and he just doesn't have a lot of experience dating and hooking up with women. He's only got a handful of good experiences so far that he can build upon. And so, in his particular case—much like a guy that's just spent 20–30 years with the same woman and they hadn't had sex for several years, the last few years that they were together—they're going to want to go out and play the field for a while and kind of get used to being single, practicing the things in my book, and getting better at them so they can become competent and very efficient at it.

LINK: https://understandingrelationships.com/life-imbalances-lower-attraction/23105

Get Ex Back: Eliminating Your Competition

"Most men do not understand women. As a matter of fact, 97% of men may know some things about women, but they don't know the things that the most successful 3% know about women. By learning the pickup, dating, and relationship skills in my book, *How To Be a 3% Man, Winning the Heart of the Woman of Your Dreams*, you will be able to successfully attract and eliminate all of your competition from other men who are richer, better looking, and more successful than you are. This will give you choice with women so you can attract the most beautiful, desirable, and highest quality women. You will also be able to make them fall in love with you and keep them in love with you so you can have an easy and effortless relationship. When you know more than most men know about women, this will give you an incredible feeling of peace, serenity, certainty, and happiness that only 3% of the world's men get to experience in their personal lives. 95% of your happiness or your misery is going to come from whom you choose to spend your time with. You deserve the very best in life. By becoming a 3% man, you will be able to manifest and experience the best that life has to offer. That's something to think about." ~ Coach Corey Wayne

Something that's shocking to most guys who have never dated the kind of women they've always dreamed of—in other words, their dream woman—is they often mistakenly think that the right woman is going to finally be the solution and key to all of their happiness in life. And while it's true, women are a great complement to a man's life, there's an infatuation period that usually lasts 6 to 12 months on average with most couples. And for guys that are unhappy, when they start dating a woman and then that infatuation period wears off, they recognize that they're still unhappy, even though they have this great woman in their life. That's why the most important thing you can do to help yourself be successful in a relationship is get to a place in life where you really love yourself, you love your life, your lifestyle, your friends, your family, the people you spend it with, and you have an absolute blast. Because that's why people say a great relationship usually happens when you're not looking for it. What that means is you're having so much fun living your life and being you, that you naturally draw a really great woman into your life, and then she becomes a great complement to it. Because if you're not happy right now being single, you need to do the work on yourself and your life to get you to the point where you do love your life and you are happy. Because only then will you be able to see your woman as a great teammate and complement your life.

LINK: https://understandingrelationships.com/get-ex-back-eliminating-your-competition-2/17727

Having Awesome Dates

"Love is about mutual bonding, connecting, excitement, enthusiasm, chemistry, attraction, giving, receiving, allowing, affection, growing, romance, acceptance, and no holding back. Most people you find attractive will not feel the same way. Most of the people who find you attractive, you simply will not feel the same way. But there's a small number of people you will have animalistic and passionate chemistry with, and this will cause you both to feel like your meeting and being together was divinely orchestrated and meant to be. Most people will never experience this kind of explicit true love, passion, and joy because they do not do the work that is necessary on themselves to prepare and become able to successfully attract their dream lover or lovers. Since they are too impatient and settle for mediocrity out of desperation and fear, they never circulate long enough to perfect their skills and reach their full relationship potential. Once you know what you want, you must be willing to pay the price to make it a reality." ~ Coach Corey Wayne

As I often say, most people encounter between one to three really amazing romantic lovers over the course of a decade, and these are people that you feel instant chemistry with, you complete each other's sentences, and you just get the internal feeling as if you've known them forever, like you already know them. And those people are rare and special. Just like, how often do you meet a new best friend? It's just not something that happens every day. And so, if you're single and searching or you just got out of a relationship, you've got to take time to get to the place where you love being single, you love your single life, it's full of friends, and family, and good things to do, good times, good fun, good activities, things you're passionate about, things that you enjoy. Because it's in the process of enjoying your life and getting to a happy place that you're a happy, whole, complete person, and then you're ready to find somebody else who's a happy, whole, complete person, so you can share your completeness with them.

LINK: https://understandingrelationships.com/having-awesome-dates/24740

I Need To Get My Life Back In Order

"Dating is supposed to be full of fun, mystery, excitement, and romance, not needy, possessive, controlling, jealous, or insecure behavior that is a constant source of drama and complications. Acting inadequate or unworthy is the quickest way to cause the other person to feel like being with you infringes upon their free will and freedom. If you have weaknesses you are working on trying to overcome, you must learn to act in ways that respect the freedom, personal space, desire, and feelings of those you love and those who you want to be loved by. Love is about giving, not possessing or controlling another person so you feel good about yourself. If you don't feel good about yourself or your life, get your shit together first, so you can ensure you're not simply looking for another person to make you happy." ~ Coach Corey Wayne

When you feel good, when you feel positive, when you feel optimistic, when you have hope, and you're able to see that you're making progress. Because success, at the end of the day, is feeling like you are making progress towards accomplishing your grandest goals and dreams, and when you feel like you're making progress, and you see incremental changes slowly but surely getting you closer to where you want to be, this gives you hope, this makes you feel more optimistic.

This also builds your confidence, and makes you smile more, and makes you happier, and makes you more inclined to work out and take better care of your body. This is going to put you into a vibrational state where you're going to be the most attractive person that you can be. Because when you're happy and you feel like you're banging on all cylinders, so to speak, and your life is going well, and you're seeing progress, you're going to be more attractive. Just simply because you're happier, you're going to smile, you're going to be more excited, you're going to notice more things in your life to be grateful for. That's why it's essential when it comes to creating attraction, that you take care of you first. Just like Jim Rohn said, "I'll take care of me for you, and you take care of you for me."

LINK: https://understandingrelationships.com/i-need-to-get-my-life-back-in-order/16867

Online Dating: A Woman's Perspective

"Learn to trust your heart above everything else in life. When something does not feel good to you, it means that you should take a second look, continue your analysis, or that your assumptions may be off. Until you get clarity about what feels right, it usually means that something is off in your assumptions or your plan of action. When you choose the path that is in alignment with your heart and intuition, this will feel right, and your fear of moving forward will disappear. Things will feel effortless, and you will be able to move forward, taking action with certainty instead of fear. Learn to respond to life's circumstances only after careful introspection, analysis, planning, and consideration, instead of reacting upon fear-based impulses and emotions. If it doesn't feel right, something is still not right. Keep searching and keep looking until it does." ~ Coach Corey Wayne

This is about learning to master your emotions and exercising emotional self-control. I remember about four or five years ago, one of my close friends came by to visit me at my office, and we went to lunch for that afternoon. And I remember he was talking about some stock trades that he had been doing, and one of the stock trades had done really well, and he had sold a bunch off. And he was using the profit to invest in some other stock that he thought was going to do really well, and then it ends up going the wrong way. What happened was, we were talking about this, about how to manage your emotional state with something like this, and so, what ended up happening is he started chasing a trade.

He made some bad trades that caused him to lose money, he became fearful that he lost that money, and then, because of it, he became impatient and wanted to do something to make that money up. And so, what happened was, he kept making trades when he was in a fearful state, which typically were not very good trades. And what ended up happening was, it's kind of like gambling at the slots in Las Vegas; he ended up losing most of his money in these trades, just because he became really impatient.

Especially when it comes to stocks, I know me, personally, is I like to buy and invest in companies that I believe in their CEO, in the vision of the company, in the product or service that they are involved in, and that it has good long-term upside. And when you do this, and you do your research, you buy the stock with the mindset that "I'm going to keep this for several years—four, five, maybe even ten years—until it gets to a certain point, and then I'll sell it off and then invest in something else." But I look at it as a long-term investment. I'm looking at stock investments to invest over several years. I personally don't get involved in day trading, even though I know there are lots of people that do it and do very well at it. If you're going to do those kinds of things, you've got to be able to manage your emotions. Because just like my friend who was doing day trading, he ended up losing multiple six figures on these trades because he got too emotionally wrapped up, got into a place of fear, and just made one bad decision after another because they were all based upon fear. It's just simply a bad way to go.

LINK: https://understandingrelationships.com/online-dating-a-womans-perspective/13788

Hacking The Girl Code

"Most of what we have been taught about life, relationships, and success is flat-out bullshit or totally wrong. Society teaches us we should conform and not try to stand out too much or create waves. The reality is, we were created to be spectacular, stand out, and reach our full potential. As Steve Jobs said, 'Everything around you that you call life was made up by people that were no smarter than you and you can change it, you can influence it.' The world is in dire need of leaders who stand out, follow the beat of their own drum, and who tear down the old paradigm of limited ways of thinking, creating, and being. The only things standing in the way of you reaching your full potential are the story you tell yourself about what you can't do, filling in your knowledge gaps, and taking the time to master your gifts, skills, and talents. By mastering and perfecting your passions into skills, you can use them to add value by providing a useful product or service. The more value you add, the higher your income earning potential will grow." ~ Coach Corey Wayne

What Steve Jobs was talking about in his quote about how life is made up by people around us that are no smarter than you or I and that we can change things is that in order to be able to change things, we have to be able to change ourselves. In other words, we come up with an emotionally compelling reason why we want to accomplish, achieve, or have some particular thing in life or experience some particular thing in life. And then, once we have a clear vision of that, then it's a matter of taking relentless, consistent action. And it takes many years and often a decade or more to really make any kind of significant progress towards creating the life and lifestyle you've always dreamed of.

Like Dr. Wayne Dyer used to say, "It's never crowded along the extra mile." What he means by that is most people just simply give up. We're talking about almost 100% of people will give up on the journey to achieving their goals and dreams. And the reason amazing people can do amazing things, like when you look at something like what Tesla has done, that company's been around for almost 20 years. It's really just been the past five to seven years that most people are talking about Tesla and what they've accomplished. They don't see all the tens of thousands of hours that Elon Musk and his team have spent in their day in and day out lives, individually, to make these things a reality. They just see the fact that he's now the richest person in the world and has all this success. But the reality is his success was long in coming.

Everybody laughed at him. Who the hell did he think he was, being some technology guy, and he's going to go up in the car industry and uproot companies like Ford, and Toyota, and General Motors, and all these other companies that have been around a long time and that's all they've done is make cars. Elon Musk is not a car guy; he's more of a business guy and an entrepreneur, or an engineer and a builder, if you really look at it. What he is really great at is using first principles. So, when Elon Musk looked at getting into rocketry and he saw the astronomical amount that it took to launch a rocket into outer space, which was hundreds of millions of dollars, he was like, "Well, what are these things made of? What do the raw materials cost in rocketry?" And what was interesting is he had to go through many contractors and subcontractors and sub-subcontractors before he finally got to somebody that actually made rocket parts. And what he realized was that most of what made rockets so expensive was all the bureaucracy and the paper pushers that didn't really build anything. And so, what he was able to do is to take apart piece by piece in his mind and approach the problem from a completely different angle.

When you look at Tesla and the fact that how does this guy build cars that are way better than anything that the car companies have been building that are over 100 years old? It's because he had a fresh mind, a fresh perspective. He didn't have all this bureaucracy, and he wasn't stuck in the past in the way of doing things. He came at it with a fresh perspective and pretty much built the best car in the world, (as of the time of this recording).

LINK: https://understandingrelationships.com/hacking-the-girl-code/26000

Leaving Behind Those Who Disrespect You

"Every person must make a stand for their own dignity, self-worth, and self-respect when it is consistently violated by those who insist on keeping us small. It is not your job or responsibility to make others feel comfortable with the real you. Other people's opinions of you are none of your business. True friends and lovers embrace, accept, and encourage the real you. Those who do not must be left behind. There is no other way. You'll never be happy or reach your full potential by trying to live up to the opinions or unreasonable expectations of others."
~ Coach Corey Wayne

Once you get to a place where you know who you are, what you want, and you're comfortable in your own skin, displaying your masculinity—displaying the real, true, authentic you without any kind of apology or regret—this is going to give you a state of peace, and ease, and delight. Because we're all surrounded by haters and people that are going to talk shit about us whether they're talking shit about our appearance, the sound of our voice, what we do for a living, how we go about life, what we say, the people we interact with, the lifestyle, or what we do for a living. The world does not have a shortage of people who are going to show up and try to convince you that you suck. That's why you've got to get to a place where you know who you are, what you want, you love yourself, and you love your life. Because when these energy vampires show up, you can tell them to go on down the fucking road and go mess up somebody else's life, that you're not interested. And all that projected self-hatred and self-loathing, they can talk to the hand, because the face ain't fucking listening.

LINK: https://understandingrelationships.com/leaving-behind-those-who-disrespect-you/16879

STANDING UP FOR YOURSELF

Banishing Your Inner Wussy

"No one will ever do or say anything to you that you don't invite them to do. When you fail to stand up for yourself, you are communicating that you don't love yourself and value yourself enough to feel you are worthy of the respect and love of others. Therefore, people will treat you in direct proportion to the amount of respect and value that you have for yourself. If you don't love, value, and respect yourself, other people won't either." ~ Coach Corey Wayne

Whatever you allow into your life, whatever you tolerate, you're sending a signal to the universe to send you more of that. It doesn't matter whether it's good or it's bad. The bottom line is, if you don't stand up for yourself and set and enforce healthy boundaries with other people, they will keep abusing you—whether it's emotionally, verbally, mentally, as well as physically. Bullies never stop until they are forced to, and you have to set and enforce healthy boundaries. Otherwise, you're inviting other people to walk all over you and treat you like a doormat. And the reason other people will treat you like a doormat is it puts you in a position that is beneath them, where they can literally wipe their shoes, their feet, all over you and project their own self-hatred and self-loathing onto you. Because if they're able to push you down lower than they are, they feel better about themselves.

There's a lot of people in this world that go around tearing down other people because, quite frankly, they feel like shit about themselves. So, if they can make other people feel like shit or make other people feel worse than they do, then they actually feel better about their own shitty lives at the expense of other people. Set and enforce healthy boundaries, and if people continually violate them, give them the gift of missing you permanently.

LINK: https://understandingrelationships.com/banishing-your-inner-wussy/14591

The Power Of Learning To Say "No"

"One of the most powerful things you can do for yourself to cause other people to start to respect, appreciate and value you, is start using the word "No." Too many people go along with things they do not like or want to put up with out of their desire to be accepted and loved. When a man won't say no to a woman he is dating or wants to date and instead allows her to walk all over him, she will quickly lose all respect for him and reject him. People who are not really your friends, users, takers, manipulative people, or people who don't really care about you will accuse you of being selfish. Say no anyway. The right people will respect you and stick around. The posers and phony people will simply find others to leech off of and manipulate, thereby freeing you up to attract even better-quality people into your life." ~ Coach Corey Wayne

This is something that, as you start to become more successful, whether it's in your career or in your business—say you're an entrepreneur and you have a business that starts to take off—once everybody else on the outside starts to recognize that you have a successful business and it has a nice, healthy cash flow, you're never going to run out of a stream of people who want some of that cash flow for themselves. They either want a job from you, want to come work with you, they want you to invest in their company, their product, their service. It's just amazing to me when I go and I look at my different email inboxes, all the people that are sending me information trying to get me to do business with them, and just the approaches that they go about it. Sometimes they start out with just insulting me or insulting my business, thinking that, somehow, I'm going to go, "Well, I really need that person my life." The first thing they do is they start acting like a narcissist and telling me that something sucks in my business that I know is working really well. I could tell these guys are using some kind of bullshit sales routine on me, and they have no idea, or no concept, or no clue on how my business functions.

It's the same thing when you're perceived in your personal life as being a fun person to hang out with—a good guy for the ladies to date, a good friend to have—is that you're going to have some people that are going to be drawn to you just because you're a good person and you've got your shit together, but they're not on the same level. That's why it's so important to look at what people do and not necessarily what they say. If you meet people, whether it's a girl or guy, and they want to hang out or spend time with you but they're always late, they jerk you around, they cancel plans at the last minute, they show up ridiculously late, they expect you to change your plans at the last minute to match theirs without any remorse or apology. When you just see little signs of disrespect, that's when you should just give those people the permanent gift of missing you. Let them go fuck up somebody else's life.

LINK: https://understandingrelationships.com/the-power-of-learning-to-say-no/17133

I'm Sorry, But You've Changed!

"Oftentimes in our relationships, out of our own desire to be accepted and loved by others, we change who we are in order to become what we think other people want us to become so we can hold on to what we want, or feel we need from them. This will oftentimes lead to one or both people saying that they felt like they are losing themselves or have lost themselves in their relationships. When you have changed so much of your life and your routines to accommodate other people to gain their acceptance, love, or approval, it can definitely start to feel like you have lost your identity. Relationships of all kinds are best when you enter into them knowing who you are, what you want, and without having to change or modify who you are. Relationships are about sharing and appreciating each other's uniqueness, not conforming to someone else's vision of who you should be or becoming something you are not to please another." ~ Coach Corey Wayne

You're never going to be happy if you're constantly bending yourself into a pretzel and jumping through your butt trying to please other people and live up to their unreasonable expectations. When you try to live your life according to the expectations of other people, there's always somebody who's going to be disappointed. I've talked to countless guys over the years and gotten countless emails where guys changed themselves and did everything that their girlfriends or wives wanted and said that they wanted, and yet, the women were still unhappy. And this is, obviously, incredibly frustrating for guys because they're thinking, "I did everything she said she wanted, and she still left me," "I did everything she said she wanted, and she still broke up with me." And the problem and what caused the loss of attraction is the guy changed who he was in order to please his woman. In other words, he wasn't strong enough with his own internal constitution to stand up for himself and what he believed in, and to set and enforce healthy boundaries, and tell his woman "No."

Everybody should get used to saying the word "No" more often. When was the last time you said "Yes" to somebody just because you didn't want to upset them and did something you didn't really want to do? We all do that too much. You'd be a lot happier if you said "No" more often.

LINK: https://understandingrelationships.com/im-sorry-but-youve-changed/14768

She Canceled Last Minute

"When you allow another to take you for granted, mistreat you, or jerk you around, you are communicating that you feel that you have no value and no self-respect. If you don't have any love for yourself or any self-respect, how do you expect another person to value you when you don't even value yourself? If you want to be loved and valued, you'll have to start acting like a person who loves and values themselves. Healthy self-love leads to removing yourself from people & circumstances that don't honor your value." ~ Coach Corey Wayne

People are going to treat you how you view yourself, because how you view yourself determines what you allow into your life. So, if you want people to be in your life who don't really want to be there, and yet you don't love and value yourself, you'll tolerate when they treat you like a doormat—when they show up an hour late, or they cancel plans at the last minute, or they do disrespectful things to you, and you just put up with it. You allow them to continue doing this to you, which simply enables their behavior. You're literally, through your actions, the tone of your voice, and your words, asking them to continue mistreating you. You've got to set healthy boundaries and hold people accountable to them.

LINK: https://understandingrelationships.com/she-canceled-last-minute/13681

Patience & Inaction Ruined My Life

"Patience is a necessary and essential component to making your dreams a reality and getting what you want in life. However, being patient does not mean that you let people walk all over you, treat you harshly, or that it is justification for inaction. You should pay more attention to what people do and less attention to what they say, as their actions reveal their true intentions and interests. So, whether it's a sales negotiation, a friendship, a romantic relationship, or making your dreams a reality, you must give other people the space and time to do what they say they are going to do and co-create with you. You can't force things or force people to do things they can't or won't do on their own. Therefore, when a person's actions do not match their words, you must let them go and continue seeking and searching until you find someone whose words and actions are congruent." ~ Coach Corey Wayne

If you don't value yourself and love yourself, you tend to ignore when somebody's words and actions are not a match, and then, you make excuses for their bad behavior or their mistreatment of you, because you're so desperate for love and attention and affection. Getting to a place where you love and value yourself is essential if you want to attract people who are a good match for you, not only to date but also to have good friendships with. Same thing when it comes to clients; if you have your own business or you work for other people, and you have a lot of clients who are high maintenance, and they're just assholes, and you put up with it, and you don't set and enforce healthy boundaries, you're inviting more of that kind of behavior and more of those kinds of people.

One of the beauties of the internet and what I've been able to enjoy in my current business versus when I was in the real estate and mortgage business is that I get to pick and choose the kind of people I want to work with. I let my political beliefs be known, I let my spiritual beliefs be known, and I interact with the world in a way that lets everybody know who I am and what I'm about. And if they don't like it, I highly encourage them to go follow somebody else who they jive with. Because the last thing I want to do is spend my time interacting with people that are assholes, who don't appreciate the way I am, or who are just constantly trying to insult and demean me because they're projecting their own self-hatred and self-loathing.

LINK: https://understandingrelationships.com/patience-inaction-ruined-my-life/20665

Why She Tries To Change Your Plans

"The proper way to respond to other people when they try to change your plans at the last minute or jerk you around is to stand up for what you want and let them know you are willing to walk away if you don't get what you want. When people don't value you or your time, they often will do and say things that communicate this. You don't get what you deserve in life, only what you negotiate. When you show you are willing to walk away and never look back when others show a lack of respect or value for you, they will either back up and give you what you want or let you go. If you feel you deserve what you want, do not compromise and take less. You'll only resent it later. Plus, others will respect you more when you stand up for yourself and are willing to walk away, even if they let you." ~ Coach Corey Wayne

So, women will often do this with guys that they're dating and they have somewhat of a low interest in, or the guy was displaying a lot of weakness and communicating that he didn't really have the balls to stand up for himself and what he wanted, including standing up to her. And so, if a woman is unsure of you—if she doesn't really think you're displaying enough dominant, masculine strength characteristics—she'll oftentimes when you try to set a date give you a "Maybe" answer, or "We'll see," or "Call me Friday just to confirm or make sure before our date." In other words, what she's basically saying to you if she communicates this way is that she doesn't really see you as a high-value male. And if she has nothing else going on, if she doesn't find a better offer, she's figuring, "Hey, well, at least I'll go out and get a free meal, because it's better than staying at home with these four walls." But 9 times out of 10, if you agree to one of these "Maybe" dates or a "Confirm to verify on the day of" date, when you finally do confirm, she's going to go, "Oh, something happened," or "Oh, my best friend had a problem, and she needs me to be there for her." You'll get some weird, BS answer.

So, if a woman is not expressing enthusiasm to set a date and lock it in, you've got to withdraw the offer. Tell her something along the lines of, "Well, if you're not sure of your schedule, we can just do it another time," and then don't say anything—see what she says to that. And if she wants to see you but was just testing you, she'll say "No, no, no, it's okay. Yeah, okay, let's definitely make plans then." She'll back up. If she's unwilling to make definite plans, you've got to withdraw the offer. And, if she still continues with the flaky, up in the air response—expecting you to just sit around and wait until the last minute to hear whether or not you're going to have plans with her—if you value yourself and your time, you're not going to let anybody else waste it.

It's the same thing when you're trying to set appointments with a client and they're giving you an "Uh, yeah, maybe I'll come by." If you're in sales, you want to be face-to-face with good quality prospects, you want somebody that's a serious prospect. And if they're not willing to make definite plans, then just tell them to get back to you when they know what their schedule is like and then, therefore, you can schedule somebody else into that timeslot who will actually show up. Because when you're in sales, your appointments that you set, as long as you prequalified these people properly, you're going to have to have a certain number of appointments and not all of those appointments are going to turn into sales. And, therefore, you don't want to be wasting your time or leaving your schedule open to people that just blow you off at the last minute. Because if you act like your time is not valuable, then other people, especially women, will treat you exactly that way.

LINK: https://understandingrelationships.com/why-she-tries-to-change-your-plans/14278

Have Some Self Respect!

"It is demeaning, unloving, and disrespectful to yourself to try and keep someone in your life who no longer wants to keep you in theirs. Relationships of all kinds are only possible when all involved parties want to be in a relationship with one another. When one or multiple parties to a relationship can't or won't make any effort to keep it going, it's time to accept the reality that it is over and move on with your life. You deserve people who would jump fences to be with you, not people who are sitting on the fence or building fences to keep you away." ~ Coach Corey Wayne

Part of what causes people to act and behave this way and to continue pursuing lovers who are not reciprocating interest is the brainwashing that we get from the mainstream media, television, and movies that teach men to act like feminine women and act like creepy, weird stalkers, and eventually, the woman will relent, and fall in love, and want to live happily ever after. If you're coming to a negotiating table and you're negotiating with somebody on the other side who's on an equal footing, you're not to going to just give everything away; you're going to make sure that you get full value for whatever it is that you're selling.

Obviously, when it comes to romantic relationships, you want to make sure that the other person values you and treats you with respect, as if you're the kind of person they want to keep you around and not risk screwing up their chances with. But when you get involved with somebody and they treat you like a second-class citizen and yet you stick around, you actually enable their behavior, and you invite more of that same kind of negative treatment. Remember, no one will ever do or say anything to you that you don't invite them to do. If somebody has a total lack of enthusiasm for you, then you should lose all of your enthusiasm for them, and move on, and find other people who express enthusiasm and who make a mutual effort.

LINK: https://understandingrelationships.com/have-some-self-respect/16756

WTF? She Expects Me To Pay Her Bills?

"You deserve to be loved by and in love with someone who appreciates you for you, not what you can do for them, buy for them, your money, social status, connections, etc. Part of having self-love and self-respect means being able to walk away from people who seem more interested in what they can get from you instead of what they can contribute to your relationship. The purpose of all relationships is that you go there to give. Only spend your time with mutual givers, not those who leave you feeling fleeced emotionally, mentally, spiritually, and physically."
~ Coach Corey Wayne

So, obviously, the intent behind that particular article is a guy that was dating a girl, and she was expecting him to pay all the bills. Now, I don't remember all the details of it because that was written many years ago, but I see this a lot when I do phone sessions with guys. Like, I just had one just recently, a guy met this girl that was long-distance; they were international. He tends to work and travel all over the world, and he likes to date women, especially Eastern European women. And even though he supposedly had been through my book several times, he really wasn't doing what the book teaches. And so, after a few months of interacting with this particular woman over the internet, he had given her a job. And then, she was actually doing the work for him and doing a good job, but instead of keeping the relationship all about dating, sex, romance, hanging out, and having fun, and hooking up, he started trying to solve her problems because he felt bad for her. And so, he's got a situation now where this girl is working for him and he hasn't even met her yet.

And then they finally met, and they hung out together in person, and they fooled around a lot, but they never went all the way. He didn't really understand two steps forward, one step back. Fast forward to when I was talking to him; it was like 6–8 months after the last time he had actually seen her in person, and yet, he had tried to get together multiple times in person, but she was never able to. Even when he was over in Europe and was like, "Hey, I'm here. I'd love to see you," she always came up with things that were more important to get done. And the mistake he made was, instead of interacting with her in a sexual and romantic way, he started engaging with her in a platonic friendship, in an employer-employee type of way, and just totally shot himself in the foot and ruined any chances he would've had to have anything romantic with her. All because he was more focused on trying to do things for her instead of noticing how much she was actually contributing to, investing in, and benefiting his life. She became a net negative, especially on his bank account and his emotional well-being. It's a bad way to go.

LINK: https://understandingrelationships.com/wtf-she-expects-me-to-pay-her-bills/13904

Is It Time To Move On?

"Breaking up is never fun, nor is it easy. Most people tend to stay in bad relationships or relationships that have run their course and need to end way longer than they should. One of our six human needs is certainty. The fear of ending a relationship and moving on is always going to conflict with our need for certainty. If you are involved with someone—be it an intimate relationship, business relationship, or friendship that needs to end—it does not serve you or them to prolong your suffering and unhappiness. Only when you create a space for someone new can you move forward and allow them to come into your life. Resist the temptation to go back and heat up leftovers. If you don't, you'll only delay the arrival of what you really want and deserve." ~ Coach Corey Wayne

I've got a good friend of mine that I've known for probably about 20 years now, and he's one of the smartest, most successful guys that I know, but when it comes to his intimate relationships—especially the fact that I've known him for a couple of decades now and known the different relationships that he's been in—as he's gotten older, as we've both gotten older, he still has the same issue, and that is he always stays in relationships way longer than he needs to. And he kind of complains about it, complains about her, complains about what he really wants, but yet it takes him years to finally end the relationship. And then, take the time to be single, and enjoy his life, and start dating again, eventually, and then, sooner or later, he meets a girl that he really likes, and they get into a relationship. And it's just interesting to watch him go through this in all these struggles, because now, as he gets older, he starts to justify staying in these relationships, even though he knows they no longer serve him.

So, the danger becomes, as you get older, you tend to get lazier; you think, "Wow, my time's running out. This is pretty good." And it's like, I've watched him over all these years, and he struggles with his desire to have somebody, to also have his freedom, and to settle. And because he gets into relationships with women that aren't really everything he wants, because part of his story is, he tells himself that he doesn't deserve to have the kind of woman that he really wants. And so, therefore, that justifies him continuing to stay in these relationships many years longer, after he already started talking about breaking up and ending it.

And, you know, as the years roll by, as the decades roll by, and he spends more and more time with somebody he doesn't really want to be with, it's like, at some point, you kind of give up; you just settle, and you go along with it. And if you're all about reaching your full potential, whether it's a friendship, maybe you've got somebody that's a childhood friend that's been in your life for a long time, but they're just a shitbird, and they're constantly doing things to violate your trust, your dignity, and just cause problems in your life. But because you've known them so long, you feel guilty about cutting them out of your life. But, sometimes, you just have to do this so you can move on and create space for better quality people to come into your life. Because when you stay in relationships with people that are low-quality, you're enabling this behavior—you're putting out the vibration to the universe that you want more of these kinds of people and mediocre relationships.

LINK: https://understandingrelationships.com/is-it-time-to-move-on/14828

Why You Shouldn't Take Her Back

"How does a guy know if he's with the right woman for him? The right woman will be supportive of his hobbies, interests, goals, and most importantly, his mission and purpose in life. Your woman should be your biggest cheerleader and advocate for what you do. A good woman will be proud of you, who you are, and what you do. She will encourage you to go for what you really want, take the necessary risks to achieve your goals, and become all you are capable of becoming. She will relish in your success and only want you to do things that make you happy. If you ever start to date or are dating a woman who tries to change you or who tries to get you to give up all of your dreams and everything that is important to you, instead, give her up and get her out of your life ASAP! Otherwise, you'll only make yourself miserable, she'll continue to be miserable, and you will spend your life living a life that is less than what you are capable of living." ~ Coach Corey Wayne

This is so, super important. In your personal, intimate relationship, the person that is closest to you has to be on board with your mission and purpose in life. If she doesn't like it, if she's against it, if she's offering you resistance, if she doesn't have positive words of encouragement, find a new woman. You can't reach your full potential if you got somebody inside your castle and in your inner circle trying to sandbag your success for whatever reason. Maybe she doesn't like what you're doing or want to do, or maybe she's just a miserable human being; it really doesn't matter. You can't have these kinds of people in your inner circle; you'll never get anywhere that you want to in life. They're like a big, giant boat anchor around your neck. Life is too short to be trying to reach your full potential with a boat anchor around your neck.

LINK: https://understandingrelationships.com/why-you-shouldnt-take-her-back/18454

How Much Contact Is Too Much?

"It's much more fun and effortless to date only people who have a high level of enthusiasm to spend time with you. Sometimes it is possible to raise a potential lover's low interest to become high interest with time and effort, but if you really feel like you are a catch, know you are a catch, and act like a catch, would you really want to spend your time with someone you have to convince of your own amazingness? I think not. The best relationships with the strongest bonds and connections happen when both people really place a high value on spending time together and like each other from the moment they meet. Trying to be liked or to get the attention of other people who do not freely give it is demeaning and disrespectful to you. It's only once you recognize your own value that other people will see it also." ~ Coach Corey Wayne

This really is an art: learning how to interact with people that you want to spend time with, that you want in your life, but also giving them the freedom, the time, and the space to choose you willingly without trying to force things. Because, obviously, if you try to force things with women—you try to force interactions with them, you're trying to figure out where you stand with them on a constant, daily basis because you're worried that they don't like you anymore—these are the kinds of things that cause you to give off the vibe that you're not worthy. And especially when it comes to women, this gets in the way of the process of them emotionally bonding to you, missing you, wanting to see you again, really starting to hunger for you and fall deeply, head over heels in love with you, and want to be with you and only with you.

LINK: https://understandingrelationships.com/how-much-contact-is-too-much/22454

Dating Delusions

"When it comes to potential romantic partners, it's healthy to have an attitude that a person is either in or out. You deserve someone who has mutual romantic interest and enthusiasm towards the possibility of being your lover. Life is too short, and there are way too many romantic possibilities and choices than you could ever explore, experience, or capitalize on. Therefore, continue circulating, seeking, and extending romantic invitations to those you desire. And only spend your time and energy with people who value and appreciate it and who reciprocate romantic interest. Getting hung up on someone who does not reciprocate romantic interest is demeaning to yourself, demonstrates a lack of self-love, and leads to unhealthy attachments that prevent attracting the high-quality partner you want and deserve." ~ Coach Corey Wayne

You want somebody who really wants to be with you. Also, if you're dating a woman and she starts talking to another guy, you're going to have to give her the choice: she's either all in with you, or she can go on down the road to be with that other guy. And the same thing with dating. If you're trying to make a date, you don't want to take or accept "Maybe" dates, because this communicates that you don't really value yourself or your time. And when you take "Maybe" dates, you're telling a woman that you're happy to be in backup position to another guy or other plans that she finds more exciting. And then, you wait around until the last minute, you kept your schedule open for her, and she blows you off for some BS reason and says, "Oh, I'm really sorry. I hope you're not mad"—some kind of BS excuse like that.

If somebody's not absolutely, "God, I'd love to spend time with you," "Yeah, fuck yeah, I'd love to go out with you," "That would be great. That would be awesome," "Let's do it, that sounds like fun," withdraw the offer. And if she won't make definite plans, move on. Same thing with friends, same thing with clients that potentially want to take up your time. The greatest gift that you can give anybody is the gift of your time. Don't let other people waste it.

LINK: https://understandingrelationships.com/dating-delusions/32048

Why Did She Blow Me Off?

"Men who make the mistake of trying to date women who are in relationships with other men are just asking to be jerked around. Women and men who cheat tend to be narcissistic, selfish, weak, insecure, and lack empathy. They show little concern for the feelings of others, and loyalty means nothing to them. People who have lots of choices with potential lovers will never become involved with or put their personal lives on hold for a cheater or a liar in hopes that things will get better down the road. When someone perceives that they have limited romantic options, they often put up with behavior and people who can't or who are incapable of giving them what they want and deserve. Settling for a life or people who are less than what you really deserve is a sure-fire recipe for failure, heartbreak, suffering, and disappointment." ~ Coach Corey Wayne

I see this quite often in my phone sessions, and that is guys trying to have healthy, monogamous relationships with women who have a history of cheating, or women who they started cheating with on their own partners and the woman was cheating on the person that she was with as well. And then the guy is surprised that she's flirting with other guys when things are not going well between the two of them. They think they're somehow going to be different than the guy that they're with because they tell themselves, "Hey, I'm a better guy. I bring more to the table. I'm going to be such an awesome boyfriend that she would never treat me this way." And yet, it predictably happens when things aren't going well.

The reality is, these people who lie and cheat tend to view everyone else as coming from the same place, and given the same circumstances, they would do the same thing. The reality is, in order to have a healthy, monogamous relationship with somebody that will actually be loyal and faithful, that has to be one of their core values. And that has to be a core value, more often than not, that they grew up with in their own family and, most importantly, that they have exhibited in all of their previous relationships. Because the reality is, if they cheat on you with somebody else, eventually when they're not happy, they're going to cheat on you with another person as well. It's just simply delusional to think that you're going to be different.

But if you look at all the movies in Hollywood, you see this all the time; people are in relationships, they're married, they start having an affair, then they each plan their getaway and how they're going to end their relationship with their current partner. And then they finally leave, and then they're together, and they live happily ever after because their love is magical and amazing and spiritually destined to happen. And this is a bunch of BS that you see from Hollywood and the media—it's not real life. When you act like a shitbird and you have a total lack of integrity, you're going to attract other people that have the same lack of integrity. Like attracts like. Water seeks its own level. So, depending on the kind of relationship you're looking to have, make sure that the people you're getting involved with actually value the same things that you do and have the same goals that you do.

LINK: https://understandingrelationships.com/why-did-she-blow-me-off/23345

Love Is Giving, Not Possessing

"Love is about giving and sharing. It is about mutual appreciation and admiration. It's about two people who are happy, whole, complete, and content with themselves and their lives coming together to share their completeness. If you feel like you are lacking something inside of you or that you need someone to complete you or make you happy, you will cause the person you desire to feel like being with you is an immediate threat to their freedom and independence. This will cause them to avoid you, friend-zone you, or reject you outright. Extend your invitation for a date, phone number, or communicate your desire, and allow the other person to accept or reject your invitation without any attachments to the outcome you want. If your vibration and souls are truly aligned, they will accept it. If not, they will reject it. Be happy and proud that you had the courage to take the risk." ~ Coach Corey Wayne

When it comes to intimate relationships or trying to just simply strike up new friendships, you have to extend your invitations to people and give them the space to say, "That sounds awesome," "That's amazing," "I would love to," or "Thanks, but no thanks." Part of being an alpha is being courageous and having the courage to go for the things that you want, and then letting the chips fall where they may. In order to make sure you end up with somebody that really loves, and cares about you, and values you, and respects you, you've got to give them the time and the space to accept you, move toward you, or to move away from you.

Because what you're really looking for is, you're looking for a match. That's what pickup really is all about: "Are we a match?", "Do we have enough in common to warrant sitting down together and having fun on some kind of playful date?" And you want somebody who enthusiastically accepts your invitation, not somebody who has the attitude of "Well, if they've got nothing else better going on, they might give you a chance." You want somebody that recognizes your value fairly quickly, not somebody that you've got to talk into liking you or spending time with you.

LINK: https://understandingrelationships.com/love-is-giving-not-possessing/16930

In Fear Of Losing, I Lost

"In order for someone else to recognize your value, you must first learn to create a life and lifestyle that supports and enables valuing yourself. It's hard to overcome the impulse to tolerate mistreatment and a lack of respect from those you have strong emotions for. Having high standards, setting boundaries, and acting in a way that is consistently congruent with them is the key to making sure you only spend your time with people who value, respect, and appreciate you. Without them, you invite and enable others to abuse, mistreat, and disrespect you. You invite what you tolerate." ~ Coach Corey Wayne

This reminds me of a situation that I used to have with my former business partners. When we all went into business together, (about 22 years ago at this point), after having worked together for almost 2 years, we each brought something to the table. One of my partners was great at finance, and the relationships that he had with our private mortgage investors, and this enabled us to get all of our properties funded in a pretty easy and effortless way. My other business partner was great at sales and selling the properties that we acquired. I was good, obviously, at acquiring and negotiating good deals on properties and figuring out exactly how much work and how much money it was going to take to fix them up. Plus, I'm very organized, and I liked running the day-to-day operations of our business. And so, we had a good synergy between us. But we had agreed to do certain things in how we set up our business and our compensation plans that ultimately weren't really fair to the way I went about acquiring the properties that I had. But because we had an agreement when we went into business together, my other two partners were unwilling to change that or modify it to be fair. And that was part of the impetus that caused me to kind of move away and, in essence, start another company within my company—where we were doing regular retail mortgages, and being a real estate broker, and selling houses, doing loans, refinancing houses, that kind of thing.

And over time, what happened was the agreement was my two partners were going to keep funding money into the retail side of things until it became profitable. Well, after only about two months, neither one of my partners liked the fact that they were investing their money into what I was doing and just basically said, "Okay, well, the retail side of things needs to be profitable and stand on its own." You can't start a business and expect it to be profitable within two months. And so, basically what happened was they altered the deal. And so, it wasn't fair, but I bit my tongue and I started flipping foreclosure properties again after several months of not having done that and leaning on my partners to focus on that and fund it.

And so, it was interesting years later when the companies were all very successful and we were talking about disengaging and going our separate ways. What was interesting was, both of my business partners felt that they owned 1/3 of what I did on the retail side but that I didn't own anything on their side. And what their reasoning was, was "You didn't build it." I was like, "Well, we actually built it together, all three of us. The two of you just continued maintaining it." But that was part of the reasoning behind why I just decided I no longer wanted to be in business with those guys. It's because it was completely unfair considering how much I did and what I brought to the table where I, in essence, had a small minority in my own company, even though 80–90% of the revenue came from the operations that I ran.

And then, years later after we had all gone our separate ways, one of my business partners, he's done quite well for himself (but not nearly as well as I've done). And the other business partner—the older one who has since passed away—he basically spent the rest of his life broke as a joke. The moral of the story is if I hadn't brought all of the value to the table that I did, and it really was their value that they brought to the table, these two would've achieved way more success on their own than they ever did with us. And, you know, I was younger, and I wasn't strong enough to stand up for myself, and I also was in business with a guy who would use physical threats to try to get his way. And after, you know, 8, 10, 11 years of that, I just finally had enough and decided I was going to move on.

But these are things, this is how you learn in life. You go through these trials and tribulations, and sometimes people that are supposed to be on your team want an unfair advantage over you. And sometimes, it's best to just disengage and go off and do your own thing. Because those first several years that I was off doing my own thing and not doing very well at it, they were laughing and snickering and sneering at me. But once things really took off, I had one of my partners—the one that's since passed away—basically wanted to come back into my life and wanted to be a 50% owner of what I had created, and on top of that, he wanted to tell me what I could and couldn't say on YouTube and what I could and couldn't write. And, obviously, I told him in a polite but respectful way that he was out of his fucking mind and there was no way, after all that suffering and all those years of investment of my own capital, that he was just going to waltz right into my life and now own 50% of everything that I built.

You know, I've said many times, people typically don't change who they are—they just become a better version of themselves. And I simply was not going to allow an energy and financial vampire to come in my life and fleece me, because I had learned that lesson before.

LINK: https://understandingrelationships.com/in-fear-of-losing-i-lost/32277

THE POWER OF CONFIDENCE

The Power Of Words

"Most people are not aware of how their negative self-talk, self-perceptions, and limiting beliefs influence their body language, voice tone, and the words they say. People who hold a negative worldview tend to put themselves down, express doubts about their capabilities, talk like they expect to fail, and communicate they lack confidence when talking about themselves to other people. Successful people assume and presuppose things will always work out for them in the long run. They also believe failure, challenges, and setbacks are simply obstacles to be overcome instead of impediments to their success. You should always talk about yourself in an optimistic and hopeful manner, even if you are fearful and uncertain of your outcomes. Successful people even talk about their flaws, failures, faults, and shortcomings as being positive, character-building, and something they are proud to have overcome. Unsuccessful people tend to be defined by their failures and flaws. Successful people tend to be defined by what they have overcome and become." ~ Coach Corey Wayne

We're going to behave consistently with how we view ourselves to be. If we think we're amazing and life is full of awesome possibilities that we can accomplish with enough time, we will act and think in accordance with that belief. If we don't think we have much to offer and don't bring much to the table, we will tell ourselves why we can't or shouldn't do what we know we need to do. We literally talk ourselves out of doing things to help ourselves to move us closer towards our grandest goals and dreams. Whatever you focus on will expand, so spend some time being present with your thoughts. Next time you find yourself bashing yourself and being unkind to yourself, catch yourself and say something nice to yourself. Be kind to yourself, and ask yourself good, high-quality questions. Because the quality of your life is in direct proportion to the quality of the questions that you consistently ask yourself.

LINK: https://understandingrelationships.com/the-power-of-words/25719

Are We Good For Each Other?

"Like tends to attract like. People who like the same things tend to like each other. If there is a part of us that is wounded, needs to be healed, that we deny or are ashamed of, we first need to learn to fully accept and love ourselves as we are, so we can allow others to come into our lives to love us. If we don't do the work that we need to do to accept and love ourselves completely, this will create problems in future relationships, because we won't allow another to love the parts of ourselves that we have not yet accepted or learned to love. If you believe that you are unworthy in some way, shape, or form, then no matter what anyone else does or says to the contrary, you simply will not accept this, believe them, or allow them into your heart. We, therefore, will often stay with people who are a bad match for us because they validate what we feel or believe is wrong with us. People will always act consistently with who they view themselves to be. It does not matter whether that view is accurate or not." ~ Coach Corey Wayne

It's amazing when you become aware of this—when you become aware of how your self-perception and your beliefs about yourself cause you to put up with people and behavior that is simply toxic and not healthy to be around. Like, I remember when I was in my mid-30s and I was getting to that point where I recognized that I no longer had the same internal enthusiasm for the real estate, mortgage, and construction industry that I once had. Now, the relationship that I'd had with my business partners had often been strained or full of drama at times, but I always found, or actually, I should say all three of us found ways to work around that with each other because we were all doing so well financially.

But as the years roll by and you mature and you get to a place where you're comfortable in your own skin and being who you are, I know I speak for myself personally that there were just a lot of people that I was in business with and who I worked with—whether inside my business or externally in my business—that I quite frankly just didn't like dealing with them. I didn't like being around them or being associated with them and putting up with the drama, because I had made so many changes in my life around the time I was 34, 35, 36 that facilitated me having more inner peace and being in a peaceful and relaxed state.

When you're trying to get into a place where you are in a peaceful and relaxed state most of the time during the day, and you get people in your life who are constantly bringing drama into your life, I just started to recognize that I still had a lot of toxic people in my life, and my business, and my personal life, and I just slowly started distancing myself from them. And some of them I booted out of my life completely. Like my business partners, we just went our separate ways. And man, I'll tell you what, after all those years, (the better part of a decade), working with those guys and being in business with them, and then waking up every day not having to focus on avoiding some kind of conflict or doing something that was going to upset either one of them or both of them, it just was very freeing. But obviously, I was starting something new, and I also had the uncertainty of when or if what I was trying to build was going to work out at some point in the future.

But the reality is, all these years later, when I look back 15-16 years beyond all those major life changes that I made in my mid-30s, I'm really grateful for where I'm at now. The people that are in my life bring peace, and ease, and balance, and delight into it. Everybody that works for me, my friends, the people I hang out with, the girls I date, just everything is set up to bring me more peace, more ease, and more delight. Because you're going to do your best work when you're in a peaceful and relaxed state, and you're going to be a lot happier and healthier if you can have as little amount of stress as possible.

LINK: https://understandingrelationships.com/are-we-good-for-each-other/14899

Be Proud Of You!

"People will tend to perceive you how you perceive yourself. As you work to create the life of your dreams, a lot of what you want to accomplish and create may be years and even decades into the future from manifesting. However, if you have an emotionally compelling vision for your life, you know what you want and why you want it, you can then focus on what you need to accomplish day in and day out to make your visions a reality. Most people never reach their full potential because they have lousy success plans, goals that don't inspire them, and simply do not believe in themselves enough to persevere long enough to see their dreams through to reality." ~ Coach Corey Wayne

The idea is to be proud of yourself—to be proud of the fact that you know what you want, and why you want it, and because you're actually taking action to make it happen. Because almost 100% of the people that you're going to encounter in life are just simply not doing that. They're working just to get through the workweek. And the difference that makes a difference between a high achiever and a low achiever is the high achiever is always taking action day after day, week after week, month after month, year after year, decade after decade. They never stop trying to improve themselves and their lives. They're always trying to grow their reserve of knowledge, they're always trying to enhance their wisdom, and they're always trying to do something to get a little better each and every day, no matter what. It is a lifelong pursuit. It is a daily mental battle with yourself. It's a daily mental battle between doing what you know you need to do and being lazy and putting it off. At the end of the day, the time is going to pass, so what you do today or what you failed to do today is going to determine your trajectory in life and where you end up.

LINK: https://understandingrelationships.com/be-proud-of-you/14759

What's Really Important To You?

"Life is a never-ending process of inventing and re-inventing who you really are and building your life around your grandest goals and dreams. You will work the hardest at things you truly love and enjoy. When you do things you love and enjoy, they seem like playing instead of work. Playing and having fun at what you do makes you become really great at it over time. Becoming great at something enables you to add maximum value, maximize your time, and maximize your income earning potential when you find a way to monetize your passions through a career or business. It's a thousand times easier to convince someone to hire you when you have little to no experience if you are excited about their opportunity instead of simply looking for a paycheck." ~ Coach Corey Wayne

As an employer who has hired and fired hundreds of people over the course of his career, when I think about all of the job interviews and people I've talked to where it didn't go anywhere versus the ones I ended up hiring and then the ones I hired who worked out really well, the best employees were always the ones who had enthusiasm, who had confidence, who smiled a lot, and who seemed really eager to come work for me. And so, just displaying enthusiasm and excitement and looking forward to potentially working somewhere, as well as taking the time to take an authentic interest in the people you're interviewing with, and getting to know them personally, and asking the questions, you're actually able to be the one who controls the job interview.

Because in every human interaction, whoever is asking the questions is the one that is in charge of the conversation.

LINK: https://understandingrelationships.com/whats-really-important-to-you/26327

Confidence & Authenticity Vs. Manipulation

"Masculine vulnerability is the willingness to take risks, express sexual interest, and go for what you want without fear of rejection or looking like a fool. True confidence and authenticity is the key to maintaining attraction over time and attracting non-manipulative lovers. Acting disinterested when you are actually interested, ignoring texts/messages/phone calls for days at a time, canceling dates to punish the other person for not doing what you want, or belittling those who you are attracted to will only attract manipulative and low self-esteem lovers, but repulse and repel high self-esteem and confident lovers. You attract how you act." ~ Coach Corey Wayne

Being authentic and true to who you are, speaking your truth, and living your truth without fear, apology, or regret is highly seductive and attractive to women. Because these are the traits of masculine men that know who they are, what they want, and they go for it relentlessly. That's why, if you want to be your most attractive self, you've got to set your life up in a way that enables you to get up every day excited about the day, excited about where you live, excited about where you work, excited about where you play, excited about the people that you get to play and spend your time with. Learning to love your life and create a great life and a lifestyle, instead of painting yourself into a corner and doing everything from the mindset of you've just got to get through the workweek to the weekend, and maybe you can have some fun on the weekend and escape from your shitty life. Women love men who are carefree, who go for what they want and feel like they deserve it. And even if they don't have it today, eventually, whatever it is that they're chasing or after, eventually, with enough time, patience, and repetition, it will be theirs.

LINK: https://understandingrelationships.com/confidence-authenticity-vs-manipulation/16938

Getting Her To Friend-Zone Your Competition

"Women are most attracted to men who exhibit the alpha male qualities of leadership, charm, humor, honor, playfulness, masculinity, ambition, certainty, and a general non-compromising, relentless approach to achieving their mission, purpose, and dreams. Men who are cocky and charming go for what they want without fear or compromise. Why? Because they know what they want, why they want it, they expect to get it and are, therefore, unwilling to settle for anything that is mediocre, second best, or undesirable in their lives. To alpha males, settling is for pussies and people who are too weak to follow their own dreams and goals." ~ Coach Corey Wayne

An alpha male has an abundance mentality, especially when it comes to dating women. Because he views himself as a catch and far superior as far as any other potential options a woman might have. He's also going to want to insist that she treats him like he's her best option, that she is actually extra nice to him, that she goes out of her way to seek his attention and validation. And what's counterintuitive about this and what the article and video talks about that this quote is originally from is, how do you get a woman who has multiple guys in her life to friend-zone the others she's dating and devote her time and attention to you, exclusively? And on top of that, she's the one that asked you to be with her exclusively. And the way you do that is counter-intuitive.

You have to control, obviously, how you show up, and be her best option, and follow the action steps that are in my first book, *How To Be A 3% Man*—going out on one date per week, being direct, decisive, getting to the point, making dates, spending less time on the phone chitchatting, those kinds of things. Because what you've got to recognize is most of the other guys that you're potentially going to be competing against, even ones that are better looking than you, more than likely don't know the information that's in my book. And so, a woman—especially a beautiful woman who has lots of choices and lots of options—she's going to have to whittle down her dating pool to figure out which guy is the most desirable, most masculine, most alpha, and most dominant. The more beta male-type of guys are in a fearful state, and therefore, they're going to try to call and pursue and text more and get her out on more dates more frequently. Whereas the guy who has lots of choices and lots of options, who knows he's a catch, already has plenty of women hitting on and displaying interest in him. So, he's got basically the same problem that she does. He's trying to figure out which girls are worth his time, and energy, and effort. And, therefore, the women he's going to spend most of his time with are also earning his attention and his validation.

So, the way that you get a woman to friend-zone all the other guys that she's dating is you're backing off enough, and you're going slow enough in the courtship—slower than the rest of the guys are—that she starts to wonder why you're not pursuing her as hard as the other guys are. And what happens is, she starts to test all of the men in her life—little tests to see if she can intimidate the guy, feign being upset to see if he backs up and apologizes for something that he really shouldn't be apologizing for. In other words, she's going to test the shit out of all the guys that she is dating and seeing. And, obviously, whoever displays the most weakness determines the pecking order.

And if you're unaffected and you're kind of indifferent to her testing, if nothing really changes how you're showing up and your level of pursuit of her, if you're a high-value man who has lots of other high-value women vying for his time and attention and you've got a girl who is kind of being indifferent and not really making that much of an effort, you're simply going to spend more time with the women who are more easygoing, easy to get along with, and who treat you better.

Whereas, when it comes to women, it's the exact opposite behavior that's going to cause attraction in her towards you and cause her attraction towards the other guys to fall, and eventually, put those guys in friends zone. Because the more she tends to pull away from those other guys that don't know any better, the more they're going to chase, pursue, and try to force things, which is simply going to literally drive her right into your arms. When it comes to dating and attraction, the turtle is always the one that's going to get the victory.

LINK: https://understandingrelationships.com/getting-her-to-friend-zone-your-competition/17130

Are Men Intimidated By Successful Women?

"Masculine energy is all about purpose, drive, mission, succeeding, accomplishing, breaking through barriers, achieving goals, being direct and decisive, etc. Successful and wealthy women tend to intimidate men who feel inferior, unsuccessful, or men who do not have a real clear sense of their ideal purpose and mission in life. If a man does not have a career, business, or purpose in life that is emotionally compelling and exciting to him, he will not feel like he is very successful as a man. He will be more in a survival mode than in a mode of success and abundance. He will have a poverty and scarcity mindset that leads him to believe that he is not enough to make his woman or a woman happy. Therefore, when things get hard in relationships, he will tend to withdraw and leave the relationship because he does not feel successful or avoid relationships altogether. If a man is happy, fulfilled, passionate, and content with what he does for a living, he will feel a strong sense of purpose, inner strength, satisfaction, and confidence. He will feel that he has plenty to offer and give to a relationship without holding back. You can't give away what you don't have for yourself."
~ Coach Corey Wayne

If you don't feel successful at getting what you want in life as a man, it's going to be really hard to create, maintain, and sustain attraction in a woman towards you, because of the fact that you don't perceive yourself as being successful. It's demoralizing when it feels like nothing is working out in your favor, and when a man feels demoralized or like he is a failure, he's going to tend to withdraw into his man cave and want to be alone so he can contemplate and ponder. And if he's not doing the work that is necessary to get his life in order, he's simply not going to be able to maintain any attraction long-term with any of the women he's dating or trying to become involved with. That's why it's essential to get to a place where you feel happy, where you feel optimistic, where you feel like things are finally starting to work out in your favor.

LINK: https://understandingrelationships.com/are-men-intimidated-by-successful-women/16671

Realizing My Own Self-Worth

"People become more attractive when they smile, laugh, or look with confidence into the eyes of someone they find attractive. The happier you are, the better care you will take of your body, the better the quality of food will you eat, the more you will exercise, the better you will sleep, the more successful you will become, the more personal and professional options you will have, and the quicker you will achieve your grandest goals and dreams. When you focus on being awesome, becoming better, and improving every area of your life that is important to you on a consistent basis, eventually, you will realize your full potential. Become the kind of person a dream lover would want to have by becoming an increasingly better version of yourself over time." ~ Coach Corey Wayne

Being 50 years old, when I look at the person that I am today versus the person that I was when I was 20, there's obviously a lot of night and day differences. When I was 20, I was extremely impatient, and when it came to my personal life, I was extremely insecure about what I brought to the table. Deep down, I felt like I wasn't good enough and I wasn't worthy to have what I wanted. And, therefore, in order to make up for that, I tried to force things way too many times. And that caused a lot of setbacks, a lot of emotional heartbreak, and a lot of struggle in my personal life, even though my professional life just seemed to be one success after another. And it wasn't until I got into my late 20s, early 30s that I was finally, as far as my personal life goes, able to fill in my knowledge gap and recognize what I was doing wrong that was consciously and unconsciously sabotaging my success and causing me to display unattractive qualities.

And then, after I had my first relationship with a unicorn type of woman that knocked my socks off, I felt free after that. I felt like I had arrived. And then, I looked back on everything I had experienced up until that point in my life, and I laughed myself. I thought how silly it was, the way I used to think, and I could see how I screwed up every good relationship opportunity with what I considered a unicorn or a really amazing woman in my earlier youth. It really was all a mindfuck—it was all part of the story that I was telling myself. But it took a lot of heartache, a lot of rejection, a lot of failure, years and years and years of failure, to eventually recognize that my approach was not working. And I continued to refine it and try new things, and eventually, enough things clicked and worked, and I was able to figure it out. And then, ultimately, that led to all of the information I put in my first book, *How To Be A 3% Man*.

LINK: https://understandingrelationships.com/realizing-my-own-self-worth/23583

Acting Neurotic Ruins Attraction & Respect

"One of the quickest ways to ruin someone's attraction towards you is to start acting desperate, neurotic, impatient, needy, controlling, or emotional. This behavior is the result of a belief system and model of the world that causes a person to believe, think, and act in a way that communicates that they do not feel worthy, adequate, or lovable. They presuppose that they have already lost and have no chance to get what they want or have what they want to want them back. This shows up as controlling, fearful, and obnoxious behavior that will repulse anyone. They feel like they have to force things in life since they believe and presuppose that no one would ever want to be with them or freely give them what they want. It can become a hopeless loop of desire and disappointment, and therefore, a self-fulfilling prophecy." ~ Coach Corey Wayne

An example I've used off and on over the years in my videos: it's like you go to the zoo, and you have a monkey that's in a cage, and he's bouncing around, throwing his turds and his food at the people in the zoo. He's acting neurotic and crazy. And sometimes people in relationships behave this way as a result of, deep down, they don't think they're good enough. They call too much, they act impulsively and obsessively, and they try to force everything. The phone calls are not phone calls or texts to see how the other person is doing—what they're doing is looking to see if the other person is still interested in them. And what this does is, eventually, typically, in a very short period of time, the other person picks up on the fact that this person is needy and insecure and needs constant attention and validation, typically because they didn't get enough strokes as a kid—they didn't get enough hugs, they didn't get enough 'I love yous,' they didn't get enough 'Atta boys,' and they grew up starved for attention and affection and constantly feeling invalidated. And so, therefore, when they become adults, they behave the same way. They're emotionally conditioned to think and behave only in that way, and therefore, they drive people nuts when they're in a relationship with them. And eventually, this leads to ghosting or being stuck in friend zone permanently.

LINK: https://understandingrelationships.com/acting-neurotic-ruins-attraction-respect/16681

She's Jerking Me Around

"No one will ever do or say anything to you that you don't invite them to do. When a woman senses weakness in her man, she will tend to pull away and test his strength. If he stands up for himself, remains centered, and passes her tests of his strength, then she will come back more attracted and affectionate than before. If he displays weakness and indecisiveness, this turns her off even more, and she will usually back away more also. If a man is fearful of losing his woman, he will tend to try and force things by contacting her more, acting dopey, more feminine, seeking her approval, and constantly needing to know where he stands with her. The confident, centered, masculine man knows women tend to behave more like cats and come and go as they please, and he is okay with that. Smart men let women come to them at their own pace. Men who don't know any better will chase women right out of their lives." ~ Coach Corey Wayne

This is why I place such a big emphasis on a man being focused on his purpose and mission in life, because if he's focused on his purpose and mission in life, he's going to be busy as hell. And all of his free time is taken up with good people, and good places, and good events. And when he's not spending his time enjoying his life, he is working, he is busy making things happen. And when your mind is occupied with the task at hand, you really don't have time to worry about a woman who is not calling you back as quickly as you would've liked or a woman who is not as receptive to getting together with you as you would like. But if you're sitting around, and you've got nothing to do, and your mind is idle, it's going to start to focus on imagining the future. And usually, when you're doing that, you're focused on the future, you're not living in the present moment, and you start to worry, and you build this perception of the pain or potential pain you may experience in the future that is totally irrational and based upon imagination instead of reality.

Just like Dale Carnegie said, "Inaction breeds fear and doubt. Taking action breeds confidence and courage." And when it comes to creating and maintaining attraction with women, being a busy alpha male that has big goals and dreams he's trying to achieve is the best way to put and keep you in that state of mind that you need to be in order to act like a masculine man acts, and, therefore, the woman will be seeking your attention and your validation instead of you seeking hers. A woman seeking your attention and validation is feminine energy. If you're seeking hers, you're acting like a woman acts, and that's why it turns women off.

LINK: https://understandingrelationships.com/shes-jerking-me-around/31107

No Defeat Is Final

"People who feel like they can't get what they want in life tend to be angry and frustrated. When they can't get what they want, they tend to look for people or circumstances they can blame to absolve themselves from any personal guilt or responsibility for their failures and lack of success. Superior people take personal responsibility for their personal growth, successes, failures, and circumstances. Self-reliant people see success as simply the result of infinite patience, sustained self-discipline, personal growth, honing their gifts, skills, and talents, constant learning and improvement, and perpetual focus on achieving their outcomes. Success, therefore, is simply a matter of time and continuous effort." ~ Coach Corey Wayne

We all tend to project what's inside of us. I remember in Dr. Wayne Dyer's *The Power of Intention,* there was a part in the presentation where he talked about an orange. So, when you squeeze an orange, what comes out? Orange juice. Why? Because it's an orange. That's what's inside. And he used the metaphor: what happens when people or life squeezes you? What comes out? Love, patience, kindness? Or frustration, irritation, anger? What about when you see somebody that's more successful than you? Are you happy for them? Do you look at their success as a reason, and justification, and belief that you can do it, also? Or do you look at other people who are more successful than you and feel envy, jealousy, and irritation that they are doing better than you? The key is what is inside of you. Because when we feel pressure in life, whatever we feel inside is what comes out. And we tend to project that onto other people, so we can disassociate from it and absolve ourselves from any blame or responsibility.

LINK: https://understandingrelationships.com/no-defeat-is-final/33146

We Project What's Inside Of Us

"People tend to project what they are thinking and feeling on the inside onto other people in order to disassociate from it and absolve themselves of any blame or responsibility. This is why we should never take anything anyone else says or does to us personally, because they are simply projecting what's inside of them. When people call you names or say mean things, they are reflecting what they think and feel about themselves. When people do nasty things to you, they are treating you how they feel about themselves in that moment. Don't take assholes seriously, and don't take their insults personally. Why? It's not about you. It's about them." ~ Coach Corey Wayne

This, to me, is one of the most powerful things that I've learned through studying different spiritual traditions and studying self-help. Because everybody that's listening to this, at some point in their life, has been treated harshly by other people who've just been absolutely nasty motherfuckers to you. It's something that we all have to deal with. And when you recognize that no one will ever do or say anything to you that isn't a direct reflection of how they feel about themselves in a moment, you start to recognize that it has nothing to do with you. For whatever reason, they perceive you as being weaker, they perceive you as being a doormat, and, therefore, you can be the object of their projected self-hatred and self-loathing. And if they're able to project that self-hatred and self-loathing on to you, and then you take ownership of it, you're influenced by it, you're diminished by it in any way, they feel better.

They then feel like they're the good person and you're the horrible person that they said all these nasty things to. At the end of the day, whatever comes out of their mouth, it is their story, not yours—don't take any ownership of it. It's like the Buddha once said, "If somebody gives you a gift and you do not accept it, to whom does the gift belong?"

LINK: https://understandingrelationships.com/we-project-whats-inside-of-us/25680

Pickup: The Non-Approach Approach

"It is a man's job to be direct, decisive, and take advantage of the opportunities that the universe brings to him when he encounters women he finds attractive, by either getting contact information or making a date on the spot. Most women are not going to ask a man out for a date when they find him attractive, because that is the man's job in the social interaction. However, most women will put themselves into a man's orbit to get his attention when they find him attractive by approaching him, asking for his advice or opinion, standing near him, asking other people about him, making eye contact while they smile, playing with their hair, or physically touching him. Guys who are shy and terrified of rejection should take the lazy man's way of picking up women: by focusing on having a good time, taking up too much space, exhibiting alpha male body language, smiling, laughing, and being 100% present with people they are engaged in conversation with. If they do, this will cause them to appear approachable, comfortable with themselves, happy, successful, content, safe, fun, likable, desirable, and like a man who is already very successful with women and who has lots of choices with them. Men who are successful in life and with women always get approached by women due to their non-hungry and abundant state of being." ~ Coach Corey Wayne

Most guys have had this experience that, when they're single, it's hard to find women to date or women who have interest in them. But as soon as they get into a relationship or have a girlfriend, it seems like women are always approaching them and talking to them and wanting to interact with them. They think to themselves, "Where the hell were are all these girls back when I was single?" What they don't realize is their vibe has completely changed once they're in a relationship. They give off a more relaxed vibe—a vibe of abundance—because their needs, their wants, and their desires are being met by the women, or woman, in their life, and other women can pick up on this. Men who have their shit together emotionally, mentally, spiritually, and physically give off a completely different vibe than guys who are insecure, who lack confidence, and don't have their mission and purpose in order.

That's why, as I stress in my first book, *How To Be A 3% Man*, being attractive to women really boils down to exhibiting attractive behaviors by developing yourself, by focusing on taking care of your body, by focusing on creating a great life and lifestyle, and having some kind of purpose or mission in life that is emotionally compelling and exciting to you. Because, as you take care of your own life and you build it out to be a great life that you're happy with, and happy about, and proud of, other people are going to take notice. You start giving off the kind of vibe that a champion or high-achieving athlete gives off. Everybody wants their attention. Just like a famous person does. They walk into a room, and everybody assumes they're an awesome person, women assume he's an awesome guy to date, because he's been able to climb the corporate ladder, so to speak, and achieve and succeed at the highest level.

That's why being successful with women is not so much about approaching them or what you say or what you do—it's the vibe that you give off that is a direct result of how you take care of yourself, develop yourself, and create a great life and lifestyle that you're proud of. When you do this, meeting women just simply becomes a side effect of having your act together as a man.

LINK: https://understandingrelationships.com/pickup-the-non-approach-approach/19028

I Never Do This!

"Men who know how to act like real, masculine men and who are comfortable in their masculine energy are very rare. This is because most men vacillate back and forth in an unbalanced way between being in their masculine and feminine energy. They are so rare, most women hardly ever encounter them, and when they unexpectedly do, they often become unsure of themselves but love letting the men take control and lead their interactions. When a feminine woman is in the presence of a masculine man who knows how to lead and be a real man, she will feel safe and comfortable enough to relax, let go, and become totally submissive to his lead. Unfortunately, most men will never get to experience this kind of submissiveness, playfulness, and sexual polarity with women. A man who wishes to become the type of man all women dream of should focus on cultivating his own masculinity by focusing on his mission and purpose in life, taking care of his body and being healthy, and creating a great life and lifestyle, full of fun activities and people. This will naturally and effortlessly attract the right kind of women into his life that match and mirror who he becomes when he is at his best personally." ~ Coach Corey Wayne

The most important thing that you can do to make yourself the most attractive man you can be, (or woman, if you are a woman), is to focus on reaching your full potential—getting to a place in life where you're doing some kind of life's work that you love, and you enjoy, and you have a passion for, and that you surround yourself by like-minded people who are also positive and optimistic. Because the happier you are—the more things in your life are there by your design and by your choice—the better you're going to feel about yourself, the more confident you're going to feel in yourself.

Self-confidence is sexy to both men and women, and we all respect other people when we see that they have a lot of self-confidence as well. Self-confidence comes from knowing what to do and doing it really well, and this simply comes from time and repetition. Time and repetition make us excellent at something. When you look at somebody like Tom Brady, when he walks in the room, he just has a presence about himself. He's confident, he's happy, he loves what he's doing. There is no place that he'd rather be on earth than out on the football field with his teammates playing football.

LINK: https://understandingrelationships.com/i-never-do-this/26589

True Friends Want The Best For You

"True friends build you up and support you no matter what you choose to do. People who are jealous of you, who want to be you, who envy your success, or who hate themselves are going to frequently get offended at you being you. You can't please everybody. Some people go through life looking for reasons to be offended. Instead of trying to change who you are or be something you are not in order that you don't offend people, be yourself and let the chips fall where they may. Why? Despite your best efforts to not offend or insult people, it's going to happen anyway. So, instead of making yourself miserable trying to live your life according to other people's expectations, be happy, and don't associate with people who always find reasons to get offended. It's THEIR PROBLEM, not yours." ~ Coach Corey Wayne

I had an old business partner of mine that I was in business with for many years back when I was in real estate. We stayed friendly after we split up and went our separate ways, and he actually stayed in the real estate business for a period of time. And then I, obviously, completely went in a new direction and started my life coaching business and becoming self-published author. And I remember when I was about four years into it and things were really starting to take off for me and things were going well, I did a YouTube video with him where I was exposing my YouTube audience to his music to help him grow what he was doing. And we'd been hanging out and having a few beers, we were having a good time, and I filmed it. And we were dropping F-bombs like we always do, because this is just how we were around each other. Ans so, he went and he posted that video on his Facebook of the four or five songs that he had played in the video. And some of his churchgoing friends saw that and heard the cursing, especially my cursing, and got butthurt and offended at that.

About a week or two later, we were hanging out, and I was expecting him to be excited about all the feedback that he got from my audience who saw it and liked it, and emailed him, subscribed to his email list, whatever it happened to be. But instead, he came out to tell me that I needed to clean up my act on YouTube. And I shouldn't be talking that way, and he was expecting me to edit out all those bad words. And he went on to tell me that he thought we should go into business together, and that we would make a lot of money together, but, you know, that I needed to clean up my act and start behaving in a way that he felt was appropriate, because he was worried about what other people thought about him.

And I was pretty stunned at this. I wrote about this extensively in my second book, *Mastering Yourself*. But he proceeded to go on and tell me that we should be equal business partners in my business, and he was basically going to have the final say on what I could and couldn't say on my YouTube channel. And this was absurd to me, because he never invested a dime. He wasn't the guy that had slept on his father's couch for 4 fucking years and waited tables for 10 months and dumped all of that money into the business to make it a success. And now that it was really starting to take off and do well, he wanted to step in when all the hard work was done and be a 50% owner and, on top of that, start telling me what I could and couldn't do.

I obviously let him know in a respectful but firm way that I really didn't care what other people thought about me, and if they were going to choose to be offended or they didn't like my language, there were literally millions of other YouTube channels that they could follow. I remember he said, "Well, what about decency?" And I said, "Well, who gets to decide what is decent and what is not?" I said, "If people don't accept me for who I am," (you know, at the time I was, like, 43 years old), "they can go fuck themselves. I really don't care."

"People either like me, love my work, or they can't stand me, and they go somewhere else. I would rather the people that don't like me, don't like how I talk, the way that I look, the sound of my voice, the way I explain things, whatever it happens to be, I would rather they go on down the road. And the people that really do value and appreciate me, those are the people that I want to work with." Needless to say, that was the last time we ever spoke, and he passed away a few years ago being totally broke and never reaching his full potential in his music career.

LINK: https://understandingrelationships.com/true-friends-want-the-best-for-you/13941

OVERCOMING STRUGGLE

Letting Go Of The Past

"Letting go of the past so you can move on in life is more of an art than a science. It would be nice if we could turn off our negative emotions and feelings so we would not have to experience them, but experiencing pain is how we learn from our mistakes and become better versions of ourselves. We must feel our pain in order to learn from it, heal it, and overcome it. It is the collective accumulation of life experience along our journey that acts like the tools and instruments of life that refine, polish, and perfect us, just like pressure and heat perfect a diamond." ~ Coach Corey Wayne

Pain is also life's way of letting us know that what we're doing or how we're approaching things is not optimized, ideal, or potentially is incorrect. Whether it is pain showing up in your body or emotional pain mentally showing up in your life, when you experience pain, it's something that you should listen to. There is a reason for it; it's showing that there is resistance. Maybe it just means there is a simpler, easier way to optimize what you're doing, and you need to be looking for other alternatives. Maybe the way you're taking care or not taking care of your body is causing pain. Just like going to the gym and doing an exercise and not using proper form, there is a good risk for injury and experiencing pain as a result of that injury. Pain is a great guard rail of life, so when you experience pain, whether it's emotional or physical, you should pay attention to that. Because if you continue to ignore it, the pain will tend to get worse, and so will the damage if you continue to ignore it.

LINK: https://understandingrelationships.com/letting-go-of-the-past/19950

I Manipulated Her Into Marrying Me?

"Life's disappointments, setbacks, and struggles are there to teach you patience and lessons essential to your success in the future. You won't see the dots connecting to your future success until you're able to look back upon the path you took to succeed once you achieve your goals. Trust that everything good and bad is happening in your life in order to shape you into the person you need to become to fulfill your destiny and reach your full potential." ~ Coach Corey Wayne

I'm almost 51 now, and when I look back on my life, everything seems like it just kind of magically lined up. It was like the perfect experience, the perfect people, the perfect circumstances all seemed to show up right on time. At the time that I was going through my life, obviously, and running into challenges, it just seemed often like life was against me—like I was going up against insurmountable obstacles and challenges. But when I look back on it now, obviously, it all seems like it was perfectly aligned, and it was a beautiful life path. But like I said, when you're going through difficult times, it's really hard to see how these bad things that may be happening to you are actually, in the long run, going to be good for you. These difficult challenges, failures, and setbacks that you have in life, they all teach you something. Oftentimes, they obviously are teaching you what's not working, what's not optimized, and what's not ideal. That's why I keep coming back to focusing on "What do I have to do today before I go to bed in order to get myself a little closer to where I want to be and get a little better than I was yesterday?"

LINK: https://understandingrelationships.com/i-manipulated-her-into-marrying-me/13732

Crazy Women You Should Avoid

"We are a byproduct of our parents' limiting beliefs, fears, biases, blind spots, and flaws. Much of our early adulthood is often spent trying to overcome the parenting mistakes of those who raised us. Most people are not aware of this truth of life, and therefore, spend no time on trying to overcome their flaws and shortcomings to become a better version of themselves and to become the person they were meant to be. This means there are countless potential toxic friends, lovers, and acquaintances we must avoid in order to reach our full potential. Finding great lovers and friends is as much about dealing with our own flaws as it is about finding and identifying the flaws in others, so we can avoid them and the toxicity they will inevitably bring into our lives if we allow them into our inner circle. A large part of our happiness or misery is the result of the people we spend our time with. Choose wisely." ~ Coach Corey Wayne

We have to be aware that, oftentimes, how we react to other people, especially in our intimate relationships, is that we're not necessarily reacting to their behavior and how they're showing up. We're reacting to somebody in our past—usually a parent, somebody close to us, or even a family member. And because we became emotionally anchored to how they showed up and are responding in the way that we learned in our family, (which is oftentimes dysfunctional), when we encounter somebody in our life when we're an adult and they make us feel the same way, we react to them in the same way that we were programmed in childhood. And you have to recognize that a lot of this is unhealthy. Because we hold people accountable to, and we blame them, for things that other people have done to wound us or hurt us in the past.

You often see this in relationships between men and women. If a guy has been cheated on, he's going to be extra suspicious of women that he dates in the future. And so, he's looking for evidence that she's being unfaithful, that she's lying to him, that she's deceiving him. And if something happens where she does something that's kind of similar to what the one who cheated on him in the past did, he automatically assumes something nefarious is going on and accuses her of it. This creates a lot of unnecessary drama and problems, because instead of reacting emotionally and having a nasty outburst, he should be calm, think about it. If he's really irate, he needs to back off and say to himself, "Well, maybe I'm overreacting. Maybe I'm misperceiving this situation. Let me talk to her. Let me ask her some questions and find out what was really going on, and we can discuss it in a calm, relaxed manner." And that's the appropriate way to handle these things.

LINK: https://understandingrelationships.com/crazy-women-you-should-avoid/37029

Contemplating Life: 1 In The Chamber

"Nobody likes to experience physical or emotional pain or to have unpleasant life events. The reality is life is not all sunshine and roses. Challenges and pain are life's way of letting you know that your current approach is not working, not optimal, or needs improvement. Pain and hitting the wall metaphorically are what usually causes us to move in a new or different direction. When you are on the right path, things seem to flow and be more effortless. When you accept your current circumstances, where you are in life, and can find joy in your journey, only then can you live in the present moment and appreciate the little things. When you don't accept your present reality and wish that it were different, you will experience pain and suffering. The best way to get out of a rut is to surrender to where you are, accept it, and keep grinding towards what you want, no matter how many decades it takes to get there. In life, pain is temporary, but quitting lasts forever." ~ Coach Corey Wayne

Over the years, I've gotten many emails from guys who are vets who literally said that my book and my work help them to keep from eating a bullet. In other words, putting the gun in their mouth, and pulling the trigger, and ending it all. The reality is, a lot of guys that go through traumatic experiences in war never have the time or take the time to really get into the emotions of whatever they're feeling and deal with it. Because when you're in combat, you don't have time to be upset. You have to focus on the process of what you've got to do to contain, suppress, and kill the enemy that's trying to kill you.

And, obviously, as men in our society, we're taught not to feel. And what happens is, as we grow up and we don't feel comfortable or safe enough in our own body to experience our own suffering and surrender to it, like I talk about in the quote, what happens is, you resist it. And what you resist persists. The only way to get out of suffering and emotional pain is to let go and surrender to it. In order to get out of pain, you have to get into the pain. And when you surrender to it, you're giving yourself permission to feel the negative emotions, the negative thoughts, the negative feelings, and by stating what you feel: "I feel like shit," "I feel like my life's over," "I feel like an ultimate failure," "I feel like things are never going to get any better," "I feel like it's never going to work out," "I feel like I have to do everything on my own."

Sometimes, it feels like nothing works. And what you have to do is you have to give yourself permission to really get into the pain—not run from it, but to embrace it, to be grateful for it— "I'm grateful for my negative emotions," "I'm grateful for feeling like I want to end it all right now." Because the reality is, these emotions are really just stuck energy. It's energy that's stuck in your nervous system that you never dealt with, and you never released, because you never gave yourself permission to do that.

If you look at how children deal with emotions, children authentically experience and embrace their emotions. That's why they're happy and giggling one moment, and then screaming and crying bloody murder the next when they get a little scratch, or they bump their knee or their head, or whatever. Kids authentically experience the emotion—the joy, the happiness, the sadness, all of it—and it moves right through them just as quickly, in a wave, as it came. And as adults, when we have years and years of trauma or unexperienced emotions that have welled up, sometimes it's good to just sit inside by yourself, put a pillow over your face and cry. Experience your emotions, speak whatever the feelings are—don't judge it, don't run from it. Just understand that it's stuck energy.

It's energy that's stuck in your nervous system, and it needs to move through your body. And the only way that it can move through your body and dissolve is to get into it. And it doesn't mean you're going to get into it, and then you're never going to feel it again. The more you get into it, and the more you give yourself the experience to just suffer and feel whatever it is, and feel like it's hopeless, and feel like it's never going to get any better, what happens is, the first few times you do this, you might be feeling miserable for 10, 15, 20 minutes, a half-hour, whatever it happens to be, but it's a process.

Think of it as a pressure relief valve on a hot water heater; you're slowly relieving the excess pressure, and once all that excess pressure has been released, you're mostly going to feel relaxed, at ease, content, and peaceful, which is really our natural state. But, sometimes, you're going to have to take the time to suffer. So, you've got to get into it before you can get out of it, because if you don't—if you resist it—it's only going to persist.

LINK: https://understandingrelationships.com/contemplating-life-1-in-the-chamber/27478

Men Only Care About Sex!

"Many women often complain that men only care about sex. It is true that some men are only interested in casual sex and dating affairs, but when a woman has a knowledge gap in her pickup, dating, and relationship knowledge, she will often consciously and unconsciously make bad choices in the men she chooses to date who are exactly the kind of men she's trying to avoid. Why? What you fear, you attract. The world would be a much happier place if everyone had a basic understanding of what causes, grows, and maintains sexual attraction in both men and women, why men and women do what they do in their intimate relationships and interactions, and how to consistently make the right choices to achieve their dating and relationship goals. When you are continually getting bad results in any area of your life that is important to you, you must realize your strategy sucks and change your approach, or you will continue to get results you are not happy with." ~ Coach Corey Wayne

Most people—men and women both—put more thought and research into buying a car than they do the people that they date and get involved in relationships with. Because human beings tend to make their decisions based upon emotions, and then they use logic and reason to justify those decisions. And so, if you don't really understand how attraction works, and you've never really studied the topic, you're going to tend to go from one emotional interaction to another. And if you grew up in a dysfunctional home like I did, your emotions are going to be dysfunctional.

When I was younger, I would get hung up on women that weren't available, because that reminded me exactly of the relationship that I had with my own mother, where I wanted love, I wanted affection, and I never got it. Most of the time, the attention I did get was when I was getting my ass kicked because I did something wrong. And so, I was starved for emotion. I was starved for affection. And so, how this played itself out in my early to mid-20s was that I would get hung up on or involved with women that weren't unavailable or had boyfriends, think I'll just be the friend for a while, and then, once it doesn't work out with the guy that she's always bitching and complaining about, then I'll finally get my chance. And then she would be single for a while, and I would think, "Well, I can't ask her out now, because I don't want her to think that I'm only interested in sex" And I would wait a few weeks, or a month or two, or whatever it would happen to be, and then, when I would finally get the nerve or the courage up to do something about it, she'd start telling me about a new guy she met. And I was like, "Damn."

And so, the belief that I had was I wasn't worthy of love, and so I became emotionally anchored to these women that simply weren't available, because it felt, emotionally, just like the relationship that I had with my mother. And it was, obviously, not until I got into my late 20s that I connected the dots, and the lightbulbs went off that I recognized how that was causing me continually to get hung up on girls that weren't available and take myself out of the dating market, because

I was waiting for a woman who was unavailable to eventually become available.

I wasted a lot of years, and I missed out on a lot of really great opportunities back then, and that's why I love when I hear from younger guys that learn from me, learn from my mistakes, they don't make all the same mistakes, and they have nothing but great memories from their teenage years, their early 20s, and so on. And it's like everything I went through, it's like it had a purpose, and it's able to help other people avoid the same stupid mistakes that I made. You can't go back in time, and you can't get that time back.

LINK: https://understandingrelationships.com/men-only-care-about-sex/23411

Pickup & Approaching By The Numbers

"In sales, success comes from knowing your product or service, creating rapport with your potential prospects, meeting their needs and asking for the order. When it comes to dating, successful guys are simply willing to fail and get rejected more than the average guy who wants more success with women. The harsh reality of life is that most employers will not want to hire you, most people you meet will not become your best friend or even an acquaintance, most women will not want to date you, but accepting the reality that you will be rejected way more than you succeed, in every area of life, will help you to accept the truth that life is most often a simple numbers game. You must be willing to get rejected and get through the Nos in order to get to the Yeses." ~ Coach Corey Wayne

You really have to take kind of a sales approach to life, to the women you date, and to the employers who you seek out employment opportunities with. The same thing comes with business if you're an entrepreneur. I remember, in the 90s I had several friends that wanted to, (or at least they said they wanted to), invest in single-family homes, fix them up, sell them for profit. And I must've gone through probably 15 or 20 different people that were either close friends or they were acquaintances who were very enthusiastic—"We're going to do this," "We're going to do that," "It's going to be exciting," "We're going to make a million dollars"—but when it actually came down to making an offer and trying to buy a property and following through with it, none of them actually followed through with it. And that was something that was interesting to me. I just looked at that as "I just haven't found the right people to go into business with."

And ultimately, if you've read my second book, *Mastering Yourself*, I finally did come across two guys who were great business partners for a lot of years despite the fact they had a lot of flaws. There was plenty of drama, and eventually, after 10 years of being in business together and making a lot of money together, we all decided to go our separate ways. But the difference was these guys stated what they were going to do, they were already doing it on a daily basis, and then they followed through with their commitments. And so, when we went into business together, we made a $60,000 profit our first month in business, because everything, all of the tasks that we were supposed to do, was very clear. We had a clear business agreement on what everybody brought to the table and was responsible for, and it worked really well together for a lot of years, but, you know, eventually, we grew, we changed, and we went in our separate directions.

It's the same thing when it comes to dating women and prospecting. You're going to be getting failure after failure, rejection after rejection. You go out on dates that really never go anywhere. You go out on three or four dates with a woman, and then you find out there's an ex in the picture, (or that's coming back in the picture), and she decides to pursue things with him, and then you're back at square one. And then, all of a sudden, after many months or a year or two of just seemingly, like, nothing really gets any traction, you meet a girl who's easy, who's effortless, who does what she says she's going to do, who means what she says, and things just kind of flow together naturally. And by that point, you've practiced so many of the things that are in my book, *How To Be A 3% Man,* that you just naturally and instinctively know what to do to no longer talk women out of liking you who are already predisposed to like you.

So, it's important to look at life, friends, lovers, employment opportunities, business, and entrepreneurial opportunities if you're in any kind of sales, is that you're always prospecting. And you have to interact with enough people on a consistent, regular basis in order to sort and qualify the people that are coming into your life, to find the right people that are perfect for what you seek to experience or create in your life.

LINK: https://understandingrelationships.com/pickup-approaching-by-the-numbers/32380

Be Happy For Your Ex

"Most people tend to stay in relationships that no longer serve them or offer them any more opportunity for growth way longer than they should. If your lover dumps you, they obviously have done you a great favor. Why? They simply recognized before you did that it was time for it to end. If you are truly honest with yourself, on some level, you know this to be true. It's never easy to move on from a breakup. It does not matter whether or not you were the dumper or the dumpee. In life, relationships, careers, friendships, partnerships, circumstances, etc., dissolve when it's time to give birth to something grander and more suited to the next chapter of your life. Your ability to recover, move on, and see the gift and value in things falling apart will determine how long it takes for someone new or better suited for you to come into your life. Before you can attract someone new, you must first be ready, willing, able, and open to attracting someone new. The more resistance you offer to moving on and letting go of the past, the more you will suffer and hinder the manifestation of someone better coming into your life." ~ Coach Corey Wayne

Most of the time, when it comes to breakups and divorce, statistics show between 70–75% of the time it's women who initiate the breakup or the divorce. And since most of my coaching clients are men, a lot of times I'm talking to guys who got served with divorce papers, or whose girlfriend up and left them, or a woman they were dating stuck them in friend zone or has kind of drifted away. So, they basically were the dumpee instead of the dumper. And what's interesting about that is when you get dumped unexpectedly, or when it wasn't of your choosing, is that it causes your interest level to double. And as the saying goes, "Rejection breeds obsession." Guys will go from being lazy and complacent and not really making an effort into their relationship, and then they get dumped and they think that they've lost the love of their lives.

One of the first things that I do with them when I'm doing a phone session is to bring them back to the time and the months leading up to the end of their relationship when they weren't putting their best foot forward. Because the reality is, if they really felt it, they'd be making more of an effort to keep the relationship together. But as it was, most of them were just kind of half-assing it and thinking everything was fine, when in reality, their lack of effort is indicative of how they really felt about the person they were in a relationship with. And as I always say, a person's actions are a true reflection of their intent, more than their words are. And so, by bringing these guys back to the time before the breakup happened, I can help them objectively look at the fact that they really weren't making the effort that they needed to, to make the relationship work and last.

And then, the question is, "Why is that?" What was missing? What was the reason behind them not making the effort? Because even when these guys eventually get these women back, they don't stay with them long term, because everything that turned them off before is still there. The woman didn't magically become a different person overnight. And so, if you're in that situation, always look at how you felt in the weeks and months leading up to the end of the relationship. And if you weren't putting your best foot forward because you weren't that into it, then just remember your feelings of feeling like you just lost the love your life is really just rejection breeding obsession.

LINK: https://understandingrelationships.com/be-happy-for-your-ex/17195

Heartbreaks, Rebounds & Moving On

"Everyone has had their heart broken at some point in life by someone they loved. Heartbreaks are a part of life. The reason why we suffer so much after a heartbreak is because we have become attached to the person we loved, and our identity becomes associated with being with them. That is why we often no longer feel like ourselves after a breakup. We suffer when we want reality to be other than it is. The key to moving on is to let go of what was and take the risk of getting hurt again by dating someone new. However, to avoid emotionless rebound relationships and unnecessarily hurting others, make sure you actually care about and desire those who you get involved with. Have empathy and concern for the feelings of others, and never lead people on or use them as an emotional crutch when recovering from a breakup." ~ Coach Corey Wayne

Any time you've had a breakup, you've got to take time for yourself to heal, to get your life back to normal, to get back to being the person you were back when you were single, before you met your previous ex. Sometimes, this takes many months and maybe even a year or two. Sometimes, if it was a shorter relationship, you can get over it in a few weeks, especially if you were the one that did the dumping. Because it always feels better to be the dumper than to be the dumpee.

Rejection breeds obsession. And when we are not the ones doing the dumping, but instead are the dumpee, what typically happens is this doubles our interest in the other person, because we don't have control over what's happened to us. And if we weren't ready to end the relationship, even though we may have been thinking about it or seen it coming for a long time, all of a sudden, now we think we've lost something that was really, super important to us. And what's interesting is when it comes to divorce and breakups, women 70–80% of the time are the ones that are doing the dumping, so most guys are usually the ones that are experiencing getting dumped. And the most important thing when each relationship ends is that you want to learn from it. What kind of wisdom can you take from it? What kinds of things or characteristics or personality traits did the person that you were with have that you loved, and what personality traits and weird quirks and kinks annoyed the hell out of you?

Because as we date and interact with other people and have relationships with them, we start to learn what's most important to us and what is really not that big a deal. And so, every relationship, every friendship, every customer we interact with, there is a gift that you have to give them, and they have a gift to you, in the form of the interaction and what you can learn from how you treat each other. And so, by learning and reflecting upon what we like and don't like, that can help us focus in the future, so we don't attract somebody with the same flaws, and we can attract somebody that had the same good characteristics that we liked and anything that was missing we can make sure that those needs get met as well. The goal in everything in life is to try to get a little better each and every day.

LINK: https://understandingrelationships.com/heartbreaks-rebounds-moving-on/14247

The Best Way To Get Her Number

"Most men mask their feelings of attraction for a woman instead of being honest, authentic, and boldly asking for a phone number or a date right on the spot. Weak men try to fly under the radar, act like they are not interested when they actually are, say they want to be friends only when that is not true, belittle or put the woman they like down, etc. They do this to avoid rejection, feeling uncomfortable, looking foolish, or because they simply lack the confidence to go for what they want. The reality is that women know that if you approach and talk to them, then you are most likely interested. Only the most confident men immediately risk rejection. Why? Attraction is not a choice. Inauthenticity and hesitation are what really make a man look foolish, weak, and pathetic in a woman's eyes. If a woman likes you, she will help you get a date with her. If she doesn't, she will offer resistance, make excuses, stall, or reject you outright. Even when you get rejected, it's a win. Why? At least she will respect you as a man because you had the guts to show up, be present, and do what most men are too weak, shy, and timid to do." ~ Coach Corey Wayne

You have to look at getting rejected when you're asking a woman out for a date or for her phone number as a win and a victory, because the reality is, 97% of the other guys wouldn't have the guts to do what you just did. That takes balls, that takes confidence, and that takes an incredible belief in yourself and what you bring to the table. The reality is, most guys are afraid to approach and talk to women that they like because they're worried about a bad interaction, looking stupid and foolish in front of other people, and getting rejected in front of other people. But the reality is, when you have the guts to go for it in a public place, what happens is other people that are observing this admire the fact that you have the courage to do it.

And even if you get shot down or rejected, there might be a woman around that notices you and sees that you got rejected, and she might appreciate the fact that you went for it, especially if you got rejected and it wasn't that big a deal. Like, if you went and approached a woman and you asked her out or asked for her phone number, and she said she had a boyfriend, and you had a very cool, pleasant, calm, collected interaction, you both walk away from the interaction with a smile on your face. You never know what's going to happen. The thing I've always found is, even after getting rejected, at least you know you can cross that person off your list, and then, you can have peace and confidence and certainty the rest of the day as you go about your life for the fact that you had the guts to take some risk and go for it. It makes you courageous. It makes you brave. It helps you believe in yourself even more.

The goal should not be necessarily to get a phone number or a date, but just to actually go through the process to do the repetition so you get better, you get more experience, and almost 100% time when you come walking away, it's always going to be a pleasant experience. Your experience of doing things is always much easier than your fear of what they would've been like before you did them. In other words, our fear of doing something is always way worse than actually doing what we fear.

LINK: https://understandingrelationships.com/the-best-way-to-get-her-number/17390

Life Equals Pain

"Problems are a sign of life. They are a sign that you still have work to do in this life. That there is more you can become, more you can give, and more you can do to make a positive difference in the world and make it a little better than you found it. Challenges and difficult circumstances are the engines through which we perfect ourselves and become all that we are capable of becoming. Problems do not last forever. Pain is temporary. Even the worst circumstances and setbacks can eventually be overcome. What would you do or begin if you knew you could not fail? If success was simply a matter of time and taking relentless, directed, and focused action towards what you want and want to create for your life? Success is not a straight line. It is a journey full of twists, turns, setbacks, wins, failures, false starts, etc. And the quickest way to ultimate success is in one's willingness to change your approach, persevere, adapt, improvise, overcome, and compensate for whatever obstacles life throws in your way." ~ Coach Corey Wayne

So, the good news is, if you've got a lot of problems and a lot of challenges in your life, it means you got a lot of work to do, and you've still got a lot of living left to do. Because it's going through life, and encountering challenges, and encountering failure that you're able to do the things that make a great life. You're able to smooth out your rough edges and become the person that you're capable of becoming. Because we learn more from failure than we do success. Success is not a very good teacher. It actually can make you complacent and soft, especially if you get a string of nothing but successes. We see this a lot with celebrities and athletes—people that are on top of the world and think they're the shit—they become arrogant and full of themselves, and then life eventually comes along and serves them a nice slice of humble pie.

When I was young—and I was really successful when I was younger—I thought my life would always continue going in an upward trajectory. And then, I went through a bunch of changes and a metamorphosis in my mid-30s, and I knew nothing but struggle and obstacles and difficulty for the next several years. And that was really hard to accept, to take, and it was incredibly humbling. You realize that in the big scheme of things, you're not any more important than a grain of sand on an infinite beach. And, therefore, the purpose of life is to find a way to enjoy it and to have fun while you're doing it, and hopefully learn some things along the way.

LINK: https://understandingrelationships.com/life-equals-pain/16614

Why Does Life Suck So Bad Sometimes?

"Life can be really difficult and challenging at times. It's not all sunshine and roses. You are a divine being having a human experience. It is a gift meant to be enjoyed and appreciated. The reality is that everyone you love and everything that you build will eventually die and dissolve. The only thing that really matters is your relationship with yourself and others. Every struggle, tragedy, disappointment, and failure are designed to help you grow into the fullness of who the Creator designed you to be. You don't always have control over the circumstances of your life, but you always have control over the meaning you give them. Choose to see the purpose, lesson, gift, and positive meaning in your struggles, instead of complaining or labeling them bad." ~ Coach Corey Wayne

You've got to accept that life is not all sunshine and roses. Sometimes, life is going to suck. And sometimes, it's going to suck for extended periods of time—maybe days, maybe weeks, maybe months. That's just the reality. Sometimes, you're going to have to do things you hate in order to do things that you love. Sometimes, you're going to have to suck it up, dealing with an asshole boss, or work at a job that's less than ideal because it's a steppingstone and a means to an end. That's why, when you feel this way, the best thing you can do is put your head down and take relentless action towards doing those things that are the most important to you. For example, if you're working a job that you hate, but you don't really like the interviewing process—you've been talking about updating your resume for last year, but you haven't really done it—when you're not working, your spare time should be used for getting your resume in order, and then finding a list of companies that you can send your resume to, and then following up with those companies with phone calls after you've sent your resume to them to find out if they're hiring. And if they're not hiring, when they might be hiring again in the future.

I go into extensive detail on this process in my second book, *Mastering Yourself,* so you can ensure that you get any job that you want. Because sometimes that job that you want, there might not be an opening for six months or even a year. And that's why you're going to have to be patient, and do things that you don't really enjoy doing, and work for people you don't really enjoy working for until you find something better. The worst thing you can do when you're not happy is just up and quit your job, and now you've got no income and no money coming in to pay your bills, which is going to stress you out, put you in a fearful state, and oftentimes, cause you to take a job that you don't really want. And this makes your situation worse because you put yourself into a bad position.

If you're working for somebody else and you want to change jobs, the best thing to do is to line up that new job, get your employment letter, put your two weeks' notice in, and then slowly transition into the new job from your old job. This will help keep you in a peaceful and relaxed state as much as possible and, therefore, this will cause all of your decisions and your actions to be more about bringing more peace and ease and delight into your life, versus doing things that stress you the fuck out.

LINK: https://understandingrelationships.com/why-does-life-suck-so-bad-sometimes/14211

Insecurities, Regrets & What-If's

"Most people live their lives and focus all of their mental energy on what may or may not happen in the future, or they obsess over what happened to them in the past. This prevents them from enjoying their lives and living in the present moment. When our mind is consumed with 'What if?' scenarios or past regrets, we suffer unnecessarily and miss the gift that life is. If you were to adopt a superior mindset and belief system to keep yourself focused on the present moment, it would be that everything that has happened in your life happened for a reason and on purpose. There are no accidents. There is no imperfection or anything wrong with you; you've only ever done what you were meant to do. What happened, happened, and couldn't have happened any other way. The only thing you would then have to do is to understand the meaning, lesson, and gift of your past, so you gain the wisdom from it that will enable you to make the right choices in the future, so you can fulfill your destiny." ~ Coach Corey Wayne

It's a pretty common thing for us human beings to look back on what we did wrong. Especially when it comes to interacting with women and realizing that we screwed up or we made a mistake. We wish we could take that text back, or that phone call back, or we could take back what we said when we maybe had a little too much to drink. Or we got into an argument and we let our emotions get the best of us, and we said things that we later regretted. The reality is, everything that happens, good and bad, it's happening for a reason. It's happening for us, not to us. And the reality is, we get feedback, good and bad. So, when we make bad choices, we get bad feedback that, hopefully, will correct our bad behavior. And good behavior just reinforces to do more good and know what is working.

Too many of us dwell on what happened in the past, and we're unable to move forward, and that inhibits us in the present moment. You see this a lot in professional sports. When a professional athlete gets a bad call against him, you see him arguing with the referee for the next two or three plays, and the whole time he's arguing and upset about a moment that happened in the past, he's continuing to make mistakes on current plays because, mentally, he's not doing what he knows he needs to do. Mistakes are going to happen, and the quicker you can catch yourself dwelling on the past and get refocused on what you need to do right now to move your life forward, the easier and more effortless your life is going to be.

Always bring it back to the present moment. Ask yourself, "What do I need to do right now? What action must I take right now, in this moment, to move my life forward?" And then, take that action. As Tony Robbins likes to say, "Never leave the scene of setting a goal without taking some kind of action towards its attainment." So, when you recognize that you have to do something, or that you should do something, take some kind of action. Even if it's putting it onto your to-do list or adding it to your schedule—do something positive to help you make it happen.

LINK: https://understandingrelationships.com/insecurities-regrets-what-ifs/20272

Wanting Reality To Be Different

"One of the secrets to enjoying your life is learning to master the art of living in the present moment. Why? When we focus on the future and what may or may not happen, or when we obsess over the past, this takes us out of the present moment and prevents us from seeing and accepting reality as it is. When we want reality to be other than it is, we suffer unnecessarily. By accepting people as they are and our life's circumstances for what they are, without judgment or wishing them to be different when we can't immediately change things, this keeps us in the present moment. When you can't change your circumstances immediately, your only choice is to accept them as they are and take action towards your outcomes, so eventually, your life circumstances will become more like you want them to be. Circulation is one of the keys to life, happiness, and success. However, when you stop circulating and moving towards your outcomes, you will become stuck and unable to achieve your outcomes. By always keeping yourself in circulation and moving towards your outcomes, eventually, everything you want will manifest in your life slowly over time." ~ Coach Corey Wayne

The more we can stay in the present moment, the happier we are going to be, because we're accepting reality as it is. We're not thinking about the way it was in the past. We're not worried about what may or may not be in the future. We're simply looking at what we have to do right now and take action upon doing that. And we're also able to look at what's currently happening in our lives. Maybe you're just sitting at the beach enjoying a nice day on a holiday. When was the last time you took a day off and actually enjoyed having personal time for yourself without any kind of feeling of being guilty that there's something else you should be doing? Can you really sit there at the beach on a day off and enjoy the beautiful sights, the beautiful women in their bikinis, the people having fun, the lovers walking down the beach holding hands, the kids screaming and playing in the water and having fun, and just enjoying the beauty of the blue sky, and the blue ocean, and the warmth of the sun, and just embracing enjoying it?

This is all part of the art of happiness: finding a way to look at what's going on in your present reality and find reasons to be grateful for it. Because there are always things in our life that we don't like that we wish were different, but if we focus on what we don't like and what we wish was different, then we're going to become really unhappy and suffer, because now we're not accepting reality as it is. If you can look at your current circumstance, maybe you're, right now, working at a job that you can't stand but, you know, in six months, or a year, or two years, you won't be there anymore. Think about how much fun you're going to have when you're finally able to leave your current job, put in your two weeks' notice, or finish your last day at work. Or take that last quiz, that last test, that very last question, the very last test that you'll ever have in your collegiate career, and when you walk out that door you know you're done with college. Think about how good, exciting, and compelling that would be.

Even if you're going through the worst hell in your life right now, just ask yourself, "If I could find something to be grateful for in my life right now, what would it be?" Would it be because you're healthy? Would it be because you got breath in your lungs? Would it be because you have lots of life left ahead of you to live? Because there's lots of people right now that are struggling to breathe, struggling to live, and that are on their last dying breath, people with all kinds of physical deformities, illnesses, injuries, and they wish they had a perfect body, but they don't. So, if you're in good health, relatively speaking, and you're having a rough day, be excited about the fact that you're in relatively good health, and in good shape, and have the opportunity to continue to change and shape your destiny, because there are literally millions and millions of people around the world that don't have the same opportunity that you do, especially if you live somewhere in the West.

LINK: https://understandingrelationships.com/wanting-reality-to-be-different/23938

She Lost Attraction & Needs Space

"Love is about giving. You share your completeness with each other. You don't complete one another. Needing another person to complete you is the result of seeking attention and validation from outside of yourself. When you depend upon external sources of attention and validation to make yourself feel whole and complete and content with your life, you deny yourself the ability to make yourself happy from within. Happiness is a conscious choice. You can either choose to assign positive and empowering meanings to the circumstances of your life and be happy as a result of where you are, or you can choose to be miserable and unhappy when people don't match your unreasonable expectations. The effort is the same, no matter which way you choose to feel about yourself and your life." ~ Coach Corey Wayne

Everything that happens in life, we decide what it means to us. We decide whether it's positive and empowering and something to learn and grow from, or we look at it as something that's negative, disempowering, and as a reason to lose or give up hope in our goals and our dreams. When you stop seeking attention and validation from people outside of yourself and from circumstances outside of yourself, you are then able to see yourself as the creator of your life. And, therefore, you take personal responsibility for everything that's in your life, good and bad, things you want there, as well as things that you don't want there. Because if you decide that things that are in your life are not because of anything you did, that it's outside circumstances, then you become powerless to change them, because you've convinced yourself it's not your fault, and it's not your problem that things are that way. And then, you wait for somebody else to come along and save you or to fix your problems.

LINK: https://understandingrelationships.com/she-lost-attraction-needs-space/36817

Becoming The Right Man

"It's easy to talk about becoming a better version of yourself. For most people who are living their lives in ways that no longer serve them or that don't offer them any more opportunity for growth, it often takes a traumatic event to get them to change their ways. A sudden divorce, breakup, cheating scandal, being fired, health crisis, economic crisis, or mid-life crisis is what dissolves who they were, who they thought they were, or what they thought life was all about. These destructive, life-changing, and life-altering events are meant to move us in a new direction. The quicker you can embrace and accept what is in your life, the quicker you will be able to recover, rebuild, and rejuvenate your purpose, happiness, and wellbeing." ~ Coach Corey Wayne

When you can accept calamity and bad things happening to you and then ask yourself good, high-quality questions like "What's good about this?", "How can I use this?", "How can I overcome this?", "How can it make me better the next time around?", "What different permutation can I try that might get me closer to my results?", when you ask those kinds of questions, you force your brain to come up with good answers. Good quality questions elicit good quality responses.

And the reality is, as you go through the seasons of your life, life is going to throw all kinds of crazy, unexpected things your way— circumstances, good things, bad things, unexpected things—and how you respond to them is going to determine what you do going forward and what you're capable of. It's like what Bruce Lee talked about: "Be like water." If you think about how water is, it's like the ultimate flexibility—it moves, goes around, and gets in everything. And if you have that same kind of flexibility, like water, and use that as a metaphor for life when challenges come your way unexpectedly, that kind of mindset can help you just get focused on "What do I need to do today before I go to sleep to move my life even a few inches closer to my goals and dreams?"

LINK: https://understandingrelationships.com/becoming-the-right-man/17220

BEING A DOER

No Longer A Wussy

"One of the greatest things you can do to enhance your success, happiness, and confidence is to start doing the things you really want but that scare the crap out of you. It means to do the things you know you need to do despite the consequences, risks, and potential for failure. Progress always involves risk. It is impossible to get to second base while keeping your foot firmly planted on first base. Unsuccessful people bullshit themselves and tell themselves all kinds of ridiculous stories as to why they should not go for what they want. They literally talk themselves right out of everything they really want and want to become in life. Instead of taking action, they make excuses. Accomplishing your goals often takes many years and even decades of consistent action, even when it seems hopeless. Taking action, learning from your mistakes and failures, adapting your approach along the way, and persevering without exception is essential to accomplishing your dreams and creating your dream life. Without employing these principles, you're just another unsuccessful dreamer, not a doer. It's the difference that makes the difference between mediocrity and magnificence." ~ Coach Corey Wayne

There's two types of people in this world: there's talkers, and there's doers. And on a daily basis, you have to decide whether you're a talker or a doer. Doers make things happen. Doers make plans, they come up with emotionally compelling reasons why they want to accomplish those plans, and then they set about the task of making those plans happen. Talkers do exactly that. They talk about what they're going to do, but never get around to actually taking any action to help themselves or to move their lives forward. Every moment, moment by moment of your life, you're either deciding to take action and move your life forward, or you're deciding to do nothing, and avoid what you want, and avoid moving towards the things you want to move towards. Based upon your actions as well as the actions that you fail to take, this is what's going to determine, and shape and change your destiny. You're going to end up somewhere, and wherever you end up is the direct result of what you do and what you fail to do on a daily basis.

LINK: https://understandingrelationships.com/no-longer-a-wussy/16837

The Boomerang Date

"Most of the time, when a woman is romantically interested in a man, she will put herself into his orbit in order to get his attention and make it easy for him to hopefully get the hint and ask her out on a date. However, since men are supposed to be the aggressors, women usually will not come right out and ask for a date. A man should understand, when a woman gets in contact with him, it's not really because she was simply just thinking about him, but because she was hoping he was also thinking about her too and would like to see her again and, therefore, make a date. When it comes to a woman who initiates contact, a man should never hesitate, but instead, make a date." ~ Coach Corey Wayne

What I teach in my first book, *3% Man*, is that men need to allow women to come to them at their own pace. Because of societal conditioning and the way we've all been brainwashed by the mainstream media, television, and movies is that men should, in essence, become stalkers and chase and pursue a woman until she relents, and gives in, and says "Yes" to go on a date. The reality is, a woman will like you more, be more attracted to you, and be more aggressive toward you if she has to earn your attention and validation. That's why it's essential, if you want a woman to fall head over heels in love with you, that you allow her to come to you at her pace.

So, what happens is, like I talk about in *3% Man*, the guy, especially in the beginning, doesn't need to set more than one date per week and call her once per week to set up one date. And as the second, third, and fourth weeks tend to roll around and a woman's attraction starts to go up, she doesn't want to wait to hear from you. She starts to call and text you, but 99% of the time, she's not going to ask you out on a date; she'll just call to tell you she was thinking about you, or that she was watching a television program the other night and one of the actors had a shirt on, and that shirt reminded her of you. Just like I say in *3% Man,* you should assume that if she's reaching out to you, it's because she wants to see you and to make a date.

But take the initiative to do that. Don't sit there and wait for the woman to bring up getting together, because nine times out of ten, she won't. Just realize that if she's contacting you, it's because she's thinking about you, and that, typically, is her invitation to you to create the next get-together.

LINK: https://understandingrelationships.com/the-boomerang-date/23920

You Stink Of Fear

"Michelangelo once said that 'Genius is eternal patience.' Genius is having the patience, care, diligence, and love to spend whatever time is necessary to perfect yourself, your work, and your life. It's a patient and relentless pursuit of perfection. If you pursue perfection, you may just reach excellence, as Vince Lombardi suggested. See yourself and your life as a work in progress. Work at overcoming your weaknesses and pushing past your fears. Success and the life you dream of is way beyond what your weaknesses and fears say you currently are and are capable of in the future. If what you want is more emotionally compelling and worth chasing than what you fear, you can, and must take action to make it a reality. Otherwise, you're just another member of the herd with wishes and excuses, not goals. A goal without a plan to achieve it is simply a wish." ~ Coach Corey Wayne

The reality is everything that you want, everything you want to build, everything you want to create, it's going to take a lot of time to become what you need to become in order to make that a reality. In our society of instant gratification, we want the perfect lover right now, we want the perfect job right now. We want the promotion, and the big pay raise, right now, even though we may not have the experience and have not developed our gifts, our skills, and our talents enough to warrant that salary increase and that increase in responsibility or position. We have to put the time in.

Obviously, if you've come to a place where you're qualified and you have all the skills, and something isn't opening up, or you're getting passed over by people that have less experience and less ability than you, maybe you haven't handled things politically, because you're not a politically correct person like myself, and you pissed off somebody that was higher up, and you didn't tow the company line. Well, if you're deserving and you're ready for that next big step, then go find a company that will give you that opportunity. And once you have a job lined up, then you can put in your two weeks' notice and move on. But the point being is that everything you want, especially if you're like me and you're an entrepreneur, it's going to take way more money than you think it's going to take to make it a success, and it's going to take you a lot longer to figure out your business model, especially if you're doing something from scratch.

That's why you have to figure out what you love, what you're most passionate about, and then pursue becoming a master of it either working for other people, or getting a college degree that's necessary in order to get the job in the particular field that you want to work in. You've got to figure out what you want, why you want it, have emotionally compelling reasons why you want it, and then, you've got to take consistent, relentless action to improve and enhance yourself every single day of the week—seven days a week, every day of the month, 365 days a year.

LINK: https://understandingrelationships.com/you-stink-of-fear/16636

Building Confidence Is A Process

"No one is born with fearless confidence. Confidence is doing what you know how to do and doing it really well. We tend to overlook what successful and confident people did to become so successful and confident and assume that they were born this way. Every successful professional athlete, CEO, entrepreneur, superstar employee, etc., got that way by taking action in spite of their fears and by accepting and embracing the fact that success only comes from trying, failing, and learning from your failures. The way to become great at anything in life is to consistently rehearse and practice something you would love to become great at. Successful people are evidence that time, practice, and repetition eventually pay off—not that you can't do it too without the same effort, passion, focus, and dedication." ~ Coach Corey Wayne

So, a good analogy—because I do quite a bit of coaching, and I see it a lot in the emails—is guys are really struggling with their confidence level, and as far as it comes to women, reading my book—the first book, *How To Be A 3% Man*—10 to 15 times really helps build your knowledge and gives you a lot of wisdom based upon my own personal experiences and the things that I wrote about.

That's why I insist that guys have to read it 10 to 15 times, because that's what it's going to take to become proficient at it. Because if a guy just thumbs through the book a couple of times, and is not really serious about things, and thinking he's different and he doesn't need to read it that many times, what happens is they get on dates, eventually, with a girl they really, super like, and then they get fearful, and they get all lost their head, and they start acting and thinking like a robot. And this makes them give off a weird vibe; it makes him do and say things that are inappropriate. And because they don't know the book, they try to come off as being too game-like and robotic in their approach, instead of being natural. When you become natural is a result of reading the book 10 to 15 times. When you get to know something so well you don't have to think about it anymore, then you've got confidence and competence at it.

A good example of this is a comedian. If you've ever watched a Netflix special or an HBO special with a very famous, well-known comedian, and they get up there in front of this big audience, and they just kill it. They deliver an amazing performance, and everybody thinks, "Wow, that was really great!" But people don't see all the hard work that goes into it. Because if you've ever been to regular comedy clubs and you frequent them enough, you're going to see the big-name guys come through, and those are the guys that do all the Netflix specials and the HBO specials. What happens is, a comedy routine is a performance—it's a memorized performance. So, they write the performance, they write all their jokes out, and then they get up in front of an audience and start performing those jokes.

And the reality is, some of those jokes are going to land and they're going to be really hilarious, some of them are going to elicit no response at all, and some of them are going to elicit a mediocre response or a mediocre laugh. And what this enables the comedians to do is they film their own performances and they record it, so, obviously, they get the instant feedback of a live audience and what they liked and what they didn't like. And so, this feedback enables them to go back and rewrite jokes that didn't land well and try to come up with something funnier, or different sounds, or noises, or facial expressions.

And then, after they practice this and rehearse it a few hundred times in front of other people and they get continuous laughing all the way through the performance, that's when the rest of us see them on their Netflix special, or their HBO special, or whatever it happens to be. We don't see all the work, all the bombing that they do in front of other people—which, obviously, if you're in front of a big crowd and you're a well-known comedian, you get up there, and you deliver a joke, and it doesn't land, and it bombs, and you get people booing or walking out on you, you're going to have to deal with that, emotionally. But the really great comedians just simply look at it as a process.

So again, when we see the final product on Netflix, or HBO, or Showtime, whatever it happens to be where we see these comedy specials, just keep in mind, there are probably thousands of hours that went into that performance—between writing it, practicing it, memorizing it, and getting up in front of and delivering it to an audience when the jokes just simply aren't landing. It's definitely something to think about and how you can apply that to your own life if you're trying to become confident and master something. Mastering anything is a process, and you have to put the time in in order to master it.

LINK: https://understandingrelationships.com/building-confidence-is-a-process/17223

Paralysis Of Analysis

"Most people in life tend to dither, hesitate and delay making important decisions or taking important actions because they suffer from the paralysis of analysis. This is caused by their irrational fears. Human beings have two primary fears: 1) fear they don't have what it takes to succeed, and 2) fear they won't be loved and accepted by their friends, family, or peer group. Taking imperfect action is always better than taking no action at all. Why? At least with taking action, you get results you can base subsequent action upon in order to refine and improve your approach. Basic science teaches us: bodies in motion tend to stay in motion, and bodies at rest tend to stay at rest. Life happens when you move; stagnation happens when you don't." ~ Coach Corey Wayne

This is what unsuccessful people tend to do—they over-analyze everything. I see this with a lot with guys who watch my videos for years and try to cherry-pick information, maybe they gloss over the book once. And then, they come across a girl they really like, and they really jive with her, but because they didn't take the time to learn the fundamentals, (in other words, they were watching thousands of videos, read the book, but never really went out and applied it or practiced it, and then a really amazing woman comes along that they click and they jive with), and since they didn't take the time to practice and make mistakes with other women, they start making all kinds of mistakes—especially when their emotions get involved due to the fears that they have.

And then, nine times out of ten, they end up doing the wrong thing and talking the girl of liking them. And before they know it, she's gone from his life forever as quickly as she came. And those really sting, because in my own personal experience, I've found that typically, per decade, you get two, maybe three really cool girls that you click with, that you jive with, that are good, long-term relationship prospects to have a good, healthy, happy, fun relationship, where you share similar goals and similar values. When you recognize that one of those comes along, (what I like to call a unicorn), and you don't really even get to date her except, maybe, a few times because you screwed up, man, those hurt like a fucking motherfucker. And it takes months to get over them, because you're always thinking about her in the back your mind.

But that's why you've got to keep moving forward. You've got to practice, because everybody starts out as a novice, everybody starts out as a beginner. Nobody comes out of the womb and is a master of something other than crying, and making a lot of fucking noise, and shitting and pissing themself. You've got to get out there, and you've got to take action. Because when you start something—you start on a new goal, or a new plan, or a new direction in your life—you don't necessarily know the whole roadmap of how you're going to get from where you are to where you want to be. But as long as you start taking action, it gets you centered, living in the present moment. When you're in the present moment and you're taking action, you're not worrying about the past, or the future, or what may or may not happen in the future.

LINK: https://understandingrelationships.com/paralysis-of-analysis/24785

Try To Get A Little Better Each Day

"Success is a process. The best and most successful athletes, CEOs, entrepreneurs, and high achievers tend to focus relentlessly on trying to get a little better each and every day. Accomplishing big goals over a long period of time is the result of constantly achieving small daily goals. Feeling like you are making progress is essential to feeling happy, fulfilled, remaining focused, and staying motivated to achieve your dreams. Time, repetition, learning from your mistakes, adapting your approach, and perseverance are essential components to achieving your grandest goals and dreams." ~ Coach Corey Wayne

All professional, high-achieving athletes are always focused 100% on trying to get a little better each and every day. Because they love what they do, and they have a passion for it, and they naturally have talent that they develop, they become very skilled at their jobs, which is what ultimately leads to them getting their large, multimillion-dollar contracts that the rest of us look at and are amazed how they continually seem to go up year after year after year. As the industry grows, as the sports organization grows, as their audience grows, they're able to reach more eyeballs, in essence. And then, therefore, the more eyeballs they reach, the more advertising dollars they can get to fund their organization.

This same philosophy can apply to your business, your career, your relationships, your lifestyle—whatever it is that you do for fun in life.

The better you get at it due to successful repetitions, (because repetition is the mother of skill), and the more you do something, the more you work at it—especially if you really love and enjoy it, or it feels like playing—you will work harder at it than anybody else that you're competing against. And when you stick with things longer and you're able to outlast your competition, as the years and the decades roll by, you get so much further ahead that nobody can really catch you.

I was just reading an article this morning about Tesla and their autonomous driving , and the fact that Tesla cars can pretty much drive themselves now, versus Apple. Apple has been flirting with and playing with getting into autonomous driving vehicles for many years. But, because Tesla has been on this long curve closing in on 20 years, they have surpassed one of the best technology companies in the world in what they're able to put out as far as their products go. And now, Apple is trying to play catch up, whereas Tesla's got over a decade and a half ahead of Apple.

LINK: https://understandingrelationships.com/try-to-get-a-little-better-each-day/22159

I've Found My People & Passion!

"In order to reach your full potential and do what you consider to be great work, you must love what you do. When you love what you are doing, you'll do it out of sheer enthusiasm and joy for the work itself. It is fun and effortless because it seems more like playing than working. When you love your life's work, you will outwork and out-hustle any potential competitor, because most others will be working for money and not for the joy of the work itself. Passion for something internally compels you to become obsessed with mastering all of the essential details required for successful and competent execution." ~ Coach Corey Wayne

The important thing to understand is that success is a process. So is discovering your purpose. Many people who don't know what they want to do should start doing something that they're curious about or interested in, or they like watching videos on it, or documentaries on it, or reading books about it, and immersing themselves in the activity or the task. Because it's only when you actually do something and immerse yourself in something can you find out what you're good at and what you're passionate about. But it always comes from an intuition—something you're curious about, something that you're excited about.

When I look back on my life, now that I'm about to turn 51, and I think about all the jobs that I had when I was younger, I was always excited about the job, and what I was going to do, what it was going to be like, what I was going to experience, what I was going to learn, how it was going to be a good steppingstone for me to, eventually, get to where I wanted to be someday. And what's interesting is all along those different paths that I wrote about in my second book, *Mastering Yourself*, it's when you get to experience the things that you're excited and curious about—your experience of finally doing those things that your intuition told you was something good to do or get involved in—some of those things, when you start to do and work at them for a while, you think, "This really kind of sucks. It's not what I thought it would be." And when those moments happen—when you start to get to the point too many days in a row where you're no longer enjoying your work, or your tasks, or what you're doing—then you know you need to make some kind of change.

So, I was doing a phone session recently with a client that was making multiple six-figures working for a very large tech firm out in Silicon Valley. And for the last couple years, he's really loved and really enjoyed his job. And so, about two and a half, three months ago, he got a promotion. He got an additional title and he got a significant pay increase over and above what he was already making. But what happened was they changed the structure of the department that he was involved in, and it went from him running things, and having people work for him, and having a team of people around him to support the objective that they were working on, now, he was working under somebody else. And because of this particular company, (and if I told you the company, you would know who it is, but I like to keep that stuff private), but what happened was they changed his structure, because part of the company's rules is that you've got to have seniority. And because this other person had four, five years at the company more than he did, this other guy had seniority, and he was forced to work under him.

He lost some of the responsibility that he had, just by the nature of the large bureaucracy that he worked at in the company that he worked for. And so, he went from loving what he was doing, and getting up and going to work every day and being excited about it, now, he was working for somebody that, as Steve Jobs referred to it, was not an A or B type player; they were a C and D type player. And the reality is, your A players—your top-tier employees and team members—they don't want to work with C and D players, and they start to resent it. And so, even though this guy got a significant bump in his pay, he got a nice title to go along with it, his day-to-day work satisfaction plummeted.

Because of some of the things, when he went through his list to figure out what his purpose was in life, a big part of it was teambuilding—being given a task and a vision, and then executing that by leading the team to do it together. And with his new position, he no longer had that same responsibility and was having to defer to somebody that he, quite frankly, thought was an idiot and totally incompetent. But this particular guy that he was now working under, he had kissed all the right ass and played the political games in the company to get the position that he wanted.

And so, what we looked at doing was strategizing on how he could go to his superiors and ask them to make a lateral move. And now, because he had this list, his driving force needs that I discuss in my second book, *Mastering Yourself*, he had, I think it was, two or three different things that were on his list that were super important to him that he went from doing on a daily basis in his job, to now, he was only doing them on an intermittent basis. And it was getting to the point where he wasn't even excited about getting up early and going to work anymore.

And so, his first goal that we decided and the strategy that we came up with, was to see if he can make some kind of lateral move in the company. Because he had a good relationship with his superiors, and he could go and sit down and tell them about what he loved, and what was missing, and what he's most passionate about from the perspective of, he wanted to be the most valuable employee that he could be to the company. But because he wasn't able to do things he really loved, and really enjoyed, and was really passionate about, it was detracting from his overall sense of well-being and enjoyment of his job.

And so, one of two things was going to happen: he was going to have a sit down to see if he can make a lateral move in the company, and if he ran into too many walls and too many obstacles, and they weren't willing to help him make the changes that he needed in order to enjoy his work like he once did, then the next option is to go find an opportunity outside the company at a different firm that he could do the same kind of work.

And so, these kinds of things happen, and what's interesting when you study corporations, and you study employees and why they leave those corporations, most of the time, money is the last thing on their list as far as importance. The biggest reason—the number one reason why most employees leave corporations and leave their jobs—is because they don't feel like their contributions matter, and that when they give honest feedback, and try to help make changes, and implement things, and grow things in the company, they're stonewalled or shot down instantly. And, therefore, they just feel like their opinions don't matter, their contributions don't matter.

And if you're going to spend 40, 50, 60 hours a week, whatever it happens to be, working at a job, you want to really enjoy that work. Because if you're getting up, and you're working that much, and you're not enjoying it, that's going to have a really negative impact on your life and your overall level of fulfillment. And you can only do that for so many days in a row, where it gets to the point where you're forcing yourself to go to work, instead of it being effortless when you jump out of bed in the morning, excited about what you're going to do that particular day.

LINK: https://understandingrelationships.com/ive-found-my-people-passion/33389

Life Keeps Kicking My Ass

"Life isn't all sunshine and roses. Your struggles and your challenges happen to you for a reason.; they happen in order to give you exactly what you need to become strong enough and wise enough to become the person you're capable of becoming in order to accomplish your life's purpose. The average person lives a life of quiet desperation because they are too afraid to go for what they really want. Only the most determined, focused, optimistic, and internally driven people will do what it takes to change their circumstances for the better by taking consistent, sustained action. Unsuccessful people make excuses. Successful people take action and succeed because they know success begins and ends with what they are willing to do." ~ Coach Corey Wayne

Going for your dreams and trying to accomplish your goals is not easy, and anybody that tells you differently is full of shit. You're going to experience challenges, setbacks, obstacles, friction, and resistance. Because when you decide to do something, or to become something, or try to experience something, or acquire something, most of the time, you have no idea how you're going to accomplish it. You may have some ideas on how to start, but the whole plan—your plan of action, your day-to-day routine of what's actually, eventually going to make it work—is something you just do not know. And as you start making attempts and moving towards the things you want, you're going to encounter things that go well and easy and effortlessly, and you're going to encounter a lot of things where you experience friction, and resistance, and things not going well.

It's through this trial and error and trying to improve the things that don't go well that you are able to measure your results and constantly change your approach until you, eventually, find the right combination of action steps that you take over and over and over again to make it a success. The average person simply is not willing to suffer long enough and persist long enough to eventually figure out the flaws in their approach and refine it to the point where it actually starts working. That's why it's so important that you have to have something that's really emotionally compelling and you're passionate about—because when things aren't working, are not going well, you're going to have an optimistic attitude, you're going to be excited about what you're learning and what you can improve the next time around.

So, make sure you're moving towards something you love and you're passionate about. That is absolutely essential. Because if you get that part wrong, as soon as you encounter difficulty, and challenges, and obstacles, you'll just give up. And that failure then becomes an emotional anchor that causes you to become risk averse. So, next time around when you have what you think is a good idea and you want to go for something that requires you to step outside your comfort zone, now, because of the major failure you had in the past and the fact that you gave up, now it's going to be twice as hard. Because you're going to look at what didn't work out in the past, you're going to be stuck in the past, and you're going to use what happened in the past as reason and justification to do nothing to move your life forward. You'll actually move away from what it is that you want.

LINK: https://understandingrelationships.com/life-keeps-kicking-my-ass/14298

Becoming An Awesome Catch

"In order to reach your full potential, you must first be willing to let go of all your preconceived notions of who you are and what your limitations are. The beliefs we hold of ourselves determine the type of walls and barriers we will consciously and unconsciously erect in between what we are right now and what we are capable of becoming in the future. If you see yourself as an unlimited being capable of learning, practicing, refining, and perfecting anything you have a compelling enough vision to become, you will give yourself reasons to take action and find the time to make it a reality. If you choose to see yourself as a limited being, your capabilities and comfort zone will contract to the point it saps your happiness and will to live. Your focus, attitude, and actions determine your destiny." ~ Coach Corey Wayne

The most important thing to focus on, once you've decided what you want and why you want it, is the action that you must take on a consistent, daily basis to become that—to fill in your knowledge gaps, to develop your gifts, your skills, your talents—so you can become proficient over time. And oftentimes, I've even found myself doing this. Especially as you get older and you get more experience, your experience kind of becomes your rules for what you are willing and unwilling to do to help yourself.

I remember when I was 39 years old and looking at the prospect of going and waiting tables. That was something that I used to have nightmares about when I was in my mid to late 20s any time I got stressed about things. I'd wake up in the middle of the night imagining that I was back working my job waiting tables. And I absolutely hated it, it was the last thing I wanted to do. But I was willing to start waiting tables, because even though the worst thing I could imagine doing I was actually going to do—I mean, after making half a million dollars a year and becoming kind of a local celebrity in Orlando, like I was with my real estate and mortgage company—here I am waiting tables again.

I went from making half a million a year to basically, depending on the night of the week and the season, $80–$150 night. That's pretty humbling when you're willing to do something like that in order to eventually do something that you love. My business was successful, and it was making money. It was making a profit, but it wasn't enough of a profit to really have a nice, comfortable living. And so, I was willing to work for about ten months to supplement my income and improve my business to the point where I didn't have to work. It gave me additional capital that I could use to spend.

And it's difficult. You work your ass off for eight or ten hours, and you make 150 bucks, and then you've got an email squeeze page that you're sending traffic to, and you literally, in a matter of minutes, you can blow all that money that you spent eight to ten hours working. And then, you get a handful of email sign-ups, and it's pretty discouraging, and it's tough to do that. But what it does do is it forces you to be very frugal and look at doing things that you were unwilling to do in the past. I mean, at that point, I was waiting tables. And so, I went back and I reexamined my approach to my business and how it was all focused on trying to sell my book, and eventually, it clicked that I was just going to start writing articles and talking about other subjects that complemented my book.

And over time, what started to happen is, I started to get more free organic search traffic from Google. People started signing up for my email newsletter more and more, I started getting more and more questions from people, and I started getting more coaching clients, and my book sales increased. So, I recognized that by creating content, and teaching what I know, and answering people's questions, I was actually causing my business to grow organically. And the only thing it was really costing me was my time, and the cost of my server, and any images that I bought, and, obviously, paying my web developers for any coding they did on my website.

But it was small, incremental change, and I was only able to figure out the right business model, because I basically got to the point where I ran out of money, and I had no choices. I didn't have enough capital to keep throwing a couple grand at my business every month to just screw around with advertising and try different things. When you're waiting tables, and you're spending 8–10 hours a night, and you only make $80–$150, and you spend that money on a paperclip campaign, you really learn quickly. It highly motivates you. And within ten months, I was out of that job, and that's the only thing I've done working for other people for the last… I think the last time I worked for somebody else was 1996, prior to that.

It was hard and it was humbling, but I was willing to do it. I was willing to suffer for what I wanted to do, because I was so passionate about it. And my clients were getting great results, and sending me great testimonials, and posting great reviews about my books.

LINK: https://understandingrelationships.com/becoming-an-awesome-catch/25476

Accepting Your Present Situation

"Life is a journey that is meant to be enjoyed and cherished. When you stay present in the current moment instead of being fearful about the future and what may or may not happen, you enable yourself to find joy in your current situation. When we want reality to be other than it is, we become unable to accept ourselves and our life situation, causing us to suffer and experience unhappiness. The more you can accept the things you can't instantly change in your life, the more you will be able to experience the beauty of what is. Besides, the only moment that exists is the now. Embrace it. Enjoy it. What you focus on will expand."
~ Coach Corey Wayne

This really is an art, and it's something you have to practice. Just like happiness is an art. As the saying goes, "There is no way to happiness; happiness is the way." In other words, you have to make a conscious choice on a moment-by-moment basis to label the things that are going on in your life as being good, as being bad—as being positive, as being negative. It's totally up to you to what things mean. Now, it doesn't mean that when something is really shitty you say, "Oh, it's wonderful." But if you ask yourself a positive, empowering question such as, "Well what's good about this?", "How can I use this?", "What can I learn from this?", "How can this make me better the next time around?", you're going to force your brain to come up with a good, empowering answer.

When we don't accept reality as it is—when things are going shitty, and yet we want them to be going well—we're going to suffer, because then we're not accepting the present moment. But if we get into it and we just accept that things suck right now, that's okay, because pain is something we should be looking at to move us away from the things that are bringing us pain, and we should move towards doing things that will bring us pleasure down the road. But it's essential that we know what we want, why we want it, and we have emotionally compelling reasons why we want it. Because when you have a goal, you'll move towards that goal, even though it involves doing things that are unpleasant.

When we take our eyes off the ball, and we sit, and we ponder, and we look at all the distance that we have to go—we look how big the mountain is in front of us that we have to climb in order to get to the top and have the success that we want—we become overwhelmed thinking about all of the unpleasant things that we're going to have to do to get from where we are to where we want to be. And the average person that does this, all it does is cause them to get out of the game, and run away from the mountain, and run away from the challenges, and the goals, and the dreams that they have, because they're simply trying to avoid experiencing pain, and discomfort, and unpleasantness in life.

The reality is when you know what you want, and you move towards it, and you have emotionally compelling reasons why you want it, you'll do what it takes to overcome those obstacles and challenges—even when it means doing things and experiencing things that are temporarily unpleasant. Focus on the present moment and what you need to do right now to move your life forward. And then, take action.

LINK: https://understandingrelationships.com/accepting-your-present-situation/14452

The Illusion Of Action

"It's much better to learn to go with the flow in life. People will often try to force things that do not seem to be going well or effortlessly. That may be pushing a client to make a decision before they are ready, asking a lover to be exclusive before you've really gotten to know each other, pushing your body too hard when trying to get into shape, or simply trying to force things to happen faster than it's possible. There are no shortcuts to success. A rose takes its time to bloom for a reason. You can't over-water, over-fertilize, over-stimulate, or over-expose a rose to sunlight to make it bloom faster. All you will do with excessive action is kill the rose. That's something to think about." ~ Coach Corey Wayne

One of the hardest things to learn and master is to be good at practicing infinite patience. Everything I've ever achieved in my life always has taken way fucking longer than I've ever expected. And I'll tell you, as the days, the weeks, the months, the years, the decades roll on, you achieve a lot of things, and you make a lot of progress, but there's also lots of things that you want to happen faster, and they just simply don't. That sucks. And part of the problem when you're looking at it that way is, you get attached to time frames and things happening in a certain time frame. And then when they don't, and then reality hits you that things are not happening in the timeframe that you set, this causes you to suffer. And you suffer because you have an attachment to a time frame.

The best way to be, (the hardest thing to do, though), is learning to live and act in the present moment. And you're able to do that when you just simply focus on taking action, even when you don't feel like it. Just like when I sit down, and I have these sessions with my sound engineer. I don't always sit down with the attitude of, "Oh, I can't wait to record this," and sit there for a two-hour session, talking into a microphone and looking at a computer screen as I'm reading these quotes. But I have a goal in mind. And my audience has been asking me for years, and years, and years to put a bunch of books of my quotes together, and I'm now finally doing that. So, I'm giving people what they want. But like I said, I know I have days where I simply just don't feel like doing it, and it doesn't seem like it flows. But yet, I force myself to sit down, start reading the first quote, put one foot in front of the other, and just start working and making it happen.

The same thing comes with my videos. Or even times when I sit down and I've got a full schedule of phone sessions to do, and I really don't feel like doing it. I just sit there, start the first one, call the first client, and just sit back and listen to what they have to say and what they need help with, as they describe their issue or their problem. And then, I just get solely focused on serving them and helping them, and within a few minutes, I become completely lost in being of service. And every single time, when I get done with all my phone sessions, I always feel good because I know I've helped people, and they appreciate me for it, and all the gratitude and the email success stories that come from that.

So, when it comes to achieving the things that you want in life, you've got to remember: you've got to practice infinite patience, but you got to do the work. You can't make people fall in love with you quicker than they're going to. You can't make the right employer hire you or give you that promotion sooner than they're ready to. And that business that you want to start, it's not going to become a multimillion-dollar business overnight. Great things take time.

LINK: https://understandingrelationships.com/the-illusion-of-action/14106

Why Tom Brady & Bill Belichick Win

"Successful people focus on doing the little things right day in and day out, despite the fact that success and victory over overwhelming odds seem impossible. Focusing on and accomplishing easy to achieve, small, daily goals and doing what's necessary accomplishes big goals. You're going to be somewhere in 5, 10, or 15 years that is a direct result of what you do and fail to do on a daily basis. If you don't take action and do what's necessary today, you'll never be where you want to be tomorrow." ~ Coach Corey Wayne

Unsuccessful people and low achievers look at high achievers and successful people like Tom Brady and Bill Belichick, the Nick Sabans of the world, and the Michael Jacksons of the world, and the people that have achieved and lived the lives that most people dream of, and what they don't see is all the struggle—all the hours in the gym by themselves, all the hours in the recording studio, on the practice field, in college, the late nights up at 2:00 and 3:00 in the morning, working while everybody else is asleep. When everybody else, the low achievers, are watching TV and escaping from their lives, they're doing something productive to try to get ahead. There's an old saying that goes like this: it took ten years for me to become an overnight success; it's because, until people become really successful, you don't hear about them. You don't know about them until they have a breakthrough, dramatic success.

So, just remember success is long in coming. It takes discipline, day in, day out, week after week, month after month, year after year, decade after decade, to eventually get to a place where your dreams are a reality.

LINK: https://understandingrelationships.com/why-tom-brady-bill-belichick-win/29931

Avoiding Failure To Ensure Success

"Not everyone you like, want to associate with or give you what you want and need is going to feel the same way. Continuous circulation is the key to life and perpetual opportunity. Focus and action towards what you want to create provides knowledge, wisdom, skill refinement, ability enhancement, practice, and results. Mastery of anything requires time and repetition; that's why there's no shortcuts to success." ~ Coach Corey Wayne

To get from where you are right now to where you want to be someday is going to be the result of a process. Every day you get up, and you have to take action. And you're either taking action to move you towards the things you want, or you're taking action, or no action at all, which is actually moving you away from the things that you want.

Everybody in our society is addicted to instant gratification. When you look at really successful people—athletes, millionaires, entrepreneurs, all those people that we look up to—none of us see the decades and the years and years of practice and failure that went into becoming that person. When somebody becomes rich and famous, we only know about them becoming rich and famous, because they became so good at what they're doing that the rest of us couldn't take our eyes off of them. And that's what self-mastery is all about; it's mastering a set of fundamentals—the fundamentals of the science of high achievement— that day in and day out, week after week, month after month, year after year, decade after decade, incrementally, and slowly, (and way slower than you expect), will eventually move you from where you are to where you want to be, so someday, you wake up and you look around at your life, and you recognize that everything you wanted and dreamed about many years earlier is now your reality.

It is simply a process. And most people that are not successful and that are mediocre don't know this process and, more likely than not, have too much emotional leverage and anchoring in themselves to avoid doing the things they know they need to do, so success is never even possible. They're not even in the game. They're not even on the playing field of life to maximizing and reaching their full potential; which is a tragedy, but that's why high achievers like me and like you, obviously, if you're listening to this or reading this right now, you're willing to do more than 97-98% of all other human beings are willing to do to help themselves. And that's why you'll get way farther than most of them ever will in life.

LINK: https://understandingrelationships.com/avoiding-failure-to-ensure-success/34002

Making Excuses Vs. Taking Action

"People who seem to be standing still in life, and not progressing towards realizing their grandest goals and dreams are prevented from reaching their full potential due to the paralysis of analysis—or their fear of things not working out, fear of rejection, fear they don't have enough education, fear they don't have the skills, fear they don't have the resources, or fear that they simply don't have what it takes to succeed. Before beginning, you must decide what you want and why you want it. The how you are going to do it is not important; the how only becomes clearer when you actually start taking action. Imperfect action is better than no action at all. You learn from everything you do, your successes and failures." ~ Coach Corey Wayne

The reality is, taking action on a daily, consistent basis is what determines where we end up in the future. Time is going to pass, no matter what we do. So, even if we're unsure, one of the best things you can do when you're unsure of your life, unsure of yourself, you're not feeling good, is to do something to take action that's positive to move your life forward, so you can start to go from where you are to where you want to be. I believe it was Dale Carnegie who said, "Inaction breeds fear and doubt, and taking action breeds confidence and courage." And I've found in my 50+ years of being on this earth that anytime I felt restless, fearful, worried about the future, or unsure of the future, busying myself taking action brings you back down to the present moment to where you're being productive. And after several hours of working and being productive, you feel like you accomplished something, so you feel better about yourself, versus just sitting on the couch and contemplating and worrying about your life and what may or may not work out in the future.

So, anytime you're not feeling good, and you're fearful, and you're worried, get off your ass and go do something positive. Take some kind of positive action that will help you to go from where you are to where you want to be, even if it's just writing down a new goal, or an action plan, or a to-do list of things that have to get done. As Tony Robbins said, never leave the site of setting a goal without taking some kind of action towards its attainment.

LINK: https://understandingrelationships.com/making-excuses-vs-taking-action/14050

Own Your Purpose, Own Yourself

"Taking action towards what you want in life is the best way to reduce your fear of the future and what may or may not go your way. Your life and destiny are shaped by the decisions you make and the actions you take or fail to take. Time is going to pass, no matter what you do or fail to do. Life evolves and changes for the better incrementally and usually much slower than you expect. Unsuccessful people give up and stop trying when their life does not radically change for the better in an unreasonably short period of time. Successful people think in terms of decades and take action, even though success seems far off or unrealistic. Taking action that is productive makes you feel good and gives you hope of a positive future outcome." ~ Coach Corey Wayne

Tom Brady talked about, in an interview, about getting yourself right emotionally—and this was after a big blowout loss where his team just got absolutely crushed. And getting yourself right emotionally really is all about managing your internal state. In other words, if something tragic has happened, or you got undesirable results, or you had a lot of failures, or one big failure, and you're feeling despair, the best thing you can do is get yourself back to a good place emotionally where you can put your head down and focus on one simple question, which is "What must I do today, right now, in this present moment to grind, to keep moving myself forward?"

Because the reality is, every day is a grind. There are things you have to get done. And there's going to be plenty of times where the future's going to look hopeless, and it's going to be in doubt. You're not going to be sure whether or not what you're doing is even the right thing. A quote, I can't remember who said it, but it's so true: "Imperfect action is better than no action at all." The worst thing you can do is nothing, because the more you sit around and do nothing, the easier it is to be lazy and do nothing. And the reality is, your life is the summation of your actions and efforts.

LINK: https://understandingrelationships.com/own-your-purpose-own-yourself/35631

ENERGY & APPEAL

Her Curiosity & Interest Soared

"No matter what women say or think that they really want, the reality is, women are more attracted to men whose feelings are unclear and guys who are mysterious, confident, strong, and unpredictable. Men who are too nice, compliant, available, who don't stand up for themselves, and who wait on women to tell them what to do predictably get rejected or the 'Let's just be friends' speech. Women test men to determine whether or not they have a spine, will stand up to them and for themselves, and to test their strength and worthiness. Women lose respect and attraction for men who let women jerk them around. Being too nice reveals that deep down, you don't think you are worthy of a woman's time, desires, or attention. This gives women no choice but to agree with you that you are not worthy." ~ Coach Corey Wayne

This is not about playing games with women. If you're a busy professional, if you're a busy man who has a full life, a full career, a business that keeps them busy—maybe you've got a side hustle going on, maybe you're a single parent—you've got to take time to work out and take care of your body. You've also got to take time to take care of yourself, you've got to take time to spend with your friends and your family, and to do activities and fun things that you love and enjoy.

Because you don't want to be working 100% of the time and having no free time to do things for yourself. You want to have a balanced life.

When you're busy and you have a balanced life, you're not going to be available 24/7 to chit chat and text all day long on different messaging apps, or texting, or talking, or FaceTiming on your cell phone. And so, when you're busy, you're naturally going to be mysterious and unpredictable to women. And guys that don't have anything going on in their lives, and then they make women the center of attention for their lives, women start to pick up on this. The guys become too predictable and boring, and they don't get their emotions stimulated by the guy, because he just simply doesn't have his life together.

And on top of that, being too nice, too compliant, too available, not standing up for yourself, just like the quote says, communicates that you don't think you're worthy and deserving of her attention and love. And women want a true equal. Ideally, women would like to date a guy that's on a higher level than they are. In other words, they have a higher socioeconomic status than they do. We all want the best for ourselves. If you're a guy, who doesn't want to date a woman that you feel like is out of your league? And the same thing for women. What woman wouldn't want to date a guy who's better looking, more successful, comes from a better family, lives in a better area, has a nicer house, and has a better life than she does?

LINK: https://understandingrelationships.com/her-curiosity-interest-soared/22314

The Moment You Start Losing Her

"Most guys who screw up perfectly good dating opportunities with the kind of women they've always dreamed of tend to fall under the illusion of action. What this means is that they believe and talk themselves into doing something in order to cause a woman to like them more or to want to date them. This really is nothing more than weakness, insecurity, neediness, fearfulness, desperation, and neurotic behavior causing them to try and make up for something that they feel they lack. In other words, they don't feel like they are good enough or deserve to have the kind of woman that they really want freely choose to love them and want to be with them. This manifests itself in the form of excessively contacting a woman, over pursuing her, and generally trying to force themselves into her life, instead of letting her come to them at her own pace." ~ Coach Corey Wayne

What's so cool is you can look back at old movies—especially movies from the 40s and the 50s, and even, like, the early 60s—where you see that the whole movie, the women are always plotting and scheming and trying to get the men to notice them so, eventually, the men fall in love, and want to live happily ever after, and have babies, and the white picket fence, and the family, and the happy home, and all of those things. A great example of this is the movie with James Stewart and Donna Reed that's always on during the holidays at Christmas called *It's a Wonderful Life*. What's great about the movie is Donna Reed's character, even when she was a little girl, always had a crush on Jimmy Stewart's character, 'George Bailey.' And George never really seems to notice this; he's kind of oblivious to it. But once he runs into her when she's, I think, a senior in high school and about to go off to college, he's taken by her beauty because, obviously, she's all grown up now—she's a beautiful young woman.

And through a series of events, what you see happening is, you know, over the course of say four or five years, as she goes off to college, and then comes back after college, and then, they hear about each other being in town, she obviously arranges through the neighborhood network, if you will, for Jimmy Stewart's character to be invited to come over and call on her. And, obviously, you could see they get together, and there's this amazing chemistry. And it's just a great movie that just shows how a beautiful love story naturally kind of comes together, because that's typically what happens in most regular people's lives. But what you look at movie-wise and media-wise over the last 50, 60 years is the exact opposite is happening. Men now act like women, the women act like men, and the men basically act like creepy stalkers. But yet, the women always seem to fall in love with them on screen, and they live happily ever after.

When you do this in the real world, you end up with a restraining order, getting friend-zoned, or a woman losing complete interest in you. So, movies like *It's a Wonderful Life,* and even the movie *Charade,* with Cary Grant and Audrey Hepburn; what I love about that movie is Cary Grant's character always does a great job with a deadpan kind of humor. He says something that's really funny, kind of serious, and also sounds kind of ridiculous and far-fetched, but he says it with a straight face. And Audrey does a great job of noticing that and looking perplexed at the moment when he drops something like that on her. And then, she's looking at him with a look on her face like, "Is he serious, or is he just fucking with me?" And as he sees this, and he lets her suffer for a little bit and be unsure of what his real intent was, then he lets her know that he's just messing with her or busting on her, or he teases her even more. And this is what's beautiful when it comes to flirtation between men and women, is that's the beauty of the art of it. It's saying something that sounds kind of funny, but it also could be kind of serious, but yet even a little ridiculous.

It's having the attitude of treating women kind of like the bratty little sister. If you've ever had younger sisters or guy friends who had younger sisters, there is always a lot of jousting that goes on back and forth between the two of them—being silly and funny, playful, kind of serious, kind of ridiculous. And it's good-natured humor. And this is the kind of thing that, this is what flirtation is—it's saying things that are a little over the top, but you say them with a straight face because it gets their attention. And sometimes you'll, obviously, take it a little too far—you'll say something that's offensive, or that's upsetting to her, and she gets a little butthurt—and then you just let her know that you were messing with her. So, you've got to have a little empathy, and you've got to have some sensory acuity to notice this, but it's really, super effective at creating attraction.

LINK: https://understandingrelationships.com/the-moment-you-start-losing-her/18587

Epic Virgin Date: Redemption

"Men who are used to getting and expect to get what they want because they are used to being successful with women take their time and practice infinite patience. They are never in a rush because they know a successful seduction is in the bag and will happen eventually. Therefore, they are able to live in the present moment and enjoy every delicious second of seducing and making love to the women they desire. Only inexperienced and unsuccessful men try to rush things, because they are fearful and because the kind of women they really want are scarce in their lives. Successful men have too many choices and are forced to be selective and take their time when deciding which woman, or women, to give the gift of their time to. If you behave in the same ways men who have an abundance of female choices in their lives do, women will see you as being desirable, sexy, valuable, rare, a catch, and a man who's worth the effort to make you theirs." ~ Coach Corey Wayne

The idea is the guy just has to go slightly slower in the seduction process than the woman. Almost 100% of the guys in the modern dating world are in a rush to make something happen, because they're worried that they're going to lose out on this unicorn that they've just come across. And what this does is it causes the woman to feel smothered and like she's losing her freedom. He's starting to act and treat her like they are in a relationship, even though they may have only been out on a few dates. That's why, by setting up just no more than one date per week, taking your time, and if you do that, just like I talk about in *3% Man*, over the course of two, three, four weeks of dating, what starts to happen is the woman notices that he's not moving as fast as the other men in her life might be moving. She starts to wonder why, she starts to think about him more, and when a woman is thinking about you, this has a positive impact on her interest level in you.

And so, when you take your time like this, she'll start to actually pull away and move away from the other guys that she may be dating and then spend more time, energy, and effort on trying to get your attention and validation. And as this happens, she starts to call you more, text you more, and then, you can simply use her initiated contact as an opportunity just to simply make the next date. Hang out, have fun, and hook up.

LINK: https://understandingrelationships.com/epic-virgin-date-redemption/24212

Submissiveness Is Feminine, Not Masculine

"Masculine energy stands up for what it believes in. Feminine energy is only submissive in the presence of masculine strength, not weakness. When a man is unsure of himself or goes along with something he's not really into in order to please a woman, he will turn a woman off and cause her to back away and not trust his masculine core. If a man won't stand up for himself to his woman, his woman will lose respect and attraction for him." ~ Coach Corey Wayne

If you look at the average television program or the average movie, what do you typically see? You see the bumbling guy, the bumbling husband that can't do anything right, and he always has the strong, stoic woman who always has the right word of encouragement and knows what to say. What's basically presented to us is this fake image of women acting like men and men acting like women. This ruins the sexual polarity in relationships in the natural world, but obviously, on the big screen and on your television set, everybody always lives happily ever after. And "Yes, dear," and doing what your wife wants, and being a people pleaser is shown to be the right way that a man is supposed to act. But when you try that crap in the real world, a woman will be repulsed by you, and lose attraction for you, and eventually move away from you.

LINK: https://understandingrelationships.com/submissiveness-is-feminine-not-masculine/16699

Staying On Purpose

"Masculine energy is about purpose, drive, mission, succeeding, accomplishing, breaking through barriers, setting, and achieving goals, etc. A man must pursue his purpose and mission above all else in life, and must never let anyone or anything, including his relationships, uncenter him or diminish him in any way. When a man allows his challenges or his woman to diminish or uncenter him, it will cause his woman to not trust his masculine core, become unsure of him, and act flakey. Feminine energy is attracted to masculine strength, but fearful and untrusting of weakness and uncertainty." ~ Coach Corey Wayne

A man is most attractive to women when he loves his life, he loves his career, he loves his business, he loves his friends, he loves his family, he loves what he does in his spare time for fun. He loves himself to the point where he takes care of his body so he can be in good shape and be maximally attractive to women. These are all the embodiment of masculine energy—purpose, drive, mission, succeeding, accomplishing, breaking through barriers, doing all the little things that average people simply will not do. This is what sets you apart from your competition. If you take care of your body, you take care of your career, you take care of your business, you take care of your personal life, you take care of all those little details, so instead of being focused on finding a woman to make you happy, you're focused on creating a great life and a great lifestyle that a woman would love to be a great complement to.

LINK: https://understandingrelationships.com/staying-on-purpose/14490

Masculine & Feminine Energy

"In any successful intimate relationship, there must be a healthy balance between masculine and feminine energy. When this balance is lacking, sexual polarity is reduced to the point that two people tend to act more like friends who are roommates and less like lovers who crave one another. The more masculine person must lead the relationship, be purpose-driven, make the plans, guide the direction, make the decisions, etc., whereas the more feminine person must be more playful, open, girly, follow more, and receive the strength and love of the masculine person." ~ Coach Corey Wayne

This is something that, oftentimes, creates problems in long-term relationships—is that the guy tends to, over time, become more submissive, stand up for what he believes in less and less, become more of a pleaser, and is more interested in following her lead. And then, what happens is the woman kind of becomes the dominant person, takes on a more masculine role, and the man becomes a more submissive, feminine type person. What this does is it ruins the sexual polarity. The man is no longer as strongly attracted to her as he was in the beginning, and vice versa; she's no longer as strongly attracted to him as she was in the beginning.

So, what tends to happen is, when you get the woman acting more masculine and the man acting more feminine, the relationship becomes more platonic, and the man continually defers to her leadership. And all you have to do is go out, sit on a park bench somewhere, or go to the mall, anywhere where there's lots of couples walking, and what you're going to see is kind of a sad state of affairs of our society, is that a lot of the men that you're going to notice are walking a foot or two behind the women, and the women are mostly doing the leading. And it's really interesting to watch. You can just see whoever the dominant person is; the one that's in control of the relationship is the one that's always walking in the front. So, you always want to walk side-by-side or a little ahead of her.

LINK: https://understandingrelationships.com/masculine-feminine-energy/14364

Unbalanced Sexual Polarity

"Knowing yourself and who you are is essential to having happy and balanced friendships and sexual relationships. When you are unsure of yourself and tend to vacillate back and forth between being masculine or feminine instead of acting consistent with your dominant natural sexual essence, you will instantly turn off your lover, and they will lose sexual attraction for you. Masculine energy tends to be certain, bold, courageous, willing to take risks, indifferent to chaos or things that are disconcerting, and similar to a rock or a mountain. Feminine energy tends to be, at times, unsure of itself, soft, submissive, emotional, focused on bonding, connecting, relationships, etc., and similar to the unpredictability of mother nature." ~ Coach Corey Wayne

This is something that is really, super important for guys in heterosexual relationships—it's continually being in their masculine. Because the longer a guy dates a woman, the more he tends to slack off and back off. And what happens is, he just starts to slowly abdicate his leadership role in the relationship. He, oftentimes, will become more worried about upsetting the woman and being a pleaser, instead of being the leader and the guy that's inviting her to join him. And when a man moves into his feminine energy in a relationship, this causes the woman to move into her masculine energy in the relationship, which is not her natural essence.

LINK: https://understandingrelationships.com/unbalanced-sexual-polarity/24640

Making Women Want You

"Loving in such a way that those who you love still feel free to come and go as they please is the key to having an abundance of choice with members of the opposite sex. When those who you desire sense or feel that you seek to possess, control, or lock them down to a commitment, they will move away from you because they fear losing their freedom. When you give a lover or potential lover the space to walk away from you forever or dare them to find someone better without specifically stating that, you create the conditions for them to choose you over all other potential lovers. To really own someone's heart and have them give it to you freely and willingly, you must be willing to let it go and lose it forever. That way, it becomes their idea to choose you and stay with you. It's the difference between using your innate irresistible power of unconditional love, versus trying to use force. True love is freedom." ~ Coach Corey Wayne

If you think about it, when you're competing against all the other guys out there, versus the '3% Man' that I write about in my first book, most of those guys have been programmed by society to over-pursue their romantic options. And what's interesting is it works in the movies and all the TV programs, but it basically turns men into a bunch of feminized wussies that act like women. And women are turned off and repulsed by guys who behave this way. Because men who have choice with women, men who have options, are not in a rush; they're always in kind of a peaceful and relaxed state and just have a "Take it or leave it," "Let's see what happens" kind of attitude. And that's why it's so counterintuitive that letting go, and backing off, and not being in a rush to push a woman into a commitment, but instead giving her the space, time, and freedom the fall deeply in love with you—to the point where she actually asks you to be her boyfriend—is always the best place to be. It's going to be putting you in a place of masculine strength and dominance, and this is what causes very feminine women to trust your masculine core, become soft and submissive, and willing to follow your lead.

LINK: https://understandingrelationships.com/making-women-want-you/17234

The Courtship Is Initiated By Men

"Men should always be clear about their intentions with women when they have romantic interest and not hide or mask their attraction by falsely acting uninterested or as if they are only interested in being friends. A man should not be focused on whether or not a woman is interested in him or seeking her approval, but instead, be focused on whether or not he is interested in her enough to want to pursue things romantically. It's the man's role to initiate and start the courtship by clearly communicating his romantic intentions and taking action to get contact information or set dates. Once the woman is made to feel safe and comfortable enough to open her heart to him by the strength of his character and actions, she will willingly embrace her natural instinctive role of wanting to bond and connect with him more and more over time. Once the snowball of the courtship has been pushed over the edge of the hill, so to speak, the woman will naturally and willingly pursue and chase him in order to receive his strength and presence." ~ Coach Corey Wayne

As I teach in my first book, *How To Be A 3% Man*, a man starts the courtship off, typically, by setting one date per week on a regular basis. Now, it doesn't mean you call her every Monday, and you make a date every Monday for some time later in the week. It just means, on average, you're going to call the girl, or text the girl, or message her no more than once per week, and that's it. And what happens is, as long as you follow the dating and seduction process that's in my book, *How To Be A 3% Man*, typically, by the second or third date, (usually week two or three), most women, on average, sleep with a guy by the second or third date as long as there's mutual interest, growing attraction, and he doesn't talk her out of liking him.

And then, what starts to happen is she doesn't want to wait to hear from him several days or a week later. And she typically will text, or call, or message him with something along the lines of, "Hey, I was thinking about you," "Hey, I had a great time the other night," "Hey, I saw a movie the other night, and this main character reminded me of you," or "I was hanging out with my girlfriends the other night, and this guy had a shirt on that was exactly like the shirt you were wearing on our last date," "How are you doing?", "How is your day going?" And those kinds of initiated contact, you should assume it's because she misses you, she's thinking about you, and she wants to see you. And therefore, be direct, decisive, get to the point, and make a date. Create the next opportunity for sex to happen. Hang out, have fun, hook up. It's a simple process.

And then, usually, as the weeks roll by, week three, week four, week five, the woman is calling, texting, messaging two to three times a week. And when that's going on, you really no longer have to reach out once a week, because every couple of days she's reaching out to you, and you just use those as opportunities to set the next date. It makes things really easy for you, and it gives the woman the time and space away from you to miss you, for her feelings to grow, to emotionally bond with you, and then she reaches out, and then you move things forward. That way, it goes along at her pace, and you never have to worry about over pursuing or smothering her and hearing the kinds of things that women say to guys that are moving too fast, such as "I'm confused," "I'm not looking for a relationship right now," "I'm not sure where I'm able to be at this point in my life," "I've got to get my head together," "I've got to work on myself first," that kind of stuff. That'll be a thing of the past.

LINK: https://understandingrelationships.com/the-courtship-is-initiated-by-men/16735

The Damage Over-Pursuing Does

"It's very difficult to change a woman's perception of you after you have over-pursued, over-texted, and acted needy while trying to date her, but been firmly stuck in friends-zone for several months. If you are able to exercise emotional self-control, and back off so she starts to pursue you and develop romantic interest, once she falls in love with you, she may start to complain and nag that she has to do most of the pursuing. This makes it almost impossible to find a healthy balance between pursuing too much—which turns her off—and not pursuing enough—which also turns her off—because now she will expect you to behave the same way you did in the beginning. The phone is for setting dates, not getting to know someone. If you violate this principle in the beginning of a relationship by texting and talking all day long, later on in the relationship, she will think you no longer care when you don't do this. Besides, when you talk constantly via the phone, texting, or messaging, you're not going to have much to talk about in person on your dates, which makes things boring and awkward." ~ Coach Corey Wayne

It's a scientific fact that women are more attracted to men whose feelings are unclear. Women love guys that are mysterious, unpredictable, and hard to figure out. Women are curious by nature, just like cats. And less really is more, especially in the beginning. Most guys that don't know any better spend way too much time talking and texting for the first few days or weeks, but very little time getting together in person where they can sell themselves to each other in person. And by the time he finally gets around to asking her out on a date, she kind of feels like he's a known quantity, that she knows everything about him, there's nothing left to discover, and sees him as boring and not really worthy of her time. It's kind of like having all your friends tell you the ending to a movie that's really popular and all the main plot points, then you think, "Eh, I'll just wait until it comes out on digital delivery," or on DVD, whatever it happens to be. Women love discovering everything about you slowly over time. Don't be in a rush to tell her everything about you; let her discover this slowly.

LINK: https://understandingrelationships.com/the-damage-over-pursuing-does/21206

Dating: Over-Eagerness & Over-Thinking

"It is a man's role in dating and courtship to create an opportunity for sex to happen. Hang out, have fun, and hook up. Unless your intentions are strictly platonic or professional, the whole purpose of a date between a man and a woman is to explore a mutual sexual attraction and dissolve any barriers to sex happening. Men should start out making only one date per week; this gives a man time to assess a woman's interest, compatibility, and emotional stability, as well as to create and facilitate sexual attraction. Men should not be making future dates on the same day that they are on a date or had a date. Otherwise, they risk coming off as desperate, needy, creepy, stalkerish, and scaring women away." ~ Coach Corey Wayne

Guys that don't know any better have seen too many movies and TV where the guy has to worry about losing his girl to some other guy. The reality is, if you move at a slower pace than most guys in the courtship because you are selective and you're taking your time to get to know her, because you haven't decided whether or not she's actually a good match for you, you're going to set yourself apart from almost all of the other guys she's going to interact with. Because if you're worried about losing her to another guy, you're going to call too much, you're going to text too much, you're going to pursue too much, you're going to try to force interactions with her, you're going to try to force yourself into her life to spend more time with her. Because you mistakenly think, "If I just spend more time around her, she's going to see what a great guy I am." And what ends up happening is, you make it feel to her like she's already in a relationship with you, when she's still trying to get to know you and trying to figure out how she really feels about you.

You have to give women the time and space away from you to wonder about you, to think about you, to miss you, and also test the strength of all of the guys that are in her life. Guys that don't know any better are going to pursue too, much too hard, and when you're the mysterious one who's hanging back and not really moving as fast as these other guys are, she's going to move towards you more, call you more, text you more, and you'll be able to use these as opportunities to set more dates, versus trying to pursue her and force her to spend time around her in hopes that you can convince her to like you. When you're in that kind of state of mind, you're seeking her attention and validation, which is a feminine trait. If you act like a woman, she's going to treat you like a woman, and lose attraction for you, and only see you as being a platonic friend.

LINK: https://understandingrelationships.com/dating-over-eagerness-over-thinking/22121

James Bond: Men Lead. Women Follow.

"It is natural for men to lead in all aspects of their lives, as masculinity is leadership energy. Feminine energy is submissive and nurturing energy. The word 'lead' means 'to go first'—to set the standards and vibe wherever they go. Strong alpha male masculine energy creates a space and the environment where women will feel safe and comfortable enough to relax and willingly submit to follow the lead of men. In order for this to happen, men must first demonstrate the right amount of charm, humor, humility, respect, and confidence that displays their worthiness and earns the respect of women." ~ Coach Corey Wayne

If you've ever watched the *James Bond* movies with Daniel Craig as the lead character, (or even Pierce Brosnan), what I love about their portrayal of this character is these guys display dangerous masculinity. They're willing to take risks. When they walk into the room, they act like they fucking own the place. They act like it's their casino, it's their restaurant, it's their nightclub, it's their party, even though, oftentimes, they are guests that have kind of snuck in there. They have a cocky, humorous arrogance about themselves. They're sure of themselves. They know they're dangerous. They're nice, and they're respectful to other people, but when they come across the bad guys or the assholes, they usually have some kind of sharp, biting wit and put down what they say to the bad guys, (or bad girls, in some cases), to kind of put them in their place and let them know what they really think of them, because they're trying to un-center the other person and cause them to lose control and make mistakes. That doesn't mean you want to go out and start shit with people; but you want to have that kind of cocky, humorous, humble, kind demeanor where you're nice to everybody that's nice to you. You're playful, but you also don't take shit from other people who are being disrespectful, and you use humor in a playful way to communicate to other people when their behavior is inappropriate.

LINK: https://understandingrelationships.com/james-bond-men-lead-women-follow/35375

Changes, Happiness & Feeling Good

"Personal and professional relationships that stand the test of time do so because of mutual respect, admiration, great communication, shared goals and values, growing together, being kind and appreciative, building each other up, supporting one another, honesty, and adding value to each other's lives. The happier you are, the more your choices will bring you people and circumstances that contribute to and expand your happiness. Spend your time with people who are easy and effortless to be with. People who cause friction, drama, and restlessness should be avoided and deleted, because they will rob you of your peace and ability to enjoy your life and reach your full potential." ~ Coach Corey Wayne

The best thing you can do to become more attractive to other people is to do things that will create a life and lifestyle that you're happy about. Because when you're proud of your life and what you're doing, how you live, where you live, and you're doing fun things with like-minded people, you're going to be happier, you're going to smile more. This makes you more approachable and, obviously, makes you more attractive. Like the old saying goes, "Smile, because it improves your face value."

LINK: https://understandingrelationships.com/changes-happiness-feeling-good/25278

Sexual Polarity & Rekindling Romance

"In order to create sexual attraction and polarity in any adult sexual relationship, one person must be in their natural masculine essence, and the other in their natural feminine essence. Without it, sexual attraction, polarity, and interest in sex will evaporate. By focusing on becoming the best version of yourself and being in your natural essence, you will make yourself more attractive to your lover or potential lovers." ~ Coach Corey Wayne

A big part of what I do when I'm doing coaching sessions with male clients is getting them to display more attractive masculine behaviors—to do more of the leading and extending invitations to the women they're dating, planning the dates out, making dinner reservations, and if they've got kids, going ahead and taking care of the babysitter arrangements—because these are the little things that communicate that you're the leader, and you're the head, or the king of your kingdom, or the head of your household, if you will. And this allows women to relax into their femininity—to open up, to receive you emotionally, mentally, spiritually, and physically.

LINK: https://understandingrelationships.com/sexual-polarity-rekindling-romance/23802

Sexuality Polarity

"In order to maintain sexual polarity, attraction, and interest, men and women must act consistently congruent with their natural dominant masculine or feminine essence. In all successful heterosexual, lesbian, or gay relationships, there is always one person who is more masculine, and the other is more feminine. Heterosexual men who act or become unsure, indecisive, and too weak to set healthy boundaries, stand up for themselves and what they want, and lose their focus on their purpose and mission in life, will cause their women to lose respect, interest, and attraction for them. This leads to being friend-zoned. Heterosexual women who try to make all the decisions, control things and generally stop being, looking, and dressing feminine, will turn their men off and cause them to lose interest in sex and romance. They then become more like roommates and friends instead of lovers. When you lose your connection, confidence, and congruence with your natural essence, you will shortly thereafter lose the respect and attraction of your lover, and therefore, your relationship." ~ Coach Corey Wayne

You can see this a lot in public these days. Especially a great place is to go to the mall and just observe couples. What you see is couples that have been together, and they've got kids that are middle school age— what you notice is the women are usually walking in front, they've cut all their hair, they don't wear any makeup, they usually have a scowl or a bitchy demeanor on their face, their husband is following several feet behind her along with the kids, and she is leading the way. They both tend to dress alike, they're both overweight, and when they sit down, they're not really talking to one another. They're just kind of roommates. They're just hanging out. It's like, all the sexual polarity is completely gone in those relationships. That's not a way to live. That's not the way you're going to live and be able to reach your full potential.

It's just amazing how that happens—is the women regress and become more masculine and, therefore, they feel unattractive, they act unattractive, and their appearance becomes unattractive. And the same thing with the men. They go from being confident, masculine, sure of themselves, and in shape to being dumpy looking, submissive, feminine, and too afraid to piss off the wife or upset her. So, they just become compliant and weak, and they do basically whatever she tells him to do. It's really sad, and it's really pathetic, and it's absolutely an epidemic in our society today. All you have to do is go out in public where people are congregating and moving around and just watch, and you can see this for yourself.

LINK: https://understandingrelationships.com/sexuality-polarity/21665

PURSUING YOUR CALLING

The 45-Year-Old Virgin

"Most people have many parts of their personal and professional lives that they are not happy with. However, they are not miserable enough to do anything to change their situation or alter their life trajectory in any meaningful way. The average person tends to major in minor things, and never comes close to reaching their full potential. Our time is limited on this earth, and we all must decide what we are willing to go to our graves having not achieved or experienced. Choose wisely."
~ Coach Corey Wayne

Believe it or not, this particular email was from a guy who, I can't remember specifically, but all I know is that he was a 45-year-old virgin, and I believe he may have, finally, after he found my work, started having sex for the first time in his life. I come across guys that oftentimes spent the early part of their life being super religious—dating, but nothing ever happening—and then they get into, usually, their mid to late 30s, and they kind of lose interest in their really restrictive religion. And by that point, they've kind of missed out on all the typical dating and courtship that most people in the West experience.

And, you know, several of these guys that had no experience just fucking go on an absolute tear to make up for lost time, because they get to a point in their life—especially, you know, when they get into their late 30s, their 40s and they think, "Fuck, I'm living in a body that's going to die, and I have all this stuff that I wanted to do, but I had all these rules that I came up with of why I couldn't do it." They recognize that their time is running out. And the reality is, the time's going to pass, and you've got to decide how you want to spend your time. And the best way to spend your time is being productive, taking action towards things that are exciting and emotionally compelling to you on a consistent, daily basis, and always trying to refine, enhance, and improve your approach, so you can get a little bit better each and every day.

Give yourself permission to be a beginner again every day. Be infinitely patient. As long as you're taking action and you're trying to get better every day, you're going to see incremental progress, you're going to feel like you're making progress. Because success is making progress, after all. Even if it's small and tiny and incremental; it's better than doing nothing. When you do nothing, it demotivates you. It makes you feel worse. And then, you just walk around with the feeling that you want to escape from your life instead of being excited about what's going to happen next.

LINK: https://understandingrelationships.com/the-45-year-old-virgin/36955

Why We Settle

"Life is too short to settle for a life that is less than what you are capable of living. We are all surrounded by people who are too weak to pursue their own dreams and goals—people who try to get everyone around them to settle for the same level of mediocrity, so they don't feel uncomfortable. The most successful people in life are successful because they have high standards for themselves, are unwilling to settle, and spend their time plotting, planning, and taking action to make their lives the way they want them to be. If they don't know something or lack something, they seek it out and model those who do. You either are choosing to take the action required to make your dreams a reality, or you are creating the circumstances to one day come to the realization that you have spent your whole life playing it safe, not reaching your full potential, and living someone else's life instead of a life of your own design." ~ Coach Corey Wayne

If you love yourself, and you love your life, and you're happy with your life, you're going to be naturally inclined to have better, richer quality relationships with everybody in your life. Your activities that you do socially are going to be fun, exciting, compelling, and you're going to be doing them with people that are fun, exciting, and compelling to be around. Also, whatever it is you do for a living—your life's work—is going to be something that sets you on fire, that excites you. The kind of cars you drive, the houses you live in, the neighborhoods that you work and play in are all going to be nicer, and better, and more facilitate the kind of life and lifestyle that you want.

When they look at people who live a long, happy life, the one common thread in all of them is they have good, high-quality relationships—not just their intimate relationships, but their friends, their family, their peer group. Those people tend to take better care of their bodies, they eat better, they exercise more, they eat healthier on a regular basis. They do the little things that regular, average people are simply not willing to do. I mean, think about it, if you're not happy, if you hate your life, if you don't enjoy what you do for a living, if you don't like the people you work with, if you don't like the people that are in your life, what's your motivation to eat better? What's your motivation to spend time with any of those people, if you don't really like hanging out with those people? Your life then becomes one of quiet desperation instead of one that you're designing and expecting to get better with time.

When you have no hope, you don't really have a reason for living. You're just existing. You're not really even contributing except in order to earn a paycheck, so you can pay the bills and get to the weekend, where you can have a little bit of peace and kind of check out from life. People that live this way live a much shorter life.

LINK: https://understandingrelationships.com/why-we-settle/16969

Not Looking For A Relationship

"You must be who you are. What you should be is not important. Life is your oyster. You can make it whatever you want. If you want to settle down, get married, and spend the rest of your life with one person, then do that. If you want to have multiple girlfriends whom you have an open relationship with, then good for you, do that. If you want to have three girlfriends and be exclusive with the three of them, then do that. The bottom line is that no matter what form of relationship you choose to have, like-minded people will be supportive, while most other people who have different views on relationships are more than likely not going to have anything nice to say. Live your truth without fear or shame and be unapologetic about it. Life is short. You should create a life and lifestyle that is to your liking and continually circulate until you find other like-minded people who share the same goals and values." ~ Coach Corey Wayne

The reality is, everybody has a slightly different idea about what kind of relationship they want to have and the timeframe in which they are expecting to make that happen or make it a reality. Society teaches a one-size-fits-all type of relationship strategy—that we're supposed to find a unicorn lover, "The One," the one perfect person who's going to complete us, and then, we're going to live happily ever after for the rest of our lives in marital bliss. Well, if that was really accurate or a good ideal for people to aspire to, we would not have a divorce rate of 50-60%.

Obviously, a lot of people in how they go about their personal life and their relationships, they're using a really crappy strategy in order to achieve that. And any time you get yourself into personal and professional situations and you settle, as the years roll by and the decades roll by, and especially, as you get into your late 40s and early 50s and start having a midlife crisis, you start getting faced with the fact that your choices up until that point in your midlife have led you to where you are. And a lot of people wake up when they hit middle-aged, and they don't like what they see in the mirror. They don't like their lives and the way they look at it, how they're living, and what's in their life or the circumstances of their lives, and they recognize that they need to change something about this.

They recognize that the way they've been living is not serving them and that they're simply running out of time; that the sands of the hourglass are running out, and there is not going to be any more sand being put in at the top. That's an incredible motivator for a lot of people. And sometimes, that's what it takes to wake them up to the fact that they've been living a mediocre life that they're not satisfied with, and they've resolved to pay the price to get from where they are to where they want to be, eventually, even though they may have spent the first four or five decades of their life living their life according to somebody else's expectations.

This is why it's so important to figure out what's really important to you, why you want it, have emotionally compelling reasons why you want that, and then you've got to resolve to pay the price in order to get it. Because at some point—whether it's your midlife or when you're at the end of your life—anything that you failed to go for that you, deep down, really wanted to go for, at some point is going to become a regret. And if you're at the end of your life, the last thing you want to be doing at the end of your life is thinking about all the opportunities and all the things you missed out on, and what you're not going to be able to do.

LINK: https://understandingrelationships.com/not-looking-for-a-relationship/19064

I Turned My Life Around Completely!

"Relationships and once very stable life circumstances dissolve for only one reason: to help you become more, grow, and create something even grander. Life is change. Life is always naturally and innately seeking a higher, more balanced, freer, peaceful, and more loving expression of itself. Anything that stops growing in nature dies and is then eliminated. Anything that grows and adds value expands—is enhanced, entrenched, and enforced. By becoming aligned with your heart's highest values, desires, dreams, and taking action, you ensure that you will also expand, grow, contribute in meaningful ways, be loved, and be valued." ~ Coach Corey Wayne

When I was young, I used to be big into model trains. And it's kind of a great metaphor for how I lived my life in that I might spend a year or two building a layout, and buying buildings, and cars, and lights, and lampposts, and track, and additional cars, and building and painting mountains, and other things. And then, once it was done, I'd spend a few months playing with the finished layout. And then, I would get bored and want to create something new. And then, I would tear it all apart, and then, spend the next year or two building and spending most of my paper route money buying new things to make the new layout. And when I look back on my life, it's kind of a great metaphor.

We're always in a constant state of creating, growing, experiencing what we wanted to create. And, eventually, what we created dissolves—whether that's in the form of a new job, or a new city to live in. Maybe it's a new relationship, maybe it's just moving to a different neighborhood, or buying and selling a different house, a different career. The bottom line is life is change. It never stays the same. And that's part of life's rhythms. You know, now, at 51 years old, when I look back at my life, there's a lot of people that once were very close to me, and I used to spend a lot of time with, and they've long since passed away—whether it was friends, or family, or people that were close to me. Everything is always changing, and nothing lasts. And the key to recognize is, once your internal enthusiasm is gone for something, or someone, or a way you were living, you know something needs to change. And if you don't change anything, what happens is that feeling of dread tends to grow and get worse and worse as time goes by.

So, listen to what your heart, your intuition, and your curiosity are telling you internally. Because if you're getting up every day and looking in the mirror and not liking what you're about to do that day for too many days in a row, you need to make some kind of change in your life, because you've stagnated on some level. You need some new stimuli, and new things, people, places, circumstances to look forward to, things that you want to create, bigger goals, bigger dreams—things of that nature.

LINK: https://understandingrelationships.com/i-turned-my-life-around-completely/23063

Maintaining Mystery & Interest

"In life, when one door closes, another one tends to open. The more comfortable you are with change and trying new things determines how smoothly you are able to traverse life's challenges, setbacks, and unexpected circumstances. Life is a continuous process of taking on bigger risks, challenges, and dreams. Stretching beyond your comfort zone is how you expand your skills, ability, and knowledge. Reaching your full potential requires you to decide what you want, why you want it, and executing a plan of consistent action, learning from your mistakes, refining your approach, persisting without exception, and getting better." ~ Coach Corey Wayne

As you go through life, the things that you love, that you enjoy, that you're passionate about today, more than likely, are going to continue to evolve and change over time. Things that you're really excited about today might not be so exciting 5, 10, 15, 20 years down the road in the future. And as you immerse yourself in things you're interested in, you're curious about, and you're passionate about, what's going to happen as you experience the things that you were once curious about and you actually experience it, there will be other opportunities that will kind of float by on your journey of life. And you will become curious about those things, and you'll be interested in those things, or those people, or those hobbies, or those interests, or those techniques, or strategies, or products, or services, whatever it happens to be.

When your internal Compass is telling you, "What is that? That's interesting. I'm really curious about that," you've got to honor that. You've got to explore that. Go check it out, and move towards it, and see where it's going to lead to. Because the more you're open to change and new things, the more you're going to easily traverse from one thing—from one passion—to embracing new passions or others. It might not mean that you completely give up all the things that you are passionate about today, but you add other things in the future as you gain life experience and wisdom.

LINK: https://understandingrelationships.com/maintaining-mystery-interest/25850

Crotch On Fire!

"Life is short, and your time is limited. Everyone must determine what is really important to them and then have the courage to build their lives and lifestyles around that. Someday your life is going to be over. What would you build if you knew you could not fail? What must you experience or achieve in order to feel like you accomplished your life's purpose and enjoyed your life? What must you change in your life right now in order to put yourself onto a better path to accomplishing your grandest goals and dreams?" ~ Coach Corey Wayne

This is something that everybody should think about: "What do I want to do? What am I unwilling to go to my grave having not experienced in life? What is really, super important?" If you're going to feel like you got the most out of your life and you feel like, "Man, that was a hell of a ride, and I did everything I could, and everything that I wanted to, and I went after all my goals and dreams. And, despite the fact that my life didn't turn out exactly like I once thought it did, it turned out amazing, nonetheless, and I'm grateful for where it is." Because the reality is if you talk to people who work in nursing homes and deal with people who are at the end of their lives, a lot of them have regrets that they didn't take enough risks in life. They wished they had gone after things that they had dreamed of, but because they're now at the end of their lives and they're out of time, there's nothing they can do about it. And so, they have regrets. They also regret not spending more time with their friends and their family, and people that were closest to them.

So, learn from people who are at the end of their lives. You don't want to be in the same position as they are, having regrets about things that you didn't go for or people that you didn't try to love or ask out. So, again, think back to "What would you do if you knew you couldn't fail?" Because remember, the time is going to pass anyway. You might as well be taking action and focusing on the process of taking action to get you from where you are to where you want to be. Because, again, someday you're going to come to a place, and you're going to realize that you're out of time. And if you've gone for all the things you wanted in life, and you've acquired and achieved most of your goals and your dreams, you can die peacefully with a smile on your face for a life well-lived.

LINK: https://understandingrelationships.com/crotch-on-fire/33243

Thinking About Making Big Life Changes?

"Sometimes in life, we come to the realization that our intimate relationships, our friendships, our career, or even where we live no longer serve us, and it's time to move on to something better or new. Most people tend to stay in jobs, relationships, friendships, careers, and communities longer than they should. Your ability to be happy and fulfilled in life is in direct proportion to the amount of change and uncertainty that you can comfortably live with. The only constant in life is change. Nothing stays the same forever. Everything you build and everyone you love will eventually die and turn to dust, including you. There comes a time when you must make a stand for who you are and what you believe in. You can either choose to take action towards the magnificent life you want to create, or you can choose to settle, be average, and mediocre. You should only choose the latter if you truly believe you can be okay while on your deathbed knowing that you never tried to reach and live your full potential. That's something to think about." ~ Coach Corey Wayne

Steve Jobs talked about one of the best things that you can do to make your life better is to always ask yourself, every day—especially if you have had too many days in a row—the best thing you can do when you look yourself in the mirror in the morning is to ask yourself, do you really want to do what you're about to do today? And when the answer is "No" too many days in a row, that obviously means that you need to change something. Some part of your life is not working for you and is not ideal, and you need to put some intention and some effort on it to make things better or to make some necessary changes, even when they're painful changes.

The reality is, what you love to do today might be boring as hell or unpleasant a few years from now. Life is constantly change. When you have an idea or a concept about something you want to create, you want to own, or you want to experience, and then, you actually get to experience it, you get the real-world wisdom of having that experience. And what that does is it gives rise to new passions, new goals, new interests, new hobbies, new things to master and get better at. This is part of life; this is the process of living life. Life and success is making progress.

LINK: https://understandingrelationships.com/thinking-about-making-big-life-changes/17057

I'm Sure She's Seeing Another Dude

"It's always best to trust in yourself, your heart, and your intuition. No one knows you better than you do. When you try to make your decisions based upon the opinions and feelings of others, instead of what your heart is compelling you to do, you are giving your power away and not trusting that you know what's best for you. It's impossible for others to truly know what's in your heart. When we make decisions for ourselves that are aligned with our heart, even if they create pain for us in the short term, we enable the universe to meet our needs effortlessly in the future. When we try to hold on to what no longer feels right, we inhibit the dissolution of circumstances and relationships that no longer serve us; this delays the manifestation of people and circumstances that are in our highest interest and of greater value and benefit to our overall well-being and happiness." ~ Coach Corey Wayne

I've always found that when I listen to that inner voice—when I listen to that inner intuition and feeling, and then I take actions based upon it—the results have always been pretty good. When I ignore that intuition, like in the case that I wrote about in my first book, *3% Man*, when I was thinking about breaking up with the woman who eventually became my first wife, I didn't do what felt right, which was to end the relationship. I was terrified of what would happen if I broke up with her, and I never found anyone better. From my perspective, at the time, when I was 25 years old and didn't have a lot of life experience, I was thinking to myself, "My God. I'm 25 years old, and she's the best thing that's ever happened to me, but yet, something still feels like it's missing."

And so, by listening to other people, because I didn't have the confidence in myself, I didn't have enough life experience, and I also didn't have enough good people around me who had experience in this particular area of intimate relationships that I could rely upon, I rolled the dice, took in all of the feedback that I got from everybody else, and did whatever everybody else told me I should do, even though it did not feel right. And I just basically talked myself into getting married when I really felt, at the time, I didn't want to get married. And so, that was just one example of many examples over the course of my life where my heart and my intuition were telling me something completely different than what my head was telling me.

It didn't feel right, but yet I did it anyway, and that, obviously, led to a lot of pain down the road when I had to go through a divorce. But I was young, I was dumb, I was inexperienced, I didn't know any better. And I know thousands and thousands of men all over the world have been saved from making that same mistake because of the fact I've written about it, and talked about it, and done countless videos about the topic over the years. Because most people are faced with similar choices and similar emotions in their life, and they often make the same mistakes. I've met countless guys over the years that did the same thing I did. I even had a business partner that did the same thing with his first wife; it didn't feel right, but intellectually he talked himself into it, and he listened to everybody else around him, (he was only 21 at the time), and he did what everybody else told him he should do, instead of what felt right for him.

LINK: https://understandingrelationships.com/im-sure-shes-seeing-another-dude/17029

I Am At Peace With Who I Am

"Life becomes easy and effortless once we learn to love and accept ourselves unconditionally. You should have the positive expectation that your actions and efforts will eventually lead to the creation and manifestation of the life you've always dreamed of. When you are at peace with yourself, you value yourself, you love yourself, and you see yourself as a gift, you will act and speak in ways that are congruent with those truths; you will also reject and move away from circumstances and people who are not aligned with your own internal truth; you will no longer care what other people think about you or how they think you should be living your life. Why? Because you live to make yourself happy first since you see yourself as a complete person who lacks nothing. And therefore, you don't try to live your life according to other people's expectations. Besides, no one else can really know why you want what you want, or your motivation and reasons why you want it. After all, it's YOUR truth and YOUR life!" ~ Coach Corey Wayne

This is one of the best things that you can do for yourself and your mental and emotional well-being, is getting to a place in life where you do what you do to make *you* happy. Whatever it is that you do for a living, your life's work, you do it because it brings you pleasure and joy and you're passionate about it. The same thing with your intimate relationships; you want to be with somebody that adds value to your life, that they are a net plus. They don't bring any drama or any kind of nonsense into your life. They simply make your life better just by the nature of them being there. Now, when you get into a relationship with somebody that's a net plus for your life and you eventually have kids, you're going to be a much better parent because you made a good choice in who you chose to be your teammate and your co-parent.

LINK: https://understandingrelationships.com/i-am-at-peace-with-who-i-am/16622

A Man Does What He Must

"Sometimes life can bring unexpected changes in career, business, and personal relationships that cause current relationships and circumstances to dissolve. Your comfort zone is where you are most uncomfortable. Why? It's how you will grow the most and reach your full potential. It does not serve you or those around you to live a life that is less than you are capable of living. Sacrificing who you are and shelving your dreams in order to please others will only make you miserable and cause you to resent those who you changed for in order to please them. The right people will love and support you, no matter what you choose in life. The wrong people, or weak people, will expect you to sacrifice your own happiness and dreams so they don't feel uncomfortable, despite the fact it makes you miserable. Life is too short to spend it trying to live up to the unreasonable expectations of others."
~ Coach Corey Wayne

I did a video this morning that I think this quote is great and kind of segues into what this particular emailer was having as challenges in his relationship. He had been with his girlfriend for about six months, and then about a month and a half ago, he ended up breaking up with her because she was getting upset with him for liking posts that some of his friends, which were actually female were commenting on, and he was liking some of their posts. And this guy doesn't have any pictures of himself on his social media at all, but his girlfriend—they had several discussions about this—was getting upset with him because he was liking the posts of other women that were just strictly friends. And these weren't even women that he had dated. And so, what's interesting is after about a month and a half after they broke up, he got in touch with her, and come to find out, she's already dating some other guy and wanted to see where it went.

And he was totally in love with this woman when he broke up with her, but they just basically had an impasse because she wanted him to mute all the women that were on his social media because, as she put it, she didn't feel safe. And these were women that he had known for years—they were friends, friends of family, coworkers, people that he knew strictly in a platonic sense—and she was demanding that he boot all of them out of his life. But when he refused to do that, she broke up with him. And then, after about a month and a half, he got back in touch, and then, all of a sudden, she's dating some other guy. And so, the reality is that he was blinded by his own interest and couldn't see the fact that she really wasn't that into him and, obviously, had all the power in the relationship.

And so, he's suffering for a month and a half after they broke up, got in touch, and she's already moved on with another guy. And the only reason that she was really getting upset with him about other women being on his Instagram and his social media is because she's obviously a liar and a cheater. So, the reality is, she probably picked this fight with him over this issue because the bottom line is, she's the one who's lying and devious and unfaithful. Because she obviously lined up this replacement guy while they were still together, and yet, she's giving him the third degree about how he might potentially be cheating on her.

Remember, no one will ever do or say anything to you that isn't a direct reflection of how they feel about themselves in a moment. So, obviously, what was going on is she was projecting her own disloyalty and infidelity onto him, and he's jumping through his butt trying to figure out a way that they can compromise, but he stuck to his principles. And so, he was thinking, "Hey, me sticking to my principles cost me my relationship," and in reality, what it really did was reveal the fact that his girlfriend really wasn't that into him.

But he'd been following me for several years and only read my first book, *How To Be A 3% Man*, a couple of times, (I think it was five or six times total that he had read it in the several years that he had been following me), so it was obvious he didn't really know the material backward and forwards and was completely oblivious to the fact that she just wasn't that into him. So, at the end of the day, him standing up for his principles, he was thinking it ruined his relationship, but in reality, it actually saved him from going too far down the road with a woman who was going to be disloyal anyway.

LINK: https://understandingrelationships.com/a-man-does-what-he-must/14060

Hopeless Messed Up Life

"Success always takes way longer than you think it will and is usually harder than you thought it would be when you first started. That is why it is essential to choose to spend your time practicing, perfecting, measuring, and refining your skills and talents and growing your reserve of knowledge for something you have a passionate, burning desire to achieve and become. Without a passion and burning desire for an emotionally compelling outcome, you'll simply give up as soon as things get difficult. Focus on what must be done today and do it to move yourself ever so slightly forward towards your grandest goals and dreams. Big dreams are built upon the successful execution and perfection of the tiniest minor details, day in and day out, especially when you don't feel like it." ~ Coach Corey Wayne

This is why most people really struggle with the science of high achievement fundamentals and implementing them into their life—is they just don't see enough results in a short enough period of time to keep themselves motivated to keep persevering. That's why it's absolutely essential before you start that you know what you want, why you want it, and you have an emotionally compelling reason why you want it. Because, without that, you won't get very far before you give up, because things are going to get uncomfortable really quick. And if you give up within the first few weeks, there is no way you'd be able to endure several years, or even a decade or more, of things not working out in your favor, or you not ultimately getting from where you are to where you want to be.

Me, personally, I've got lots of goals and lots of things I've wanted to do in my life that I haven't yet been able to experience, and quite frankly, I thought I was going to experience these things years ago and achieve these things years ago. But the reality is, I love what I do for a living. I love the fact that I have ownership of my time. And I've got a lot of big, audacious goals that I still want to accomplish. And quite frankly, some of them feel like they're way off in the future and it's going to take years and decades, and sometimes, I wonder if I'll even be able to achieve them. But the bottom line is, no matter what happens on a daily basis I'm still grinding, I'm still moving my life forward, I'm still trying to get better each and every day.

Because the reality is that time is going to pass, so you might as well spend that time doing things that are productive, things you're passionate about, things that you enjoy doing, because the more you work at it, the smarter you're going to get, the more wisdom you're going to have, and the better you're going to get at it. And when you get better at things, you get more efficient at them. And as you get older and you become more efficient, you're able to work smarter and not harder. You're able to spend less time earning more money and less time invested to get really great, big, outsized results.

LINK: https://understandingrelationships.com/hopeless-messed-up-life/36849

Success Attracting Women

"Success is most often due to simply showing up, taking consistent action, learning from your mistakes, refining your approach, and refusing to quit until you find a way to accomplish your grandest goals and dreams. Succeeding at what you want in life usually takes way longer than you thought it would and way more money than you expected to spend or invest. The impulse to quit and give up for immediate comfort and peace of mind will always be strong, and most people you encounter along your journey will encourage you to quit and settle because they have also chosen the less difficult path. That's why you must find what lights you up on the inside and creates a deep, burning desire to achieve or become what you want—something that is more emotionally compelling and motivating than simply quitting and seeking immediate comfort." ~ Coach Corey Wayne

Everybody must have some kind of purpose in life—whether you're a mom and you just want to raise your kids, that's your purpose, or you're an entrepreneur and you want to build a great multimillion-dollar or billion-dollar company that impacts the world and changes lives around the world. Or you just want to be a superstar employee, or superstar athlete, or the best person that washes cars for a living. Everybody has innate gifts, skills, and talents. We're all different, we're all unique, and we're all made for a specific purpose. Everybody must have some kind of purpose and some kind of life's work that is exciting and compelling to them. Even if it doesn't earn a lot of money, as long as you're getting up every day and doing something that brings you joy, that you look forward to, and that when you get home at night and you put your head on your pillow, you feel a sense of accomplishment, and peace, and contentment, because this is what gives your life meaning.

LINK: https://understandingrelationships.com/success-attracting-women/36990

Beaten Down By Life

"If you really want to get to a place in life where your days are spent doing the things you really want to do and doing it with the kind of people you really want to do it with, you have to start somewhere. Follow your passion, curiosity, and intuition when trying to discover what your purpose in life is. It is wise to assume it will take decades to design and create the kind of life you've always wanted. Most people don't become an overnight success. Your path is your path. By having something emotionally compelling to strive for, your passion will keep you motivated to keep trying and adapting your approach, even when it seems hopeless." ~ Coach Corey Wayne

Many guys struggle when it comes to figuring out their purpose in life because, like with most things, they are extremely impatient. They think it's just something that you flip on like a light switch, and you know instantly what you're supposed to do. For me, when I was 18 and choosing to major in Construction Management, I had 18 years of exploring, going to school, being curious about things, studying things I was curious about, experimenting with things with my hands, building things that I saw in my mind to the point where eventually they existed in my physical world. So, I was always moving towards what I wanted. And then, when I was looking for a degree that would enable me to do what I really wanted, (which was buy, fix, and sell single-family homes for a profit), when I was looking through those different degree programs, it just jumped right out at me because so much of that degree involved me putting my mechanical mind to work in a career.

In other words, I found a way to monetize my passions—by getting a degree which would give me a background that would help me in the construction industry. Now, when you fast-forward 16, 17 years into the future, by the time I was 34, 35, 36 and coming to recognize that I no longer had the same internal enthusiasm for the real estate, mortgage, and construction industry, I started moving towards something that I had been immersed in and obsessed about for decades, which was self-help. I originally started studying self-help because I simply wanted to learn how to be more successful. How did millionaires become millionaires? How did rich people become rich? Obviously, there was something that they were doing differently than average people.

When you study rich and successful people all throughout history, like Tony Robbins says, "Success leaves clues." You start to see a lot of different commonalities in their mindset, the way they approach problems, the actions they take, and how they deal with setbacks, challenges, and failure. Successful people learn from their mistakes. They get excited about failure and what they can learn from it, because their failures are what make them better. Failure is the best teacher; success is not. Success tends to cause you to get more into your ego and think that you're amazing, and usually what happens is, down the road, your ego gets too blown up, and then you get brought back down to earth when you have a bunch of failures again. It really helps you learn balance and moderation in your life.

LINK: https://understandingrelationships.com/beaten-down-by-life/13856

Discovering Your Purpose, Passion & Mission

"Life is too short to spend it working at something you hate or do not enjoy only because it pays your bills. People who choose careers or who start businesses doing something they really believe in, love, and are passionate about will work much harder than their fellow employees or competitors. Repetition is the mother of skill. When you repetitively work at improving your focus, skills, talents, and expertise by consistently applying yourself at maximum effort level, you will outdo and exceed all others around you who can't match your passion and effort level. When you can outshine and out-hustle all others in your field, you will maximize your income earning potential, success, happiness, and fulfillment in life." ~ Coach Corey Wayne

A big part of the reason why I have been able to succeed in multiple businesses and multiple careers over the course of my life is that I'm self-motivated, I'm a self-starter, and I've always applied myself at things I love and enjoy. And I'm somewhat competitive in nature. I kind of have the attitude that I can do things better than other people around me. I might not necessarily be the smartest guy around, or the best-looking guy around, or have the most talents or skills, but what will never happen is I simply won't be outworked by other people who are trying to compete at my level.

When you love what you're doing, and you're really passionate about it, and you're obsessed about it, working really is like playing. It's fun. You naturally have enthusiasm that comes from within. And therefore, even though there are often tasks and duties and things that have to be done in order to make your career or your business successful, because you have such a deep passion and emotionally compelling reasons why you do what you do, the work is going to seem more effortless and come easy to you. Whereas when you're competing against somebody that doesn't have the same level of enthusiasm, they're having to force themselves to work and put in the effort.

When you look at it, when you're doing something that you love, you're exercising your natural, personal power. When you're doing something that you dislike or even something that you hate, you're having to force yourself to use it. In other words, you're using excessive power and force to motivate yourself to do something that doesn't come naturally. Power comes naturally because it feels right. But forcing something is just like swimming upstream when you don't want to. Eventually, your competition is going to wear out. And just like Wayne Dyer used to say, "It's never crowded along the extra mile." So, make sure whatever you're applying yourself at is something you love, enjoy, and you're very passionate about.

LINK: https://understandingrelationships.com/discovering-your-purpose-passion-mission/17377

Problems Are A Sign Of Life

"Life isn't all sunshine and roses. Your ability to remain balanced and happy through difficult and challenging times will be tested. Challenges and problems are a sign of life. They are a sign that you still have work to do in this life. Life is change. Nothing stays the same. As you progress through the seasons of your life, people and circumstances that no longer serve you or that will hinder your progress will dissolve and fall away. Let them. Never try to keep people in your life who don't want to keep you in theirs. What you lose will create a space for something new and more aligned with who you are becoming to manifest." ~ Coach Corey Wayne

I've noticed that as you go through life and you're moving in the right direction, and you're following your heart, your curiosity, and your intuition, things tend to flow and feel more effortless, because so much of what you're experiencing and what's coming into your life is aligned with your desires. When you start experiencing a lot of friction and a lot of brick walls and obstacles that are in your way, you really have to re-examine either your approach about how you're going about things or maybe that your heart has changed and is pulling you in a new direction.

Once I realized back in 2004, 2005, 2006, that my heart was no longer in the real estate, mortgage, and construction industry, and I was moving in the path towards becoming a full-time life coach basically, in essence, making a career out of something that was once just a hobby to help myself, and later on help my employees, I was the last person to realize and recognize that my heart wasn't in my business anymore. And I remember having a conversation with my bookkeeper when we were closing out the companies and telling her that my heart wasn't in it. And she said, "Yeah, I could tell about a year, year and a half ago." I was stunned at this, because I was the last person to recognize and see this, but people that knew me well enough could tell. And what she told me was like, "Yeah I could tell. You were just kind of going through the motions, and your heart was no longer really in it."

But because my identity, and obviously my income, was all tied to this particular business and industry, I had a really hard time of letting go of that, and moving on, and moving in a new direction. It was only once I got to a place where I was experiencing a lot of friction, (because the industry was starting to go through a lot of turmoil leading up to the crash of 2007, 2008), that I recognized that in order to stay viable in the business as a business entity, I was going to have to change the business model. But because I no longer had a passion for the industry, I simply wasn't willing to do all those things again and go back and re-create a business model that worked with the changing market conditions. And so, I thought to myself, "Well, if I had to start all over, what would I do?" And then, obviously, that's where the life coaching popped in my mind, and I started moving in that direction that I detail at length in my book *Mastering Yourself*.

LINK: https://understandingrelationships.com/problems-are-a-sign-of-life/14517

FURTHERING SUCCESS

The Happiest I Have Ever Been

"Success is being able to spend your life in your own way—to be able to have complete ownership of your time, so you can spend it how you want and with whom you want. Happiness and success are a result of feeling like you are making progress towards accomplishing your grandest goals and dreams. Successful, happy, and fulfilled people perpetually focus on reasons to be excited, hopeful, and grateful for their lives as they are while they continue the pursuit of their outcomes. Happiness is a choice, not a destination. It is the result of constantly choosing to assign a positive, empowering, and hopeful meaning to the circumstances of your life. You don't always have control over what happens to you, but you always get to choose what it means to you. Choose wisely." ~ Coach Corey Wayne

This quote reminds me of back when I was in college. There was a sheet that I got from the college of engineering and design, and it had all of the classes that I had to take to finally graduate and get my Bachelor of Science degree in Construction Management. I still have this piece of paper to this day. And what it illustrated is, as each semester would wind down and I would get my grades, I was able to fill in the little line that was next to each course on what my grades were. And so, as I went through college and I filled these out and put my grades in, the amount of classes that I had taken and gotten out of the way was growing, and the amount of classes that I had to take the finish my degree was getting shorter and shorter. And so, I was able to see the progress, even though it wasn't but every four, four and a half months from the beginning to the end of the semester when I ultimately got my grades that I can continue filling in this sheet. And the sheet was from a four-year degree, but it took me seven years to finally complete it, because it took so long for me to get into my college and get my prerequisites out of the way, that by the time I finally got them all out of the way, the program had changed. And because I was not in upper level yet, even though I was allowed to take upper-level classes, it basically added close to a full year when they changed all of the classes that were required. So, this added about a year, year and a half to the time it took to get my degree.

You can imagine, a four-year degree taking seven years, partly because I was lazy and I would take semesters off, I dropped a lot of classes, early on, and it was all the result of my own doing. But that little sheet of paper—seeing myself make progress on it month after month, semester after semester, year after year—enabled me to see that I was making progress. And because I was making progress, I felt successful; I felt that sense of accomplishment. And so, whatever you're doing, whatever you're striving for, you've got to be able to measure the results that you're getting and see that you're making progress. Because without progress, you're not going to feel very successful. And if you don't feel very successful, you're not going to be as happy as you could.

LINK: https://understandingrelationships.com/the-happiest-i-have-ever-been/33302

Self Perceptions

"Our success or failure in life is directly related to how we perceive ourselves. When we perceive that we have abundant choices, we tend to not become attached to things, people, circumstances, mediocrity, or settling. When we perceive our choices are scarce, we tend to try and force things and will often settle for a life that is less than what we are capable of living. We were born into this world to be magnificent, not mediocre. Mediocre is always the result of impatience, low standards, and giving up too easily. Magnificence is the result of having high standards, infinite patience, and being unwilling to compromise in one's own ideals, even when success appears far off or hopeless. Once you settle for mediocrity in any part of your life, the impulse to settle and give up will creep into all other areas that are important to you. Settling, like succeeding, is a habit formed by your actions. You either choose to settle by giving up, or succeed by refusing to quit once things become hard or seem hopeless." ~ Coach Corey Wayne

Since our society has the mindset and is constantly pushing the irrational idea of instant gratification—that if you don't have success right away, if you don't become a millionaire right away, that beautiful woman doesn't fall in love with you right away and want to marry you, or you don't get that job right away, then there's got to be something wrong with you and, therefore, you just have to settle and take whatever you can get, (which is usually nothing for most people), and do the best you can to tough it out, get through the workweek, and maybe you can have some peace on the weekends, as you space out and try to escape from your life.

Self-reliant and self-actualizing people must be what they can be. To them, to settle, to give up, to be mediocre, to stop moving towards the things they want is ultimate failure and death to them. It literally feels like dying to think of giving up on their goals and dreams. Self-actualizing people feel alive when they're moving towards the things that they want. And as they learn, they see small, incremental progress, this continues to give them hope that someday, someway, eventually, they're going to figure out enough of the right ways to do things and eliminate the wrong ways from their approaches, and eventually, it's all going to come together. And then, one day, they'll finally be at the destination they've worked for so many years and decades to get to.

Focus on the process, always: "What do I need to do today before I go to bed to move my life forward and make some kind of small, incremental progress towards making myself better and making a little forward progress in my momentum?"

LINK: https://staging.understandingrelationships.com/self-perceptions/32986

The Science Of Achievement Fundamentals

"Most people tend to major in minor things in life. High achievers are high achievers because they have mastered the fundamentals of high achievement. The science of high achievement is a set of fundamental behaviors, beliefs, actions, mindsets, and a relentless commitment to excellence, learning, and self-improvement. Average people are focused on earning a living and getting through the week. High achievers are focused on designing a life by incrementally improving their gifts, skills, talents, and acquiring new knowledge. Average people work just hard enough to get by. High achievers are always pushing their boundaries and stepping outside of their comfort zone to become more and get better." ~ Coach Corey Wayne

High achievers are always looking for an edge. They're looking for an easier way to do complicated tasks. Because high achievers recognize that they have a finite amount of time, and if they can find better and more efficient ways to do things in a shorter period of time, (because at the end of the day, everybody has the same 24 hours in a day), they can spend less time doing something that mediocre people and low achievers spend a lot of time doing. And if you get a lot of the little things out of the way, you're just simply able to do more; you're simply more productive.

Your action steps, the things you do, the things you say, the time you spend immersing yourself and doing things is way more efficient than a mediocre person and, therefore, you achieve your results in a much quicker time, which often appears easy and effortless to average people who don't know any better.

LINK: https://understandingrelationships.com/the-science-of-achievement-fundamentals/28135

Men Are Not Soft

"Masculinity is strength, courage, and virtue. It is fearlessly charging towards one's goals and dreams in an unrelenting fashion, no matter what the odds may be. It is following your heart's desire because nothing will feel more right than becoming what you feel internally compelled and driven to be. It's aligning your life with your true calling, instead of a steady paycheck. When you are passionate about what you do, in love with what you do, and you become a master of it through time and repetition, only then will you be able to maximize your income earning potential. The bigger the problem is that you solve for humanity, the bigger your potential financial reward will be. Before you can help others, you must first help yourself." ~ Coach Corey Wayne

When you're trying to figure out what your purpose and your mission in life should be, especially if you're an entrepreneur and you want to start a business, you should be looking at, "What kind of pain does my product solve or resolve?" In other words, "What type of pain does my product or service resolve or solve that a lot of people have?" Many entrepreneurs make the mistake of painting themselves into a corner and limiting themselves to a very small demographic of people who have the problem, or the solution to the problem that they know how to solve. The more people you can help through your product or service, the larger your demographic, the larger your potential customers, and the more income earning potential you are going to be able to have if you're doing something at scale. That's why when you're trying to determine what the best product, service, career, or business to go into that you choose something you love, and you believe in, and you're good at, and that solves a very common problem that a lot of people have.

LINK: https://understandingrelationships.com/men-are-not-soft/31639

A Better Playbook For Success

"Success equals progress. Happiness is the result of making progress towards your grandest goals and dreams. Goals and dreams are accomplished by disciplining yourself to take action every day on the small daily goals that eventually result in the achievement of your big, long-term goals. Goal achievement is a long process of usually decades that only happens after you develop your talent and passions into valuable skills that enable you to add value to others through a useful product or service. Modeling the success of others and being mentored by or working for those who have achieved what you want is the key to speeding up your success and learning how to do it from those who already have done it." ~ Coach Corey Wayne

This is what we call "success factor modeling"—modeling the successful people that you want to be like. So, whether that is a job internship, when you're young and in college, or sitting down for a lunch or dinner or coffee with somebody more experienced or successful at what you would like to achieve and picking their brain, this is how you go about achieving your grandest goals and dreams in the shortest amount of time possible—is to find other people, instead of trying to reinvent the wheel, who have already figured things out, who've already done the difficult task, had all the failures. They know where the landmines are and the pitfalls are that will hinder your progress.

A prime example of this I use in my own life was back when I was in my 20s, and I was buying foreclosure properties from a company in Orlando, and all they did was find and identify foreclosure type of properties that were good investments for what they called real estate dealers—people like myself would buy a foreclosed property that needed to be fixed up into like-new condition. And I was great at fixing properties up, but I didn't know anything about how to sell them. I didn't know anything about how to finance my end-user, and I didn't know much about the hard loan business, which is the type of loan that I used the finance my property when I had purchased it from them. And so, what I did was to go work for them after two or three months of buying properties from them, so I could learn the acquisition side of the equation, how to find good deals. I could learn the hard equity industry, and I could also learn the real estate and the mortgage industry, so I ultimately could sell my fixed-up properties and get them financed to end-users.

And these particular guys had been in business for almost seven years at that point, and so I got the benefit of all of their successes. But most importantly, I got the benefit of all of their failures and the wisdom that they learned from those failures, so I didn't have to go out and make the same mistakes over the course of seven years before I finally figured out how to make money in the business. That's why, when I went into business with my business partners and we all left that company, we went from making 33% commission from them to making 100%, from literally one month to the next, and that's why we were able to make a $60,000 profit in our first month of operation.

LINK: https://understandingrelationships.com/a-better-playbook-for-success/30829

Stay Together Or Breakup?

"It's never easy to end a relationship with someone once you realize that it has run its course, or you simply do not share the same goals and values. Our fear that we won't find anyone better, we will never find anyone else, the next person will not be as attractive, as fun, or simply won't love us as much can paralyze us into inaction. Therefore, we live a lie and stay in a relationship that, deep down, we know no longer serves us or them. It takes guts, faith in oneself, and faith that, in time, someone better and more suited to us will come along. If you know yourself, believe in yourself, and can get to a place where you are okay with the possibility of never finding someone else or someone better, then you can lose your attachment to relationships that need to end. Then, and only then, will you be ready, willing, able, and open to successfully attract someone more suited to the next grander version of yourself that you are destined to become." ~ Coach Corey Wayne

Nobody likes going through a breakup. They're simply not pleasant. And it's always better to be the dumper than it is to be the dumpee. Emotional pain, and fear of the future, and fear of experiencing pain in the future keeps us stuck in place and not moving forward towards the things we want in life. This fear robs us from taking any action and ultimately achieving our dreams, because everything we do is trying to avoid what we fear and what feels uncomfortable, or potentially uncomfortable, and unpleasant.

That's why it's critically important, in order to overcome obstacles, challenges, feelings of doubt, feelings of fear, and uncertainty, that you have a really exciting, emotionally compelling goal, and vision, and mission that you want to accomplish for your life. Because when things feel like crap—when you feel hopeless, when it feels like things are never going to work out for you—and you think about all the things you want to do and you want to accomplish, and how emotionally exciting and compelling it will be to achieve and experience the things that you want, your passion and your enthusiasm for the things you want will help override the fear and the negativity and the self-doubt that you have towards achieving the things that you want.

And when you bury your head, and you start moving forward and taking action, even when you don't feel like it, you're eventually going to get closer and closer to the things you want. Like, for example, I got up this morning, and when I started working on a video that I had to publish today, I really was not in the mood, and I didn't feel like doing it. And I was telling myself that "I think I'll just blow off doing a video today," but that costs me money. Obviously, my audience expects a new video today, and I knew nothing but bad things would happen from being lazy. So, about 10–15 minutes into it, I actually felt pretty good about it, and then after I was done with the video and got it uploaded, I had that feeling of satisfaction. And so, if I hadn't known any better and didn't understand the science of high achievement fundamentals, I would've just gone with the feelings of how I didn't want to do a video and avoided it and not done it. And then, I would've felt worse all day, because it would've cost me money, and I wouldn't have taken action on it, and then my audience would've been disappointed because I didn't deliver when they were expecting me to deliver. So, instead, I took action. And because I immersed myself and lost myself in taking action, I was able to do it. And 10–15 minutes in, I was actually enjoying it and having a good time.

This is a microcosm of what happens in our minds on a daily basis when we get challenged with things we don't want to do, don't feel like we want to do, but yet we have to do. So, the key is to keep taking action and moving forward, even when you don't feel like it. Just like Dale Carnegie said, "Inaction breeds fear and doubt. Taking action breeds confidence and courage." Anytime you feel horrible, and you feel like not doing what you know you need to do, just take action anyway, and 10–15 minutes in you'll lose yourself in the process. And then, after you're done, when the day is over, you'll have a great sense of accomplishment and a great sense of inner peace. And that's what you're looking for. You want to think about, "How good is this going to make me feel if I take action and do what I know I need to do?"

LINK: https://understandingrelationships.com/stay-together-or-breakup/17142

Young Lust, Love Or Delusion?

"Life has an amazing way of giving us a reality check when we become too full of ourselves and our capabilities. It usually starts to happen when we have become too enamored with our own success, importance, or value. It's always better to let other people sing your praises, instead of trying to tell or convince others of your own greatness. All we really have control over in life is how we show up in each moment and the action we choose or don't choose to take. Success and getting from where you are right now to where you want to be is the result of continuous effort and action, not inflating your own ego or self-importance. If you become too full of your ego and self-pride, life will inevitably serve you up a giant helping of humble pie." ~ Coach Corey Wayne

I remember when I was younger and I started having a lot of success in my 20s and, especially into my early 30s; from my perspective at that time, my life only knew one trajectory, and that was upwards. When I worked for other people, I was always, with each change of employer, earning more money, and taking on more responsibility, and growing. And the same thing happened in my entrepreneurial ventures. Because I did a good job of modeling the success of other people and learning from other people who had already made all the mistakes doing what I wanted to do and become really good at it, I was able to speed up my success. And when I went into business for myself, and eventually, with my business partners, I started doing really well, really quickly.

Success tends to make you a little cocky, it tends to make you lazy, it tends to inflate your ego and cause you to be a little too full of yourself. And where this was a detriment was several years later, when I got into my mid-30s, and I was recognizing that I no longer had the same internal enthusiasm that I once did for the real estate, construction, and mortgage industry. But because of all the success that I had and the fact that it had kind of blown up my ego, there were so many things that, looking back on it now, I could've done differently that would've saved me a ton of time, a ton of effort, a ton of money, and a ton of frustration. I had associated my success with my own competence, and this created blind spots in my life. And so, it took several years to kind of unlearn what I had learned and recognize that everything I was trying was not working, and things I was unwilling to look at actually ended up being the right way to make my current business a success.

Whereas, when I was in real estate and mortgage and the construction industry, everything was about selling the client on us and selling our products or services. When I took that same philosophy toward selling books, yeah, the advertising worked, but it didn't bring in enough revenue to justify the cost of that advertising. And so, when I finally let go of my ego and my need to be right, I was willing to write emails and articles, and later on, do videos and give away a lot of free content that just simply taught the things that I knew. And also, on top of that, giving away my books for free by letting people read them on my website, by simply subscribing to the email newsletter at UnderstandingRelationships.com, and they could read them all for free.

And my ultimate goal really was to coach and teach people these things, but because I was focused on how much money I was going to make from sales from my books, it actually got in the way of the process that people needed to go through. Because what's different about the internet is that people are there for information, and so you have to give them the information first and let the information speak for itself, versus doing a sales letter or sales video talking about how great your stuff is or how great your work is. By letting people examine it themselves and teaching people for free, eventually, when they do the things that you suggest, they see that it works. In this way, the work actually sells itself.

But it took a long time to get to that place. I had to eat a lot of humble pie, and it literally cost me several years. I would be much further along today if I'd known these things back then—if I'd had access to a book like *3% Man* or *Mastering Yourself*—and I could've avoided all of these things. But that's part of life. You live, and you learn. And because I went through that, it really helps me help other people that I'm doing phone sessions with or when answering emails online or doing a YouTube video.

LINK: https://understandingrelationships.com/young-lust-love-or-delusion/21473

At A Crossroads In My Career

"In every business deal, investment, career move, and personal relationship, you should always know your downside. In other words, what is your downside risk if things do not go as you planned? It's essential to be optimistic and go for the things you want in life in order to be successful, but you should do it in a balanced way, with minimal risk to your career, business, health, and emotional well-being. Making progress towards your grandest goals and dreams always involves risk, but you should never risk more than you are willing or can afford to lose. Incremental progress is a smart, steady, sure, and balanced way to succeed, but recklessly gambling in hopes of an instant payoff is like thinking you can "beat the house" in a casino where the odds are never stacked in your favor." ~ Coach Corey Wayne

This is really, super important. If you're not happy in your job, and you want to find a new job, and money is tight for you, the worst thing you can do is just get fed up with your current job and up and quit, because now you've got the added stress of potential financial problems if you don't find a new job. The smart way to go about this is to line something up—get your employment letter, get a commitment when they want to hire you, what your salary is, and what your start date is. And then, when you have all of that in order, then you go back to your current employer, and you put in your two weeks' notice.

The same thing if you're starting a business. Most people start a business, and they've only got a few months of cushion for capital in order to lose money. Ideally, you should have two to three years of reserve cash if you're starting a business, especially if it's something that is very capital-intensive to start up. If it's something simple and relatively inexpensive that you can start in your spare bedroom, then you can take your time. Figure out a budget that you can afford to lose every month on your new business until you figure out your business model, and then just commit to invest that money every month so you can try things. You can try different advertising, you can develop your product, your service, whatever it happens to be.

It's the same thing with relationships; it's not all or nothing. The first date shouldn't be looked at as so much the Super Bowl, and the "be-all, end-all," but, obviously, you've got to handle yourself well on a first date in order to get a second date. Moderation in these kinds of things is always the best way to go. The same thing goes when you're trying to start working out if you're out of shape. You don't go in the gym and work out one time and then come out looking like Mr. Olympia. It's a process. So, if you never worked out before, you don't go in and work out with the full weight and the full amount of repetitions and sets that you're going to do, because you're going to be extremely sore to the point where you won't even be able to move.

I've seen some of these examples in the past when I was trying to figure out my business model for my life coaching business. I had a bunch of capital, but because I was worried about running out of capital, I actually spent a lot of money on a monthly basis in advertising that wasn't really working, because I was trying to get to a place of success and positive cash flow. So, I ended up wasting tens of thousands of dollars on ineffective advertising, instead of having a smaller budget and just spending the same amount of money month in and month out to just let the commercial run over several months, and even a year or two. Because I was impatient, I ended up costing myself a lot of money, and it took longer, ultimately, to get from where I was to where I wanted to be.

LINK: https://understandingrelationships.com/at-a-crossroads-in-my-career/22494

The Attraction Of Indifference

"In life, it's always better to work smarter and not harder. Focus on being productive instead of busy. The average unsuccessful person tends to fill up their day with activities that make them feel like they accomplish something, but unfortunately, the tasks they tend to occupy their time with are busy tasks that don't really move them towards accomplishing their dreams and goals. If what you're doing is not moving you towards what you really want in life, then why are you doing it in the first place?" ~ Coach Corey Wayne

When it comes to time management, this is absolutely essential. Everybody tends to have a long to-do list, but successful people prioritize their to-do list in the order of which of those activities on their to-do list have to do with their most important goals. So, if you've got 40 things on your to-do list, not all of those 40 things have to be done today. And so, if you have all of your goals written down and you order them in list of their importance to you accomplishing them, then what you're going to do is you're going to start with goal number 1, (obviously, goal number 1 is the most important goal to you). Therefore, on your to-do list of 40 things, you're going to put a number 1 next to all of the things on the to-do list that correspond to achieving goal number 1. And then, when that's done, then you're going to go through and put a number 2 next to everything that corresponds to your second most important goal, and so on and so forth with the third, the fourth, and the fifth goals, and so on.

And when you do this, this causes you to prioritize your activities doing the most important things. And therefore, at the end of every day, you're going to feel like you were really productive, because you focused on doing things that were most important to you. And what happens is, over time, and over the weeks and months as they go by, you're going to be much more efficient than the mediocre person who is just doing things that seem easy and feel good. Because remember, people do more to avoid pain than they do to gain pleasure. And the average person that doesn't know any better, when they're looking at their to-do list, they're going to be focused on doing things that are easy, and feel good, and give them a sense of accomplishment, but they're not necessarily productive things that are important to achieving their goals.

A lot of times, the things you have to do to make your goals happen is going to involve doing things that are unpleasant and that you're not really that excited to do. That's why it's so important that you prioritize your to-do list based upon things that are important to achieving your goals.

LINK: https://understandingrelationships.com/the-attraction-of-indifference/13768

New Year's Resolutions

"Studies show that 95% of people who make New Year's Resolutions have given up on them or quit trying to achieve them by the 15th of January of the new year. In other words, most people have already quit after only two weeks of trying to achieve them. In order for your New Year's Resolutions to stick so that you stay committed to them and achieve them, you need to have four key ingredients: 1) know what you want, 2) know why you want it, 3) have an emotionally compelling reason why you want it, and 4) have daily success rituals that you accomplish, so you can take the action you need to take in order to achieve the little daily goals that ultimately lead to and enable accomplishing the resolution itself." ~ Coach Corey Wayne

Rituals are really important. Getting yourself on a schedule—and maybe something as simple as waking up every day at the same time to go to the gym. Or maybe, you're getting up an hour or two every day earlier than you need to so you can spend some time working on your side hustle for yourself. And then you go on to work. Maybe it's doing meal prep if you're serious about working out and taking care yourself. Like, in my case, I always make sure I get a green juice in the morning and a protein shake, and that's the way I start my day every day. It causes my red eyes to turn nice and white and bright, it makes me feel better, it moisturizes my eyes, it softens my skin up. I have a noticeable change in my physical body when I put good, healthy, green foods into my body. I feel it right away. And because I like the way it makes me feel, when I have those days where I feel lazy, and I need to make juice, or I need to make smoothies, or nuts, or eat a certain way, I think about how I physically feel and how it will make me feel when I ingest these good, healthy foods.

So, success rituals are critical—having routines, things that you do day in and day out, day after day, week after week, month after month, year after year, and decade after decade. It's a daily battle. And even if you failed yesterday and were lazy, today's a new day. The slate is wiped clean. So, give yourself permission on a daily basis to be a beginner again. Think of life as like the old Etch-a-Sketch toy, where you just shake it up, the screen is blank, the slate is clean, and every day you wake up is a new day. The past really doesn't matter. Like Tony Robbins often says, "The past does not equal the future." The only thing that matters is what you do right now in the present moment.

LINK: https://understandingrelationships.com/new-years-resolutions/14879

Trusting Intuition & Inner Voice

"Our birthright and natural state of being is one of abundance, courage, and success. We literally were born to succeed and already have within us all we need to accomplish our grandest goals and dreams. The only way you can accomplish your grandest goals and dreams is to be brave enough to step outside of your current comfort zone and move towards the things you want. But fear might not be possible. Success only comes after you pay the price on your journey by taking action in spite of your fears, putting in the time to improve yourself, developing your skills, learning from your mistakes, adapting and refining your approach, and becoming what you need to be, so reaching your full potential is simply a matter of time and repetition." ~ Coach Corey Wayne

Our greatest two fears—our primary fears, if you will—are fear that we're not enough, (in other words, that we don't have what it takes), and the fear that we won't be loved and accepted by our friends, family, peer group, or when it comes to women, being loved by the woman that we desire. And the reality is, we were built to succeed. We have everything within us to take action, to learn, to grow, to learn from our mistakes, to refine our approach, to get better, and continually move forward towards the things we want in life. Because when you look at very successful people who came from a background where they had every disadvantage that they could possibly have, and then you see other people that came from a background where they had every advantage—they grew up in the best families, went to the best schools, had the best opportunities—and yet, still, they just turned out to be average, mediocre people, you recognize that it definitely has an influence on the average person, (meaning their environment does), but if that was the be-all, end-all, then you wouldn't have people coming from the poorest, most unsafe and dangerous countries to live somewhere in the West and becoming a billionaire, even though they never really had a formal education.

It really boils down to our choices—what we choose to believe about ourselves, and the story that we tell ourselves about our capabilities. Successful people have really emotionally compelling goals and reasons why they want those goals. And unsuccessful people never really take the time to develop these, or focus on them, or learn them all because of the story that they tell themselves. If you don't think you're smart enough, and you don't think you're capable enough, or you don't have the resources, or the time, or whatever it happens to be, that's your story, and your story will become your reality. So, make sure you choose something positive and empowering, and act upon that positive and empowering story on a daily, consistent basis.

LINK: https://understandingrelationships.com/trusting-intuition-inner-voice/24603

The Freedom Of Having Options

"Most people you encounter in life are making romantic, career, business, life, personal, friendship, health, and lifestyle choices from a position of scarcity, fear, lack, and poverty. People who believe and act this way are detrimental and dangerous to your success and happiness, because their desire to avoid fear, pain, and uncertainty is so overwhelming that they need validation for their scarcity mindset and poor choices by trying to sabotage you, so they don't feel bad about themselves, and to justify their continued mediocre lives. This is the exact opposite of your true divine nature of abundance, unlimited choices, and options. When you have awakened to the fact you are an unlimited being with unlimited potential and options, you realize you can be, do, and have anything your mind can conceive. Patience, persistence, perseverance, non-attachment, and energy can eventually overcome any obstacle, limited worldview, and thinking with enough time." ~ Coach Corey Wayne

Ideally, you want to hang out with people who are better than you in every area of your life that you are either weak in or that you need significant improvement. Because when you spend your time with other people that are better than you at certain things, you're able to see what they're doing successfully and model their success. That helps you speed up the process to getting from where you are to where you want to be. If you have nothing but people around you that are negative, and mediocre, and living a life that is less than they are capable of living, if you've started your own business or you're going to college and nobody you know has gone to college or is going to college, it's going to be very hard to get good support from the people that are not doing the things that you want to do or living at the high level that you want to live at. That's why it's so important to make sure that you only allow people into your inner circle who make you better; who are good for you and who are good to you; who say what they mean and who mean what they say.

LINK: https://understandingrelationships.com/the-freedom-of-having-options/25082

Dating: It's All In The Numbers

"Most people you will encounter in your life journey are never going to reach their full potential. As Dr. Wayne Dyer says, "It's never crowded along the extra mile." Most people give up and are too afraid and run by their fears to ever become all that they can. If you are reading this, then you are likely in the rare 3% of people who have high standards for themselves, want the best that they can get, and are unwilling to settle for a life of mediocrity and disappointment. Unfortunately, the world is full of people who are sleepwalking through life and who will try to drag you down to their level. Therefore, you must remain ever vigilant and only allow people into your inner circle and spend your time with those who have the same high standards, drive, and desire for greatness." ~ Coach Corey Wayne

Your peer group has an outsize influence on your life and what you're capable of. In order to reach your full potential, you've got to have people in your life who push you, who nurture you, who are good to you, good for your soul, and when you're having a down day—where you're down upon yourself, and you're doubting that you can achieve the things you want—they're going to have a positive word of encouragement. The wrong people are going to be telling you what a stupid idea it is and how stupid you were to be thinking that you could accomplish whatever it is that you want to accomplish—"Oh, I told you I thought that was a dumb idea at the time," "You should never have started that." You can't have people like this in your inner circle when you're taking on big, audacious goals.

Some people you're just going to have to manage the distance if they're too much of a negative black hole. Because if you allow them into your life, they will suck you into the black hole, and all of your dreams and your hopes will be sucked into the black hole with that negativity, and they will be successful at bringing you down to their level. Because the reason people try to bring you down to their level is it makes them feel really uncomfortable when you go for the things that you want in life, because they know they should be doing the same things that you're doing, but don't have the guts and the inner testicular fortitude to do what you are doing. As the old saying goes, "You become like the five people who you spend most of your time with." So, choose wisely.

LINK: https://understandingrelationships.com/dating-its-all-in-the-numbers/21628

Think, Walk, Talk & Act Like An Alpha

"Life and living at your personal best is to be found living in the present moment, taking action towards becoming all that you are capable of being. The action you take or fail to take today is what will determine what your future becomes. Winners expect to win and take the actions required to eventually manifest their grandest goals and dreams, despite the fact that success lies far off in the future or seems unrealistic to others. Losers quit and give up on their dreams when the first sign of difficulty or challenges arise, and then, they seek to sabotage the dreams of those around them, so they can convince them to give up like they have, and so they can feel better about their lack of success. Misery loves company. Your inner circle ideally should consist of people who are just as committed to their own greatness as you are to your own, and who celebrate and encourage your victories and continued perseverance." ~ Coach Corey Wayne

Life is hard enough, and reaching your full potential is hard enough without having multiple people in your inner circle who are constantly trying to sandbag your success and hold you back. The reality is, you're going to have lots of days where the future is in doubt, especially when you've been on the journey and on the path for several years. You're going to have those days where you're not going to feel positive and optimistic. Maybe a bunch of failures add up, and you're starting to doubt yourself. The last thing you need is somebody in your inner circle going, "I told you that was a stupid idea," "I told you that would never work," "I told you, you shouldn't even have started on this path." Because they're trying to reinforce their own story in your life, and if they can get you to give up, then it justifies their continued inaction.

That's why it's so essential when you're stretching way beyond your comfort zone to go for the things you really want in life, is that you've got to have people in your inner circle that, when you're having a down day, they've always got a positive word of encouragement—"Hey man, it's just another day. Tomorrow, better will come," "Tomorrow, the slate is wiped completely clean, and you get a chance to start all over," "Better will come. Keep your chin up, man. You can do it," "You've been at it for this long. Just keep going, dude," "You know, as the expression goes: if you're going through hell, keep going."

LINK: https://understandingrelationships.com/think-walk-talk-act-like-an-alpha/34602

Creating A Social Life Of Abundance

"Like attracts like. People who like the same kinds of things tend to like each other. If you are single and want to meet other single people who are looking to have a good time socially or hook up, you have to live and hang out where similar like-minded people are highly concentrated. Then, no matter where you go, it will be easy to strike up conversations in elevators, the grocery store, etc., because you will constantly be around and interacting with other single people who have similar goals and values. Your conversations will flow better, and members of the opposite sex will be eager to interact with you and help you succeed socially and sexually." ~ Coach Corey Wayne

This is really important if you find yourself questioning, "Where do I meet really good quality women?" You've got to think of your life, and especially your social life, as setting it up to stack the odds in your favor. Like the quote says, you want to live in an area where a lot of like-minded single people, especially women, are going to live, work, and play. And, therefore, it's important to understand who you are, what you want, why you want it, and what's most important to you. This also is important in where you choose to live, work, and play. Because if you're living in an area that you hate, you don't really like your job too much, and it doesn't give you a lot of options socially, you're basically going to be limited to online dating or chance, if you will.

So, here's a good example to follow from today's social media environment; and this is something that, if you've ever heard of Dan Bilzerian, (who's really big on Instagram), and I've seen several interviews where he talked about this, he wanted to set up his life where he could meet a lot of beautiful, single women. And as he started to do well in playing poker and winning lots of money, and on top of that, living in Vegas as well as living in L.A. where, obviously, there's a lot of beautiful people, a lot of models, a lot of people trying to make it, what he started doing was he set things up. Because, if you're familiar with my book *How To Be A 3% Man*, women are more attracted to guys who appear to be successful with other women. And so, what he started doing was having these modeling agencies send over their most beautiful women, probably, (he didn't go into detail, but more than likely), you have to pay these women to come to the parties, and they just hang out.

And so, what Dan does is he has these modeling agencies send over their most attractive female models, obviously, probably, that match a set of criteria that he was looking for, especially if he was going to be paying them to come and basically get paid to go to a party. And he's in the cannabis industry, and so he's kind of incorporated his cannabis business into his lifestyle, and he's kind of like the modern-day Hugh Hefner. But he has these parties, and what he used to do was have 100 or 200 beautiful women, and maybe like 10 or 12 guys there. And so, if you stack the deck in your favor with a lot of beautiful women and just a handful of guys, obviously, the women are going to want to talk to you, because you're the only guys there.

And on top of that, women then start competing for your attention and your validation, because there are so many other women competing for you. So, you should borrow from that philosophy and that mindset. It doesn't mean you go out and you hire a bunch of models to come to your parties and stuff; obviously, if you can afford it, hey, more power to you. But you want to think in terms of, "How can I set up my social life to create a lot of options and a lot of potential interactions with the kind of women I really like?"

For me, personally, that's how I've set my life up, is that I'd like to be near the water, near the beach, near where there's lots of beautiful, single women, lots of people hanging out and having fun together, lots of restaurants, lots of bars, lots of fun activities, lots of boating. And the same thing with my place in Orlando, (which I've recently relocated), is I tend to live in a more family-oriented type of neighborhood—lots of single people, especially lots of beautiful women here. Because beautiful women want to live in a safe neighborhood; they don't want to be getting harassed by homeless people and mentally ill people, kind of like it was like when I lived in downtown Orlando. And so, there's no homeless people, there's no mentally ill people or people walking around causing shit in this particular neighborhood. And it's really nice, it's really beautiful; a lot of people out with their families, very social, and people are friendly and outgoing, and it's really easy to meet people this way.

LINK: https://understandingrelationships.com/creating-a-social-life-of-abundance/14313

REACHING HIGHER

Ending Unhappy Relationships

"Ending a bad relationship or marriage should be done with love, care, and concern for the other person as well as yourself. Most people tend to stay in unhappy and unfulfilling relationships long after they realize that they need to end them. This is due to fear of the future, fear they won't find someone better, or fear that the next person will be worse. It's never too late to become the person you were meant to be. Wouldn't you much rather spend your senior years looking back upon your life with gratitude, instead of regret that you never tried to reach your full potential?" ~ Coach Corey Wayne

This whole mindset is what kept me in my first long-term relationship with my first real girlfriend that ultimately led me to go ahead and propose marriage, get married, only to a year later divorce and leave my wife. It was all because, deep down, I was so fearful that I was never going to find anybody better or somebody that treated me as well as my wife. Even though, as great as she was, she just simply was not what I was really looking for. And since I was inexperienced and I didn't come from a family that taught anything good regarding relationships and something that I considered healthy and happy, I had no good examples to follow. All I had was what I saw in movies and on TV shows. And this fear of not doing what I wanted to do—because I was young, I was inexperienced, I didn't really have anybody else around me that I looked up to or thought that they had what I considered a great relationship or happy, long-term marriage—caused me to ignore what I felt internally, and do everything to please other people, even though, deep down, it wasn't what I felt in my heart.

It really sucks to recognize this when you're a year into your marriage, and you recognize that everything you've done is really based on pleasing other people and not disappointing other people, and trying to live your life according to everybody else's expectations, and putting yours last. But luckily, I had the inner strength to do it and leave my wife, and have an honest conversation with her, as hard as it was. It was probably one of the most unpleasant conversations I've ever had to have. And to her credit, she was really gracious about it, but she also kind of knew what was coming, because my supposed best friend, who I had been confiding in, had already told her everything. And so, she knew it was coming, and she knew how I felt. And it actually did, in some ways, make it better, but it really pissed me off because I felt betrayed by my supposed best friend at the time.

But it ultimately led me to a much happier life. And the big lesson, the big takeaway for me, personally, was to live my life according to my own expectations and what made me happy. Because if you can't make yourself happy, there's no way you're really going to be able to create sustainable happiness in your partner through what you give to them.

Because if you're not happy, you can't give away what you don't have for yourself.

LINK: https://understandingrelationships.com/ending-unhappy-relationships/13762

Trying Too Hard Vs. Not Trying At All

"It is essential for every man and woman to exercise emotional self-control in all matters of the heart. You should not make promises when you are elated and happy. Why? When you come down from that temporary happiness high, you often will regret what you have committed to. It's better to take your time and contemplate all of the consequences and possibilities of your commitments before making them. In your intimate relationships, you should enjoy your strong feelings of love and desire, but pay attention to the level of reciprocation from the other person. That way, you will never continue to do too much or give too much to the point that you put yourself in a position to be taken advantage of or hurt. Healthy relationships are based upon a balance of mutual giving and receiving." ~ Coach Corey Wayne

You definitely should take your time when it comes to dating new women. Too many guys are in too much of a rush to run off to the altar of marital bliss and relationship, and they're just glad to have a girl that kind of likes them, is somewhat into them, and that they have some fun with. And what happens when you behave this way is you end up making commitments to women you shouldn't have made a commitment to. Much like if you commit to things when you're intoxicated, you're often going to regret it later. Take your time. There is no rush.

It's like the analogy of the tortoise and the hare; when it comes to dating and relationships, the turtle is always going to be the one who wins, because he takes his time, he's selective, and he's in no rush. Because, just like the rabbit loses the race, you rush in too fast, haste makes waste, and by the time you are several months down the road, or a year or so down the road, and the infatuation wears off, you recognize that the person has a lot of red flags and you don't really like them too much, but now that you've got all his time in with them, you talk yourself into staying and putting up with things that you should've recognized after a couple months of dating and just simply moved on. The longer you're with somebody, the harder it is to leave the relationship, unless you're really, super unhappy.

LINK: https://understandingrelationships.com/trying-too-hard-vs-not-trying-at-all/20107

You Are So Different

"In order to get what you want in life, you must set yourself apart from all others. This is especially true if you are trying to influence someone who has many choices to choose you over all others. How does one do this? By communicating with your words and actions that you are their most valuable choice and not being attached to them or your outcome. Scarcity creates value. When you know your true value and self-worth, you will not tolerate being around those for very long who question or doubt your value. A person of value will walk away and never look back from someone who takes them for granted or does not fully appreciate their value proposition. People who view themselves as being unworthy will chase, pursue, and try to force themselves upon others. People who know they are worthy know it's demeaning and take it as a personal insult to waste their time with those who do not reciprocate interest or see their value." ~ Coach Corey Wayne

What's interesting is, as I really started to learn the things that I talk about in my book, *3% Man,* and apply them, I started having experiences that I had never experienced or even dreamt about in my life. I was actually rejecting really attractive women who, just a few years before, I would've done anything to have a date with. And now, as my skills advanced and I was able to create, maintain, and grow attraction, over time, I actually got to spend time with these women that I used to kind of put on a pedestal. And then, I got to see them for what they really are, and I came to realize that it was all in my mind. I was basically mind fucking myself into thinking that just because she was beautiful and hot that she would be a great dream woman, without really having to consider the fact of, "What's she like?", "Do I enjoy having a conversation with her?", "Is she fun to talk to?", "Is she interesting?", "Am I interested in her life, and her hobbies, and what she is all about?"

These are questions that the average guy never really gets to experience or ask himself, because he's typically just fighting for scraps and hoping that somebody will go out with them. And typically, what happens is they end up with women that they're really not that into, and this actually enables them to display all the male strength characteristics that women find attractive, because he's really not that into her. But when he meets a girl and he's really into her, just like I used to do, they put her on a pedestal, and they're extra nice and compliant to her, and displaying lots of weakness that causes her to eventually back away, lose interest, and eventually ghost the guy, friend-zone him, or reject him outright.

LINK: https://understandingrelationships.com/you-are-so-different/30585

Avoiding Relationship Pitfalls & Mistakes

"When a man gets jealous of the attention his woman gets from other men, this makes him look insecure and weak, which diminishes her attraction for him. A man who's comfortable in his own skin and who loves and values himself will actually get the feeling of satisfaction and being proud that his woman is so desirable to other men, but yet, she belongs to him. If you give your woman the freedom to come and go as she pleases, and don't come totally unglued and lose it when you see other guys hitting on her, or she shares stories of other guys hitting on her, she will never leave your side. She will also happily tell you about the attention she's getting, because she wants you to know how special you are and how loyal she is to you. Plus, you'll have some good laughs over the bad pickup artists that predictably crash and burn when they try in vain to rip off your girl. The reality is, if your woman wants to cheat, she's going to cheat, and there's nothing you can do about it. Weak, insecure, and disloyal women cheat. Strong, confident, loyal, and healthy women communicate like adults to work things out when their needs aren't being met, or they are unhappy." ~ Coach Corey Wayne

If you do a good job of opening up a woman emotionally and you become her rock and her mountain, you become the man, and the person that is number one in her life that she's going to share all of her problems, all of her concerns, her feelings, her desires, her wants, and her needs. And you have to create a space where she feels safe to do this without judgment. If you act like a needy, insecure jackass and you fly off the handle every time she tells you about a guy that was hitting on her, you're communicating, deep down, that you don't value yourself and you don't believe you deserve to be with her. And eventually, over time, this causes her to not tell you what's going on in her life, because she doesn't want to deal with any of the drama that you create. This is, eventually, going to push her away, lose attraction, and, eventually, she'll start questioning whether or not she wants to stay in the relationship with you.

The reality is the only thing you have control over is how you show up in your own actions. That's why, in the initial stages of the first three or four months of dating and courting a woman, you have to keep your eyes open, because you're looking for red flags. Because people can hide who they really are for about the first 90 days of a relationship. And women who are loyal and faithful will not be displaying any red flags; women that are not will be constantly seeking out attention and validation from other men. And if you've been dating for three or four months and she's constantly hiding her phone from you, flipping it over when you see lots of messages coming in, those are things that are indicative that she's got something to hide, and she has a deviousness streak.

Guys make the mistake of thinking, "This girl's the hottest girl I've ever been with, and, therefore, once she finds out what a great guy I am, she won't do these things to me." The more time you spend with a woman, the better you are able to determine whether or not she's a good catch and somebody who will be loyal and faithful to you. That's why you can't get carried away with your emotions too much, especially in the beginning. Because if you allow yourself to go into La-La Land and get drunk on your emotions, once you start seeing these red flags, you'll just talk yourself into putting up with it, which always ends in disaster later.

LINK: https://understandingrelationships.com/avoiding-relationship-pitfalls-mistakes/17588

Never Put Others On A Pedestal

"You should always trust your own judgment and heart above the opinions and advice of all others, even those who you look up to and respect. Why? No one knows what's best for you than you. No one else can understand your internal motivations for why you do what you do. When you put other people on a pedestal, you open yourself up to being manipulated and taken advantage of. Listen to many voices but speak with your own. See yourself as a person of high value. Act as if you deserve what you want and be willing to walk away from situations and people who don't appreciate the value you have to offer. This will enable you to create a space for the right people and circumstances to show up and give you what you want freely. The right people and circumstances will stay unconditionally. The wrong ones will only stick around as long as you continue allowing them to take from you while giving very little in return." ~ Coach Corey Wayne

No matter who you are or where you're at in life, it's never a good idea to put your guru, somebody you look up to, a favorite teacher, a friend, or that girl you really want to date on a pedestal. Because when you put them on a pedestal, you're basically telling yourself that you're not as good as they are, you're not worthy of being in their presence. And, especially when it comes to a guru, or a teacher, or even me, as a matter of fact, if you happen to look up to me for whatever reason, what I always tell people is, "Don't put anybody on a pedestal," (and that includes me). Because when you do that, you then start valuing somebody else's opinion over your own. You should always take feedback, listen to what other people have to say based upon their life experiences, but you've got to measure it internally with how you feel about yourself and your own goals, dreams, values, and your own personal life experience to decide what's right for you.

When I was younger and I didn't know any better, I tended to put people on a pedestal that I learned a lot from and that had helped me. And what I realized is that, even when you get to the top and you get to hang out with these people that you look up to, everybody's got flaws, everybody's got faults, everybody's got weird idiosyncrasies. And when you put yourself in that kind of a position where you give somebody ultimate respect that you don't know personally, but because they've gotten great results in whatever field it happens to be, what's happening is, you're putting that person's experience and recommendations above your own. And if you're involved in doing business with these people, it oftentimes will cause you to be less skeptical than you would be otherwise. So, that's why it's always important to understand, why are you doing what you're doing? What is your personal motivation? And these other people, how do their motivations and their goals and dreams and values line up with your own? How well do they complement yours? It's important to pay attention to these things, instead of just automatically giving somebody credibility because of the reputation that they haven't earned.

LINK: https://understandingrelationships.com/never-put-others-on-a-pedestal/14308

Relationships: Casual To Committed

"Women do not approach dating and relationships the same way men do. Most men have been incorrectly taught to make a mad dash to the relationship finish line by proving themselves and getting women to commit as quickly as possible. The reality is, women fall in love slowly over time. If a man is too focused on locking her down to a commitment, she will feel overwhelmed, pressured, and most often reject, friend-zone, or ghost him. A man's job is to create an opportunity for sex to happen by planning definite dates, having fun, and leading the interaction by focusing on getting to know her as a human being. A man should pursue in the beginning by setting one date per week. As a woman's interest, attraction, and connection grow, she will start to reach out to bond and connect more and more, as she feels safe and comfortable with him. This usually happens after 2 or 3 weeks. Then, the man can simply wait to hear from her and make the next date when she reaches out. This way, it becomes her idea. Most women typically will be in love by the 7th week and bring up the exclusivity talk when men allow women to come to them at their own pace, instead of incorrectly trying to force things before women are emotionally ready."
~ Coach Corey Wayne

Just like the title of the article says, all relationships are the result of casual dating—dating without any attachments, without any commitments, without any deadlines, without any kind of brinkmanship as far as making a commitment. You're either in or you're out today, or you're either in a relationship or you're not. It's having the attitude of, "Let's just see what happens. I'm not too sure about this girl yet. Yeah, she's beautiful, and she seems fun to talk to on the phone, but let's see what it's like when you're sitting across the table having a drink, or eating some food, or shooting some pool with her, or taking a walk in the park or on the beach," or whatever it happens to be, whatever you do on your dates for fun.

By having an attitude of, "I'm going to be pre-selective. I want to see what this girl is really like over time. I'm not going to get too excited about her, because, again, I don't know her that well and people can hide who they really are for the first 90 days of a relationship," you're going to take your time. You're not going to be in a rush. And most of the other guys that have interest in the woman that you're interested in are going to be in a rush.

LINK: https://understandingrelationships.com/relationships-casual-to-committed/25295

Why She Didn't Want To See You Again

"A woman wants to know that the guy she's dating is there because he likes her personality and cares about who she is as a human being, not just because he wants her body. Nobody likes to feel used, manipulated, or taken advantage of. In order to seduce a woman successfully, you must make her feel safe and comfortable in a non-attached way, so she feels free to stay or go without hassle. A man can accomplish this by going with the flow, diffusing tension with humor, and not taking things personally." ~ Coach Corey Wayne

If you're a man who has lots of choices and lots of options in life, you're not going to be in a rush. Just like the beautiful woman that has lots of guys that want to date her—the successful alpha male has lots of choices and lots of options with women, and he wants to make sure he gets himself a top-tier woman as well. And in order to figure out who's a top-tier woman and separate all the women who have pretty faces from the average and mediocre women to find the unicorn, or the high achieving, top-tier woman that he's looking for, he's got to take time to ask questions and get to know her and look at the dating process as kind of like a job interview, if you will. Not that you want to sit there and act like you're interviewing somebody, but you want to be asking the kind of questions that they would enjoy answering.

Because you want to know, after you're tired of all the sex you've had over many months and years of being together, do you genuinely like listening to the other person? Do you like the way their mind works? Are they interesting to talk to and to listen to? Do they have fun, exciting hobbies and interests that you like hearing about? When you share things with her, when you give her a podcast to listen to or a person to follow that she claims to be really interested in the subject and that she's definitely going to check it out, then when you go out on the next date and you ask her about it, does she not look any of that stuff up, or did she? These are the kinds of little simple questions that you're going to ask, you're going to give feedback, and then, you've got to sit back and wait and see what happens. Because a woman who tells you all the things that you're telling her, how she loves and she enjoys it, and she's going to check it out, and then, she doesn't actually follow through on any of it, well, what does that tell you about the things that she says and commits to?

People who mean what they say and say what they mean, their words and their actions match. And this is something you should be looking out for in the dating process. Especially if a girl goes out of her way to tell you how excited and how interested she is in something that you just shared with her, and she's definitely going to check it out. And on top of that, the next time you guys get together, she's going to tell you what she found out. And then, say a week or so later, you get together, and she doesn't even remember the conversation. That's the kind of thing that should cause you to go, "Hmm, sounds like she's got a habit of making promises and commitments and not following through."

Me, personally, as a high achiever, dating women that say one thing and do another, that talk about all these things they're going to do and then they don't do it, that irritates the fuck out of me. And when I see women doing that and not following through, I lose respect for them. Because, if you allow a lazy woman into your life, even though she's really hot and really attractive, her laziness, over time, is going to cause you to start being lazy, because you're tolerating this in your inner circle. And so, that's why it's really important when you're in the first few weeks of dating that you're paying attention to these things—"Do I like this girl?", "Do I actually like listening to her?"—instead of being so focused on getting into her pants and hooking up.

LINK: https://understandingrelationships.com/why-she-didnt-want-to-see-you-again/37461

Dating Fantasy Vs. Dating Reality

"There is a societal myth that there is only one perfect person for you, and if you lose that person or screw it up, you'll never find someone better or as good as the one you lost. This is romantic nonsense perpetuated by ignorant people who have no real success and who don't know how to attract many options with members of the opposite sex. The truth is we live in an infinitely abundant universe with unlimited romantic, career, business, and life possibilities. How do I know? Simply look at nature. There is life everywhere you can see. There is also microscopic life that is hidden from your eyes you can't. You truly can create anything you really want in life. Once you decide what you want and start taking action, the universe will slowly bring you people, places, and events so you can create your dreams—as long as you don't get attached to anyone or anything and push them away with needy and unworthy behavior. Getting attached stops your progress and prevents you from seeing all of your infinite options. The truth is the right people will show up and stick around SLOWLY OVER TIME. The wrong ones will come and go; let them. The key is to not get attached to anyone, time frames, or any outcome to enable the universe to bring you exactly what you want and need." ~ Coach Corey Wayne

This is especially true when it comes to dating women, because if you took a poll and you asked most people, they're typically going to tell you that they don't enjoy being single. They don't enjoy the process of dating until they find somebody they really click or jive. Because the reality is, most people have a terrible strategy on how they go about attracting and keeping members of the opposite sex in their lives. And, typically, what happens is people are so desperate to have somebody that, when somebody comes along that has a lot of qualities that they like but not all of the qualities that they like, because it's taken so long to get a really good quality prospect that they jive with and they enjoy hanging out with, they usually talk themselves into staying and sticking around longer than they really should.

If somebody's not exactly what you want and it doesn't feel right, the hard thing to do is to keep being single and to keep searching. Because it might be many months or even a year or two before you find somebody that you really click our jive with. The reality is, it's better to be alone than in bad company. All you have to do is look around at society and look at our divorce rates being over 50%. Most people, when you look at the numbers, are simply making really bad choices with their partners. Just like the title of my book says—*3% Man*—only about 3% of couples are really, truly happy, in love, fulfilled, and glad to be with each other. The rest of the people are not unhappy enough and they're not miserable enough to do anything about it, and they just talk themselves into sticking around. This is not a recipe for success in a long, happy, healthy life. Just look at the obesity epidemic in the West these days. Most people deal with their problems by overeating and overdrinking foods that make them fat, and obese, and shorten their lives.

LINK: https://understandingrelationships.com/dating-fantasy-vs-dating-reality/14243

Date Outside Of Your Comfort Zone

"When we date people who are "safe" or below our level of confidence and success, over time we will lose respect and attraction for them, especially if they are unable to grow and step up to our level. Like attracts like. You should date in your own demographic. If you are a successful Wall Street executive, CEO or entrepreneur who enjoys business functions, talking about politics and world events, it's highly unlikely you will find a suitable romantic partner in a bar or night club. You should spend your time around like-minded people who have similar goals and values and who have the same passions, hobbies and interests as you do. If you date in your demographic, your success, close ratio and romantic life will be much higher and fulfilling, than trying to hang with drunk college kids whose only goal is to get drunk and party."
~ Coach Corey Wayne

If you have some limiting beliefs that cause you to perceive yourself as not being worthy of the kind of women that you really want, you're going to date average and mediocre women that you kind of play it safe with. In other words, you're always kind of in control, but you're never really challenged, and your emotions are never really engaged with these kinds of women, because you just don't have the passion for them. And then, when you actually go out on dates with women that you really like and you're into, you're so worried about her liking you that you completely act different than with the ones you really don't care that much about.

The reality is, you've got to treat all women the same. And if you have a habit, (like I used to in the past when I was younger), to put women on a pedestal, treat them like a celebrity, you've got to get in the habit of thinking differently: "How would I think about this girl if I was already bored by her?", "How would I think about her if I was already kind of turned off and maybe skeptical on whether or not I should continue dating or seeing her?" You wouldn't be in such a rush to make everything happen now. You'd be willing to take your time, spend some time to pause, reflect, and see how things go. You would be in a non-hungry type of state.

I oftentimes use the analogy with Tom Brady and his wife, Gisele. How come Tom Brady didn't marry and date some girl that just works in a small diner in a small town somewhere? Well, he's a high achieving alpha male, he's at the top of his game, and he married one of the richest, most successful supermodels in the world. She obviously had a similar shared experience, as did he. And that's the point I was trying to make with this quote, is you want to date people that are on the same level as you. Because if you're dating somebody that's on a much lower socioeconomic scale than you are, over time, you're going to get irritated with their lack of drive. You're going to get irritated with the fact that they're irresponsible, and they don't always follow through on the things that they say they're going to do.

High achievers don't like mediocre people, and mediocre people typically don't like high achievers. If you're a high achieving man, find a high achieving woman. It doesn't mean she's got to be CEO of a company, but she has goals, she has dreams, she has things that are important to her, and she makes those things happen. She operates from a place of integrity. When she says she's going to do something, she goes out and does it.

Two different girlfriends I've had in my life, one of them—one of the most amazing women I've ever known in my life—when she said she was going to do something, she would go out and do it. Because she was health and growth oriented, I'd make a green juice, I'd hand it to her, she'd be excited to drink it. I had another who was a gorgeous Brazilian but didn't look at things the same way. When I first met her, she'd told me how healthy she was, and how she was into healthy eating, and I remember when she first came to visit me in the States and I gave her some green juice, she smelled it, and she's like, "That's disgusting, I'm not drinking that." She had no interest in any of the things that I did, health-wise. She ate the way she ate, and she wanted to be that way.

The same thing when it came to working out; she supposedly worked out all the time, but when I got to know her, her idea of working out was walking on the treadmill for 10-15 minutes a week. And she had a beautiful body and a beautiful figure, because she lived in Brazil and walked up and down those hills there in her high heels and had an amazing body because of it. But when it came to working out and doing things I liked to do, it's like, she had zero interest in any of that. And on top of that, she was always breaking my balls and belittling me about it. Whereas my other girlfriend who is growth-oriented and health-oriented, and eventually became a doctor, she was always open to doing these things. On top of that, she loved it because it made her feel well.

She would juice, she would make smoothies, she co-created with me. And so, I never felt like I had to drag her along with me to the finish line, so to speak; she was there running next to me like a teammate and an equal.

It's just hard to find people who share the same goals and values as you do. And it's really helpful if you date people that have the same goals and have the same values because, otherwise, they're going to be in conflict. Whereas, you know, the one girlfriend that I shared, she was open to everything. And the other one was totally close-minded. And we laughed about it, we joked about it at first, but as the months rolled on, I got irritated with it—especially when she started insulting me, and putting me down, and saying negative things about it. Because at that point, then she was trying to demotivate me.

And, obviously, I just didn't stay with that particular girlfriend for very long. Whereas the other one, the English girlfriend, I mean, almost 20 years later she's still in my life and we talk several times a year. Every time I talk to her it always reminds me of why I always seek out great, high-quality people and I don't settle. Because great, high-quality people are absolute fucking gems, and they will be with you for your whole entire life when you meet the right people. Again, you've got to continue to circulate, and interact, and meet as many other people as you can until you find what you're looking for.

LINK: https://understandingrelationships.com/date-outside-of-your-comfort-zone/16975

Is She Just Shy, or Not Interested?

"Our egos can be a blessing and a useful tool when it comes to believing in ourselves taking risks and achieving goals; but when it comes to romance, our egos can be a little delusional and blind us to the reality that some lovers are simply not interested in us romantically. Ideal candidates for dating are members of the opposite sex who are ready, willing and able to date. That means that there are no exes in the background, they are divorced, single, unattached or not confused about how they feel about someone else. They have a clean slate and space in their already complete and whole lives for you to potentially fill. Only people who have a low self-esteem, who are shy or structured, cheaters, liars, or who are messed up in some way, will have interest but are unable or unwilling to show it or act upon it. Take the path of least resistance and spend your time with potential lovers who are ready, willing and able to date you without any messy drama going on in the background." ~ Coach Corey Wayne

What you're ideally looking for, if you're a guy looking to date a cute girl, is you want a woman who, when you ask her out, you ask her to dinner, to meet for drinks, go rock climbing, whatever it happens to be that you plan to do on a date, her attitude is, "Hell yeah, I'd love to go out with you. That would be great!"—not a woman who offers you resistance, who hems and haws, who has to get back to you, who expresses a total lack of enthusiasm and monotone in her voice. Because think about it, if it's hard to have a conversation with a woman when you first meet her and it doesn't just flow easily and effortlessly, then going out on a date with her is going to be a waste of your time.

So, you're looking for chemistry; you're looking for a woman who is open to talking to you, who likes talking to you, who expresses enthusiasm for talking to you and getting to know you. Too many guys waste too much of their valuable life and time on women who have low to no interest, trying to convince them to change their mind or develop romantic feelings. Women know within two to three seconds of meeting you whether or not they would sleep with you.

LINK: https://understandingrelationships.com/is-she-just-shy-or-not-interested/16676

Attraction, Pursuing & Interest

"In order to maintain and grow mutual sexual attraction and romantic interest, there needs to be a healthy balance between pursuing and making sure both people are making the effort to make each other feel wanted and desired. It's a scientific fact that women are more attracted to men whose feelings are unclear. Under normal circumstances, a healthy woman will do most of the calling, texting and pursuing when the man makes dates when she reaches out, and he also continually makes the effort to make her feel appreciated, wanted and desired. Should the man or the woman ever experience that they are being taken for granted or not be as appreciated as they were in the past, the healthy response is to back off and give the other person space to miss them. When a man or a woman pursues too much and ignores the fact that the other person is no longer appreciating, pursuing or valuing them as much as they once did, not backing off will lead to the end of the relationship. When you love and value yourself, you will only put in as much effort as the other person and will instinctively back off when you sense, see or feel that they are taking you for granted." ~ Coach Corey Wayne

This is a hard concept for the average guy to accept, because they've been taught that they almost have to act like a stalker to get a woman to like and fall in love and want to have a relationship with them. The reality is, you're looking for reciprocity. You're looking for a woman who has mutual enthusiasm for you, and when you first meet, she's already attracted to you. Within 2 to 3 seconds, she knows whether or not she would go out on a date with you and potentially sleep with you. And as long as you're not doing or saying anything that makes you look weak and unattractive, if you get her phone number, or you make a date on the spot, or you message her a few days later after you've gotten her number and make a date, she will be excited and enthusiastic about setting the date. And that's part of the prequalification process when you're trying to set dates.

Women who really like you are going to be very flexible about their schedule and making time to see you. Women who have lower attraction or who have no attraction for you will often give you their number figuring that they'll be able to just reject you later on. It's easier than to do that in person than reject you to their face, because a lot of guys just simply can't take "No" for an answer and they get butthurt. But despite this, these guys make dates and take women out and go to these expensive places trying to impress her, when she really doesn't even want to be there in the first place.

If you see a lack of enthusiasm, if you see a woman who is not willing to make a mutual co-creative effort to facilitate the two of you getting together, why would you want to waste your time going out on a date and spending money on a woman who just has a "Eh, well, I guess it's better than staying at home looking at the four walls," or "Eh, at least I'll get a free meal out of it. Maybe I'll meet one of his friends and I'll click with him and I can date him. Maybe I'll meet another guy in the restaurant or at the bar where we're having drinks, and I can date that guy"? You have to be very selective. The guys who are in a scarcity mindset are just happy to have somebody spend time with them. And, more often than not, they're spending time with a woman that has no interest in them and has no chance. The things I talk about my book, *3% Man,* can really help you screen out the good, high quality dating prospects from the time wasters.

LINK: https://understandingrelationships.com/attraction-pursuing-interest/19398

Should I Break The No Contact Rule?

"Never blame yourself for the actions of someone else. You're only responsible for your own actions. Choose to be strong enough to walk away forever from someone who violates yourself and your dignity. This demonstrates self-respect, high value and is the strongest negotiating position to get what you want or to be treated the way you want. Otherwise, you're simply enabling and encouraging their continued mistreatment of you. When you tolerate bad behavior without standing up for yourself, this devalues you further in the eyes of the other person and leads to a loss of respect. Self-respect means walking away from that which no longer serves you, helps you grow, or helps you to achieve your outcomes." ~ Coach Corey Wayne

Maya Angelou said, "When someone tells you or shows you who they are, believe them the first time." You always should look at people's actions and what they do, not so much what they say. And whether it's a friendship or a client or a girl you're dating, when you notice that people are taking you for granted, the best way to get somebody else's attention is to remove yours and see how they react. Call less, talk less, text less. In other words, if you no longer highly value that person, because of the level of effort or lack of effort that you're getting in return, you're going to give them less of your time and attention. Because the greatest gift you can give anybody is the gift of your time, and if people are not valuing it and appreciating it, well, then they're going to get more of the gift of missing you. And this is how you ensure the people that are in your life actually care and make a mutual effort and want to be there. It also causes them to respect and value you, because it requires mutual effort on their part to maintain what you have. Good people, good friends, good lovers are going to cheer your success, and celebrate your success with you, and be glad that you're doing well, and want you to do well, and have positive, encouraging words that help you do well.

LINK: https://understandingrelationships.com/should-i-break-the-no-contact-rule/28803

Weaknesses Are Revealed After Heartbreak

"Everything you do matters. All of your mistakes, failures, challenges and setbacks happen on purpose to help you grow and become all that you are capable of becoming. The key is to not let any setbacks or failures define you, but instead use them as fuel for change, so you can learn from them and overcome them to prevent you from making the same mistakes in the future. When you don't get the gift or refuse to see the gift of your failures and grow from them, you'll keep yourself stuck in the same level of consciousness that attracted them in the first place, instead of transcending them to become even greater than you were before. Life will keep giving you the same type of circumstances, failures and lessons until you make the right choice to grow beyond them. In order to get to a place of consistent inner peace, happiness, abundance, success and balance in all areas of your life, you must learn to consistently grow, adapt, improvise, improve, overcome, refine and learn from your experiences, instead of staying stuck in the past, repeating the same mistakes, and not getting to where you want to be, or making any measurable progress." ~ Coach Corey Wayne

This has really helped me to have a good attitude and look at everything that's happened in my life as happening on purpose. When you think about how mysterious it is when you meet somebody and they become a close lifelong friend, or a girlfriend that you may date for many years, and then you agree to go your separate ways but you always stay in touch even though you may be in relationships with other people, the both of you—even though both of you may be in relationships with other people—always stay in touch and have a kind word for each other. Now that I'm almost 51 years old, what I really appreciate at this point my life is good relationships—good people that are good for me, good to me, and good for my soul.

It's like, when you're younger, you have a lot of acquaintances and people that you think are your friends, but as soon as you go through some difficulties or challenges, those people that you thought were your friends tend to disappear. And the people that are really your friends, they're there because they care about you, not what they can get from you or what you provide for them. And as you go through ups and downs in life, you start to find out who is really on your team and who is not. And the reality is, as you get older your circle of really close friends gets defined and it gets very small. This is the way it's supposed to be. All those other people that never really made the same level of effort for the relationship that you do, they tend to fall by the wayside. But those people whose goals and values and are spiritually aligned with you, you just always find a way to stay in touch and make the effort, because they're just such good people that you always find a way to be in each other's lives. And that's the most important thing in life, is showing up for those you care about and those who care about you.

LINK: https://understandingrelationships.com/weaknesses-are-revealed-after-heartbreak/16826

When Your Family... Sucks!

"You should love your family but choose your peers. If you come from a broken family, a dysfunctional family or a family full of self-hating and self-loathing losers who never have anything positive, uplifting or encouraging to say, you should remove yourself from their presence immediately or as much as possible. Weak, miserable, unhappy and unsuccessful people are always going to try to drag everyone else around them down to their level so they can feel better about their shitty lives. When they are successful at destroying other people's dreams and bringing them down to their miserable level, this will actually justify their model of the world, their limiting beliefs and the dysfunctional way that they live their lives. It's essential to your sanity and your overall success in every area of your life, that you only associate and spend your time with people who appreciate you, love you and value you." ~ Coach Corey Wayne

We don't always start out in a great place in life. Many people, myself included, came from a very dysfunctional home environment. When you grow up in a dysfunctional family, you have wounds and you have issues that you need to heal, and you're not even aware of how they're negatively impacting your personal life, your social life, and your professional life. That's why it's so important to do a lot of personal growth study, personal introspection, and reflection, and looking at the things that you want to do or have wanted to do, but up until that point your life, have felt like you haven't known what to do, or haven't been capable to do it, or really taking the initiative to make changes and go after the things that you want in life.

I know, from my own personal experience, when I was in my my early 20s, that's when I really started to recognize how the upbringing that I had had influenced my self-esteem in both positive but also a lot of negative ways. So, the positive ways it had influenced me was, deep down, I had this desire to prove my parents and my family wrong—that I could be a success, that I could succeed, that someday, I would really make it great. And the negative ways it had influenced me was how I viewed myself, that, deep down, I didn't feel very lovable, I didn't feel loved, and I didn't feel worthy of love. And anytime I met a woman I really liked a lot and she liked me, it really brought all those fears, those insecurities, and those doubts to the forefront of my psyche, where I had to actually deal with it.

It wasn't until several years later that I was able to recognize how that had influenced my self-esteem in a negative way. So, how that showed up in my dating life, my personal life, is because I basically had a tape playing, or a broken record playing, or a scratched DVD or CD in my head playing, or just a corrupted digital computer file. And the way that manifested itself was I just simply didn't think I was worthy. And I automatically assumed that I wasn't going to get a call back, that she was going to lose interest in me, that once she got to know me, she would lose interest, that things wouldn't work out.

And just like I've talked about in *3% Man*, that caused me to try to force things—to call too much, to text too much, to try to get these women to spend more time in my life than they were ready for. And every single time, especially in my early to mid 20s, it's like, I literally chased these women right out of my life to the point where I, eventually, just got ghosted and blown off and they ignored me. Because I didn't have any game. I couldn't see what I was doing right and what I was doing wrong. Everything was just simply confusing to me at that particular point. It was all because I hadn't realized how negatively the lack of love and hugs and hearing "I love you" and "I'm proud of you" as a kid had a negative effect on my self-esteem.

LINK: https://understandingrelationships.com/when-your-family-sucks/18865

Dating Unhappy People

"When people do not feel good about themselves or like they are good enough for someone or something, they often will either sabotage their relationships or their life circumstances. It is not your job to fix a potential lover's problems, fix them or save them from their crummy life or circumstances. Unless someone realizes and admits they have problems or challenges that need solving and are open to doing what's necessary to fix them, there is nothing you or anyone else can do to help them. You should not care more about someone else's success than they do. You can't do for others what they can and should do for themselves." ~ Coach Corey Wayne

I see this quite a bit, guys dating women that have a truck load of problems—problems that have to do with exes in the background, their fathers of their children that they're having problems with, dating women that just don't make a lot of money, or they're not good with money, and they're perpetually broke. And the longer time you spent with them, the more they start asking you for money, (which typically, often starts out, the guy starts volunteering to help her out, because she shares her sad story of how she can't pay this bill or that bill). And what ends up happening is, instead of dating a teammate and an equal, it's like, now you're dating somebody that you have to take care of, almost like you're taking on another child.

For me, personally, in my own life experience, I like women that have the wherewithal to go out and get a good paying job, to start a business, they're good with money, they pay their bills on time. They keep their cars clean, they do something that they really enjoy for a living and they earn good money with it. Any time I've dated women that are perpetually broke, or you have a couple of dates with them and then it comes out that they barely have the money to pay their bills, nine times out of ten, they typically, at least for me personally, are too irresponsible. I like women that can pay their bills and pay their rent on time and aren't always stressed out about money, because I always have money in the bank and my bills are always paid. And the same thing with all of my friends. I have very successful friends and family, and I don't hang out with people that are constantly complaining about money, or not being able to pay their bills, or you suggest something to them and they're like, "Oh, I can't really afford that," or "Oh, I'm broke." You know, that's just a place where I personally don't live, and so, for me, I just don't want to date women that are like that.

When I was younger, I had a girlfriend that came from a very wealthy family. She was the baby of the family, and they just spoiled the shit out of her. And the problem was that she had basically spent her paycheck every week before she even earned it. And so, she was always broke and she never had any money, and she was constantly going to her parents for money. And then, she hardly had the money to do anything nice for me. It was like, I was always paying for everything. And it's amazing, because she couldn't exercise self-control, and so, when she got her paycheck, she was at the mall buying crap.

I remember we, we had a bedroom that was just stacked from floor to the ceiling with all this crap that she had bought—stuff to decorate with, just trinkets and things—and she'd never opened any of that shit up. She would buy it, put it in a room, and eventually, it just filled the room up. And I remember when we went our separate ways, it's like, all the crap that was in that room, she didn't take any of it with her. It all went out to the side of the road. If she threw it all away, it was like thousands and thousands of dollars for the stuff that she had bought with her paychecks. That shit drove me up the wall. It's one of things that ultimately really turned me off about her. And why I didn't stay with her long term is just because she was always broke and she wasn't good with money. If I gave her access to my bank account, she would just spend all the money in there. I was smart enough not to do those things.

LINK: https://understandingrelationships.com/dating-unhappy-people/23877

EMBRACING THE UNCOMFORTABLE

Quick Ways To Improve Attraction Skills

"One of the most important skills you can develop to succeed in life is overcoming what you fear. Fear is the single biggest thief of people's dreams. Therefore, what you fear, you attract. What you look at and face will disappear as the illusion that it is. Your fear of something is always greater than actually doing what you fear. Fear only exists in the mind. Most people let their fear of success, fear of failure or fear that they don't have what it takes hold them back from taking the action they know they need to take in order to accomplish their goals and dreams. Go for what you want, and especially go for it if it terrifies you. Your playing small serves no one." ~ Coach Corey Wayne

Someday, your life is going to end. What are you okay with going to your grave having not experienced, not achieved, or not attempted? That's a difficult thought for a lot of people to contemplate. Most people avoid those kinds of thoughts, but it's reality. Because the last thing you want to do is end up on your deathbed with a bunch of , wishing that you could live your life over. And when they do interviews and have done studies with people who are at the end of their lives, they all say the same things. They wish they would've taken more risks, they wish they would've changed jobs, they wish they would've started that business, they wish they would've made more of an effort to stay in contact with their friends, they wish they would've taken more risks.

So, you obviously don't want to end up in a place where you get to the end of your life and then you finally realize that you've been playing small and not going for the things that you really want. Because when those moments come, it's going to be too late. And when you think about the pain of that, of potentially being on your deathbed and looking back on your life with nothing but regrets about what you did or didn't attempt, that's not a good place to end up. You're going to end up on your deathbed eventually, but hopefully when you get there you have a sense of peace and contentment. And if you're listening to or reading this right now, you're way further ahead than 97% of the other people who are going to have nothing but regrets when they come to the end of their lives.

LINK: https://understandingrelationships.com/quick-ways-to-improve-attraction-skills/13954

Am I Being Used?

"Too many people in this world settle for a life that is less than what they are capable of living. They often will date, marry or have relationships with people who are "safe," where they don't really risk getting hurt emotionally because they're simply not into that person. They also will hold onto relationships that really need to end out of their fear that they will never find anyone better. This behavior is exhibited by people who constantly dump and then go back to the person they dumped when they become fearful that they won't find anyone else or anyone better. Not only do they settle in their relationships, but this pattern of mediocrity shows up in their careers, businesses, friendships and the life and lifestyle they lead. Deep down, they simply don't think it's in the cards for them. If you truly love, respect, and value yourself, you will not tolerate this kind of weak behavior from your potential lovers, friends, business partners, etc. People who are weak and who constantly settle lie to themselves and others in order to maintain their illusion. You have to become really strong as a person to not only walk away from these kinds of people and situations, but to prevent them from trying to drag you back into their illusion and down to their level of mediocrity." ~ Coach Corey Wayne

Fear really does rob people of their dreams, and their hopes, and eventually, their lives. Because the average person really doesn't enjoy being single, and what prevents them from ending relationships and moving on is the average person doesn't have a good strategy for dating and relationships. And they think about how long and how hard it was to find somebody that they are either currently with or were with up until recently, and as they go through several months of being single and trying to date and meet new women and it doesn't go well, and they're experiencing a lot of friction, instead of recognizing that their dating, pickup, and attraction strategies suck, they start to delude themselves into thinking, "I broke up with the most amazing person that I've ever been with. She's the one. I've got to get her back." And then, they go and they get her back, and after a few months, all the things that turned him off about her are still there. And, eventually, he still ends up leaving her again.

It's the fear of the unknown. People will hold out for a few months, and then when the fear starts to overwhelm them, they start to have panic attacks and they start to worry that they're never going to meet anybody better. Because, naturally, human beings want to have a sense of peace and ease and delight in their life, and one of our essential six human needs is certainty, they don't want to wait until some unknown time in the future that somebody better comes along. And then, they just go back to what wasn't working, or they stay in a relationship that's not working, because, in their mind, it's better than being single.

It's the same thing when it comes to what people do for a living. If they're really unhappy and miserable, the average person, typically, doesn't do anything about it, because they don't enjoy interviewing, they don't know how to put a good resume together, they don't know how to go about finding a really good job. And what's interesting is, years ago when I was in real estate, I would post a lot of job opportunities for people that were graduating from the local university in my city, in Orlando. And I would put in there, specific instructions of what I wanted them to do if they felt that the job opportunity was right for them and they really wanted a chance to interview. And almost 100% of the people that applied for this job just emailed the resume in, even though I told them in the letter that once they sent the resume in to call the receptionist and to schedule an interview. Almost 100% of them never would even follow the instructions in the letter. I was making it easy for them to get an interview with me. And we had a very successful company that was all over TV, we were well known in town, and these people were all college graduates that had spent tens of thousands of dollars getting degrees, and yet, they couldn't even be bothered to pick up the phone and call to get an interview. They just blindly emailed or mailed a resume in, and it never went beyond that.

I never would call any of those people. And, occasionally, the ones that would actually follow the instructions, they were the ones that would get the job interviews. And out of those, only a handful of them would turn out to be good enough to hire. It was just interesting that just hundreds and hundreds of people sent resumes in that got these expensive degrees, and they couldn't even follow simple instructions.

LINK: https://understandingrelationships.com/am-i-being-used/16618

I'm Afraid To Get Rejected

"Our fears around doing things that scare us are always worse than actually doing what we fear. Since people will do more to avoid pain than they will do to gain pleasure, irrational fears are the number one cause of people not achieving their dreams and reaching their full potential. Human beings have two primary fears: 1) fear that we're not enough, in other words we don't have what it takes to succeed, and 2) fear that we won't be loved and accepted by our friends, family, or peer group. We're all living in bodies that are one day going to die. In order to become what we want and achieve what we want, we must be willing to do the things that we fear or that scare us. Otherwise, our destiny is a life of mediocrity and one day being on our death bed regretting what we didn't do or try to do." ~ Coach Corey Wayne

That's the thing that's so interesting about fears, is that when we imagine potential pain in the future, or we fear an event or outcome happening that's undesirable, is that it can become overwhelming. And what we feel we want to do is avoided at all costs. But what's interesting, what I've found is that what you fear you attract, but what you look at disappears, meaning when you face your fears and you actually experience what it is that you fear, that event, the actual fear that you feel in the moment, is always way less intense than you imagined it to be. In other words, fear only exists in the mind. It's like we psych ourselves out and we're so afraid of failure or looking bad or having a bad outcome or experience in the future that we avoid doing anything to help ourselves to move our lives forward. We actually will take action that will move us away from our goals and dreams and towards a destination that is less than ideal and is not where we want to be. Your dreams, your goals, all the things that you want in life are always on the other side of experiencing the things that you fear.

LINK: https://understandingrelationships.com/im-afraid-to-get-rejected/17939

No Longer A Sad Case

"Fear is the greatest obstacle that prevents most people from reaching their full potential. We will act consistently with how we view ourselves to be and what we think about ourselves. It does not matter whether this view is accurate or not. Successful people tell themselves an empowering and positive story about themselves. They also monitor and catch themselves when they notice negative self-talk or thoughts. We become what we think about and what we act upon. Everyone has personal doubts about themselves, but successful people take action even when success seems hopeless or impossible. Change the story that you tell yourself, and you will change your life." ~ Coach Corey Wayne

If we see ourselves as amazing, and smart, and resourceful, and look at life as full of possibilities, we will move towards the things we want in life. If we're overwhelmed with fear and we doubt ourselves, what happens is we tell our mind to find reasons to be fearful and not take action. Because people will do more to avoid pain than they will do to gain pleasure, and when you're overwhelmed with fear—fear of the future, fear of things not working out, whatever it may be—we're going to not do anything, because our fear causes us to believe that doing something or moving towards the things we want will equal pain.

Successful people are able to overcome this because they use their fears inversely, meaning they look at it from the position of getting emotional leverage upon themselves. Instead of looking at the negative consequences of taking action or the pain you may experience, the way successful people look at the future is they think to themselves, "If I don't take action and I don't do these things I know I need to do, even though it may end in failure and heartbreak, or being upset, or frustration, or anger, whatever it happens to be," they think in terms of "What am I going to miss out on? What is this going to cost me five years, ten years, fifteen years, twenty years down the road, when I'm not able to achieve the things that I want in life, when I'm not able to live the life that I want?" And so, they associate more pleasure with doing the things that they know they need to do, because it's going to result in helping them to get from where they are to where they want to be.

LINK: https://understandingrelationships.com/no-longer-a-sad-case/31186

Teaching Old Dogs New Tricks

"Most people, by the time they hit their thirties, have stretched outside their maximum comfort zone limits of who they think they are capable of becoming and will not go any further. From that point forward they tend to major in minor things due to their fear of the unknown, fear of success, fear of failure or fear that they won't be loved and accepted by their friends, family, peer group or potential lovers. Everything in nature dies when it stops growing. The only way to truly live and expand who you are is to continue to learn and grow beyond your comfort zone. Why? You're either growing, expanding and becoming more, or you're slowly dying... little by little... piece by piece." ~ Coach Corey Wayne

This is something that I noticed over the course of my life, is that when you're younger, you tend to be open to trying new things, trying more things. And as you go through life, you gain life experience, the years roll by, you tend to get set in your ways a little bit, and if things are working for you but they're not optimal, you tend to get attached to the way things are. That, oftentimes, especially in business, makes it difficult to be open to trying new things or trying things that may have slightly worked in the past or you didn't enjoy doing. The point being is when you become set in your ways, you become opposed to being as open as you once were.

This really came to a head when I was in my late 30s and still trying to figure out how I was going to have a successful business model to get it to work when I became a full-time life coach. Because I had been at it for several years, and everything that worked when I was in real estate—to advertise, to bring in new leads, to convert sales—we were selling a very high-ticket item product, whereas, if you're selling a $300,000 our house, you're looking at maybe $20,000–$22,000 commissions between the loan and the real estate commissions. And so, it's very easy if you're spending $40,000-$50,000 a month on television advertising—it didn't take too many deals from those leads to easily pay for the advertising.

But when you are trying to sell a $20–30 book, you've got to sell a lot more of them, and advertising tends to reach the same amount of eyeballs, if you will—whether it's television advertising or on the internet. And so, especially with the internet, you've got to be very efficient in your message and make sure you're showing it to the right people because, obviously, with television or radio versus the kind of targeting you can get on the Internet with computers, you can get way more targeted with the options that are available from the different digital advertising platforms. And part of what made my current business finally a success and enabled me to have the breakthroughs I needed was letting go of everything that I had learned from the television industry, the radio industry, advertising on billboards. I kind of had to unlearn what I'd learned already, in order to get rid of assumptions that were kind of getting in the way of exploring and doing things that I told myself I didn't want to do.

I went from trying to sell my book to having a business strictly focused on adding value through articles, through videos, through podcast-style media, Instagram media—just constantly putting out teaching, and work, and lessons related to my books and articles. And as people started to follow along with me and they started applying the things that they were learning for free, eventually, that caused them to have the confidence. Plus, I also let them read my books for free on my website; all they had to do was subscribe to the email newsletter. Once they did that, it built an incredible level of trust with people because, even to this day, nobody really that's at the same level I'm at does that with their books, because they're too worried about how many sales they may lose.

But, overall, when you give your best stuff away, if you look at the biggest platforms, like Facebook and Instagram and all these different digital media platforms that we all use today, everything is free to use. And on some of them, if you have good enough content, you can actually make money on advertising from it. I was only able to get to that point where I connected the dots and things work, because I was able to finally let go of everything that wasn't working for me in the past.

Sometimes you've got to let the past die, but for the average person, when they get into their late 20s their early 30s, they've kind of formed an opinion of themselves, their capabilities, and what the world is like, and once that happens, they're not really open to learning anything new and advancing beyond where they were. And that just basically becomes the baseline of how they live the rest of their lives. And so, the average person, by the time they're in their late 20s, early 30s, their dreams are completely dead, because they painted themselves into a box and they've come up with all these rules and things that prevent them from moving forward at all or taking any action to move towards what they want.

LINK: https://understandingrelationships.com/teaching-old-dogs-new-tricks/14459

How To Build The Life You Deserve

"Our greatest triumphs tend to often come from our greatest tragedies and setbacks. When parts of our lives dissolve, it can feel like it's the end of the road. The reality is that life is like peeling the layers of an onion. We shed the old to expose new possibilities, new realities and get a fresh start to become better than we were before. Sometimes life feels hopeless and like it's never going to get any better. As long as you keep moving forward, taking action towards your grandest goals and dreams, learning from your mistakes and refining your approach, success is simply a matter of time. It's easy to be weak and quit. It takes courage and strength of character to persevere in spite of overwhelming odds. Victory only comes after you refuse to quit." ~ Coach Corey Wayne

This reminds me of back in late 2005, early 2006 when all of the changes that were going on in the real estate and mortgage industry were really taking a toll on my business and my plans for the future. On top of that, I was wrestling with the fact and struggling to admit that I no longer had the same internal enthusiasm for the real estate and mortgage industry that I once had. And, based on all the calamity, and the things going on, the difficulties and the struggles, I was faced with the choice: completely change my business model and focus on a different way to sustain the success I had in the real estate and mortgage industry, or if I had to start all over and do something completely differently, what would that be? What would I do? And by asking myself that kind of a good quality question, an answer popped right into my mind easily and effortlessly. It just dropped right in there, and I remember thinking to myself, "I'd like to mentor and teach and coach people."

So, that started the ball rolling on a process, because at that point in my life, 35 years old, I'd been on that path since I was 18 in that business. And then, the other thing that struck me when I thought of that was, "How do I let go of everything I've done, everything I've known, everything I've built my life around, and now do something completely different? To take something that was a hobby to help myself, so I could achieve the things I wanted to, and synthesize that into a successful business that I could earn a good living and good income from?" So, I was excited about the possibility, but also, I was terrified of it. Because that meant liquidating all the property that I had, completely doing something different, and having no idea when things were going to take off and be really successful, even though, at the time, I believed it would only take me a year or two to figure out my business model and really make the business a success.

If you've read my second book, *Mastering Yourself*, you realize that took me about four years, because I went through about four years of letting go of limiting beliefs and the way I used to do things. I was attached to what worked in the past, and I had a really hard time accepting that what worked in the past was not working in the new business. It was only after I let go of all those rules and the attachments to the way things I thought should work, that I was able to look at doing things completely differently. And it was amazing; once I let go of the wrong way of doing things, it only took a matter of months of instituting a new business philosophy, and blogging, and writing, and putting content out, and growing my email list that things really started to take off for me, and I recognized that, finally, I found the way.

Even though I knew about how to have a successful marketing strategy through email, I just didn't want to do that because I believed that if I just focused on selling my book people would buy the book and they would see how great it was. But what I didn't understand at the time was the way that the internet worked, that people don't go to the internet to buy something, usually; they usually go to the internet to do research, and then once they've completed their research, then they go ahead and make their purchase.

LINK: https://understandingrelationships.com/how-to-build-the-life-you-deserve/36486

Life, Work & Relationship Balance

"Most people do not feel comfortable enough in their own skin to stand up for themselves, what they want and how they want to be treated. When their beliefs and how they view themselves are in conflict with their goals, dreams and outcomes, this makes it impossible to create the life and lifestyle they really want. The story they tell themselves gets in the way and prevents them from taking the action they need to take, in order to move towards what they want and overcome the challenges and obstacles that are always a part of everyone's journey to achieving their grandest goals and dreams. Since we tend to do more to avoid pain and discomfort than we will do to gain pleasure and success, we must always be aware of our self-talk and limiting beliefs, so we can take action that will move us towards our outcomes and goals. Otherwise, we will make excuses and take actions that only move us away from our dream lives and lifestyles." ~ Coach Corey Wayne

This reminds me of what I was struggling with in my late 30s transitioning out of the real estate and mortgage industry into the life coaching industry, and the fact that the way I went about marking my business in the real estate, mortgage, and construction industry, none of those methods worked when I was advertising my life coaching services and my books. And the key shift for me is that I had spent years trying to find a way to sell my book profitably. And because of the success that I had had in all of my previous interactions in business up to that point, I was kind of stuck in that belief and the idea or the thought of writing lots of emails, or an email autoresponder, or a newsletter, or writing articles on my website was the last thing I wanted to do. And, eventually, once I had spent hundreds of thousands of dollars over the years on different advertising strategies and marketing strategies that just simply were not profitable, then I came to recognize it really doesn't cost a lot, other than your time, or you know, your web hosting, and maybe you're buying stock images for the articles.

And so, I started writing articles, publishing them, sending them to my email list, (which I think, at the time, I had probably only 1,200–1,300 people in my email list, at that point), and what I noticed after about 30 days is my books were selling more, I was getting all this new, free organic search traffic to my website, people were starting to send in more questions, and I wasn't even spending any money on advertising. I was like, "Well this is great. My costs are basically a couple of dollars when I buy some stock images for the articles, and that's it." And so, it became more profitable right away. Once I started doing this and it just started clicking, after a couple of months—because I had taken on a part-time job waiting tables when I was 39 years old and sleeping on my dad's couch—within a couple of months of just changing my approach and letting go of the old way I was doing things that weren't working, you know, my beliefs about myself, about business, and the way to go about selling a product completely changed. I had to let go of everything that I knew, and once I let go of that, the obvious solution was right in front of me. As I did more of it, it was basically free marketing to sell my products. And it obviously took off from there, and here I am today.

LINK: https://understandingrelationships.com/life-work-relationship-balance/25423

Are You Good For Me?

"The quality of your life is in direct proportion to the quality of the questions you consistently ask yourself and the quality of the people who you consistently spend your time with. Here are some great questions to continually ask yourself regarding who you should let into your inner circle and life experience and who you should delete: Are you helping me achieve what I want? Do you inspire and encourage me? Are you a good influence upon me? Are you a giver or an energy vampire and taker? Do you leave me feeling happy or do you leave me feeling emotionally, mentally, spiritually and physically fleeced? Are our goals and values aligned? Are you an honorable and trustworthy person? Do you keep your word? Do you celebrate and appreciate me, or merely tolerate me to get what you want? Are you a net contributor to my life, or merely a consumer of my life-force, resources and energy? Do you make consistent effort to make me feel loved and appreciated?"
~ Coach Corey Wayne

These are all great questions that average, mediocre people never think to ask themselves of the people that are in their lives. It's essential to make sure that you're continually sorting and qualifying the people who you spend most of your time with, because, as the old adage goes, we become like the five people who we spend most of our time with. And whomever you're going spend your time with, ideally, if you're trying to be a high achiever and become better, you want to spend your time with people that are more successful in other areas that you're weak in.

If you look at all the most successful, wealthiest people throughout history, that's one of the things they've been able to identify—their own weaknesses and things that they're not good at—and then find people who love those things that they're not good at, who have a passion for those things that they're not good at, and either go into business with them, hire them, or get them on their team. And what this allows you to do is to focus on your core competencies in life.

Everybody has flaws and faults; not everybody is perfect. And you may have, like I do, some friends that are really great, very successful in their own lives, but they really don't take very good care of their bodies. And so, being around me is a good influence on them in getting them to be more concerned about health and taking care of their body. Whereas, they may have other qualities that I might not be so great or balanced in and being around them helps me balance out my essence. I tend to be a risk taker, and when I was younger, a lot of the risks that I took were a little too risky. You never want to take more risk than your downside. In other words, you don't want to risk more than you can afford to lose. Because you're going to take risks, and there's risk of failure, especially when you're putting your money at risk. You have to know what the downside risk is to that so you can mitigate that. Because if you put all your chips on the table and give yourself either "I succeed greatly" or "I just completely fail and lose all my money," well, after you do that a couple of times and you lose all your money, you're going to recognize that you should really take more moderate, measured kinds of risks.

LINK: https://understandingrelationships.com/are-you-good-for-me/14540

Effortless Seduction

"How would your thinking and the action you take on a daily basis change if you knew that not only could you never fail, but that success is simply a matter of time, repetition, learning from your mistakes, refining your approach and persistence? Unsuccessful people take action based upon the assumption of playing it safe, since success is simply not in the cards for them. Successful people take action based upon the assumption success is inevitable. Failure is an inevitable part of life and a necessary precursor to success. Unsuccessful people typically give up when they fail. Successful people simply look at failure as something from which to learn, grow and improve." ~ Coach Corey Wayne

I think it was Henry Ford that basically said something along the lines of "Failure is simply the opportunity to begin again, this time, more intelligently." When you think about what Henry Ford accomplished in his life, that success quote sums up his philosophy and his mindset towards failure. He looked at failure as an opportunity to begin again more intelligently. Well, more intelligently because, hopefully, you learn from your mistakes, you learned what didn't work, and now you have an opportunity to try something else which may also not work, but each time you try something and you have a failure, you learn from it. Just like Thomas Edison, you get closer and closer to finding something that does work. This is the difference between high achievers and how they think and how mediocre people think. Mediocre people think failure just means that it's over, it's not in the cards for them, it's too painful, and, therefore, they never really try to stretch beyond their comfort zone ever again.

LINK: https://understandingrelationships.com/effortless-seduction/25831

The Subtle Nuances Of Attraction & Seduction

"Life will test your resolve and dedication to achieving your dreams. Once you know what you want to accomplish in life, why you want to accomplish it, and you have a plan of action that you are consistently executing to achieve it, success is simply a matter of time and repetition. Obstacles, challenges and failures should be looked upon as necessary experiences to help you continuously adjust, adapt and refine your approach. This ensures that you mold yourself, and your life, into finely tuned instruments to create and experience your ideal life. Your weaknesses will attract life circumstances that help you turn them into strengths. The stronger you become, the more experience you gain and the more your confidence grows, the more you are willing to risk and do in order to make your dreams and dream life a reality. A never-ending journey of self-improvement, perseverance, performance enhancement, and simply trying to be a little better today than you were yesterday is the key to becoming fearless enough to accomplish your dreams." ~ Coach Corey Wayne

What you're going to realize as you get older and you go through life is that, as you continually stretch outside of your comfort zone, it's like, that builds confidence muscle, if you will. In other words, each time you step outside your current boundaries of what you're used to and what you think you're capable of, you recognize that you're capable of more than you thought previously. So, your comfort zone expands, your confidence expands. And so, as you take on responsibilities, and tasks, and goals, and take risks, and overcome challenges, the challenges and the risk that you take as you get older become bigger and bigger. Ideally, you want to take them in a measured-risk style approach where you never want to risk more than you can afford to lose.

So, just keep in mind, a good analogy is a guy who is afraid to talk to women or who is scared to talk to women. Say he doesn't have so much a problem talking to women he finds unattractive, but when he talks to a woman he finds really attractive, he tends to freeze up, doesn't know what to say, and he gets overwhelmed. And so, what needs to happen is he's got to get outside his comfort zone, but not so much that he overwhelms himself and just runs away like a dog with its tail between its legs. So, you want to do measured steps. And one of the things that I came up with for guys like this was a video that I did years ago that I reference in *3% Man* called "Improving Your Social Skills." And what it does is it takes guys through a process where they can kind of go at their own level. If they're afraid and they're intimidated talking to really beautiful, really attractive women, in the video, there is a step-by-step process they go through, and each one requires them to step a little further outside their previous level of comfort zones.

They're not getting totally overwhelmed. They work up to getting to the point where talking to a really beautiful woman is just like talking to an average stranger on the street. Because that's what it really is, is striking up small talk in conversations no matter where you are and using your surroundings to come up with things to talk about. So, if you've got a guy that just gets too overwhelmed by talking to the beautiful women that he really likes, you've got to get him to slowly work up to that.

Because, if he just goes and tries to talk to really beautiful women, he's going to have a series of really unpleasant experiences internally for himself, and the risk he runs is, as he does that, like a lot of guys do, they just get so scared and so overwhelmed, and it just doesn't go well, that they just quit and they give up.

And, obviously, if you're not willing to talk to women that you find pretty and attractive, it's going to be really hard to get a date. So, that's a good analogy that you can apply towards anything in your life, whether it's working for somebody else, or just like working out with weights. You know, you start out, you're not very good, you're not really coordinated, and then you kind of get the rhythm down, the form down. And then, your strength grows, your muscle starts to grow, you take on more risk, you do different exercises. You get more well-rounded in your training; you get more focused on the diet. There's just a bunch of different things that become part of the process. And so, growing your strength and your confidence really is part of a process of taking measured steps, but not to the point where you completely overwhelm yourself and then you do nothing. Because the idea is you want to keep moving forward and make incremental progress, because success is making progress.

So, if you're overwhelming yourself, take a few steps back and don't take such a giant risk next time around. Just take a smaller risk that you feel comfortable with; it causes you to try a little harder. And you're going to experience some fear, but you don't just completely overwhelm yourself to where you shut down and you do nothing.

LINK: https://understandingrelationships.com/the-subtle-nuisances-of-attraction-seduction/16632

I've Always Been Intimidated By Women

"Our fears of what we are afraid of taking a risk to do or experience are always worse than actually doing what we fear. Fear of success, of failure, that you don't have what it takes to succeed or that you won't be loved or accepted by your friends, family or peer group, is what keeps most people from doing anything to overcome their fears so they can attract the kind of people they want and the kind of life and lifestyle they want to experience. Success lies beyond what scares us. Until you decide to become brave enough to overcome your fears and take action in spite of them, you're going to struggle to achieve any kind of real or lasting success at getting what you want in life." ~ Coach Corey Wayne

The reality is everything you want to achieve is on the other side of experiencing what you fear. And so, when I look back at my life when I was in my early 20s versus now where I'm basically about to turn 51, is that back when I was young and I didn't know any better, I had my dreams, I had my goals, I had my vision of the way I wanted my life to be, but I didn't have a ton of life experience. And so, there were a lot of things that I had to do, whether it was just simply going in for a job interview, meeting with a client that I was intimidated by, getting to school on time, getting my work done on time, having a balanced life. I was stressed a lot when I was younger because I had so many balls in the air, but what kept me going through it and kept me focused was I had a vision for what I wanted, I knew what I wanted, I knew why I wanted it, and I had emotionally compelling reasons for it.

And even though everything I was doing was outside of my comfort zone and I didn't have any life experience really to guide me—I just had my inner tuition and my desires, my hopes, my dreams, my goals, my fantasies of what I thought my life would be like in the future—I just put my head down and kept taking action. I had too many things on my plate at the time, really, to be worried, because my whole day was scheduled out, from the time I got up in the morning at 6:00–6:30 in the morning until I went to bed at night at 11:00. And I was just so busy I really didn't have the time to sit up look around and be afraid of what may or may not happen. It goes back to what Dale Carnegie said: "Inaction breeds fear and doubt; taking action breeds confidence and courage." The best thing you can do, the best medicine for being afraid of the future, is to get busy being productive taking some kind of positive action that moves you slightly closer towards your goals and dreams that you want to accomplish.

LINK: https://understandingrelationships.com/ive-always-been-intimidated-by-women/20981

Attraction Turnaround

"Reaching your full potential requires the freedom, time and space to be who you really are and people who nurture, encourage and celebrate you being you. Fear, worry, and doubt causes most people to play it safe, hold back, and be too risk averse to step beyond their current comfort zone and take the actions that are necessary to make their dreams a reality. Success is the result of sustained discipline, focus, perseverance and a relentless pursuit of emotionally compelling outcomes. You're either willing to pay the price to achieve what you want, or you're okay with making excuses and settling for a life that is less than what you are capable of living." ~ Coach Corey Wayne

Striving for the things that you want in life isn't all sunshine and roses, especially your big, audacious goals that are ten years or more in the making. There's going to be a lot of days, a lot of hours, a lot of weeks where you're just feeling like it's never going to get any better. Things seem to be dragging on—you're looking for evidence of success and progress, and you're just not seeing very much of it. And then, when you're in one of those moods when you're having a difficult day and some jackass comes along to tell you how stupid they think your idea is, your business, your video, your post, your product, whatever it happens to be; when you're feeling at your worst is when you see one of those shit birds show up that try to make you feel bad.

That's why it's so super important, and necessary, and essential to have something that's emotionally compelling that you want to do. Because on those days when you're having doubts yourself, when one of those shit birds shows up and tries to project his self-hating and self-loathing on to you in order to make himself feel better about his shitty life, it's doubly more difficult to keep persevering on. But if you have an emotionally compelling reason in the back your mind, that's in your heart, that you feel in your soul as to what's driving you and why you're doing what you're doing, you're able to persevere and continue taking action even when you feel like shit. And that's the hard thing about success and achieving your grandest goals and dreams, is there's going to be a lot of days, hours, weeks, months that you're going to be feeling like crap and things are just not going to seem like they're working out in your favor. It's the emotionally compelling goal, the reason, your emotionally compelling "why" you're doing it, that helps you to keep taking action.

LINK: https://understandingrelationships.com/attraction-turnaround/34974

Sexual Frustration

"In order for any personal and professional relationship to work long term, all parties must share the same goals and values. It's hard to live your truth in a world that is constantly trying to get you to conform to what society says you should be. If you settle and compromise your values, goals and principles, you will always be wondering, "what if?" The purpose of life is to enjoy it, to fully live and experience your grandest goals and dreams. The only way you can reach your full potential is if you spend your time with those who support, encourage and share the same goals and values. Have the courage to let go of who you are by seeking what you want. When you find those whose goals and values match your own, it will feel right. Until then, find a way to enjoy your journey while you pursue all that you want. As long as you take consistent action to improve and refine your approach, success will not be a matter of hope, but simply a matter of time." ~ Coach Corey Wayne

Success is a grind, and as long as you've come up with an emotionally compelling reason why you want what you want, and obviously you know what it is that you really want, and you have a burning desire to make that happen, that's the fuel that you need to keep persevering even when things seem hopeless. This is the thing that most people don't really understand about reaching your full potential, is that there's so many days, weeks, months, and years where things seem totally in doubt, like they're never going to work out in your favor, and that the success and the dreams that you want are just way off in the future. And so, you have to get good at learning to endure being uncomfortable, to endure not feeling like it's working out for you, to endure it feeling like things are hopeless, to endure feeling like your life's never going to get any better, to endure the insults from other people who are trying to sandbag your success.

What's interesting is, people that try to sandbag your success, they always tend to show up when you're feeling like shit and you're having a difficult day. Like attracts like, and so if you're giving off that vibe, the universe seems to be nice enough to send you somebody else to help you experience that kind of a vibe, so you can endure it and you can transcend it over time. But that's the biggest thing that I've seen in my own life, is that big goals, big plans, they take a long time. And almost 100% of the people that you're going to encounter life just simply don't have the internal testicular fortitude to persevere and endure when they're feeling like crap and it feels like it's just never going to work out. So, being able to persevere when you don't feel good really is a superpower. It's a mindset. It's learning to manage your internal state and persevere anyway.

LINK: https://understandingrelationships.com/sexual-frustration/32560

Time Is On My Side

"Most people tend to seek out and expect instant results in their career, business, romantic relationships or the success that they seek. Learning to practice infinite patience in all matters of life and the heart, is essential to the prevention of suffering when things don't go according to plan. Persistence, perseverance and adaptation of one's approach as you take action towards your goals and dreams, will move you forward to eventual success. However, if you are impatient because you do not have the results you want right now, you will not enjoy your life journey as much as you will when you practice infinite patience as you take daily action. When the right opportunities and people come along, they will fit like a glove and just feel right. All others should be viewed as essential obstacles to be overcome, acquisition of skills and knowledge, preparation and practice that are necessary precursors to establish the right conditions, so your dreams can SLOWLY and effortlessly manifest." ~ Coach Corey Wayne

This is one of the greatest things you can do for your overall health and well-being is to adopt a mindset of infinite patience, recognizing that all great things take a decade or more to accomplish. Because it's hard; we're surrounded by everybody who has this idea that society has taught us that everything is supposed to happen right away or that you're supposed to succeed after two or three attempts or tries. The reality is most people give up on their goals and dreams as soon as things get difficult or they start encountering obstacles and challenges. And so, they run away from the pain and the fear of failure to try to salve their ego and not experience anything that's uncomfortable. Well, if you want to achieve all of your goals in life and accomplish great things, you're going to have to get used to being uncomfortable.

So, you should look at all obstacles and challenges and failures as teachers, because we learn more from failure than we do successes. And you have to get used to asking yourself really good high-quality questions when things don't go your way or you have failure: "What's good about this?", "What can I learn from this?", "How can this make me better the next time around?" Every challenge, every setback, every person you meet has some kind of gift for you and you for them. So embrace it, accept it, go with the flow, and remember to trust your heart and your intuition when it comes to sizing things up and sizing opportunities up, because when something doesn't feel right inside and yet you do it anyway, typically, the results are less than ideal.

LINK: https://understandingrelationships.com/time-is-on-my-side/17116

I Thought She Was "The One"

"The universe works in mysterious and unexpected ways. It will deliver the perfect people into your life to exploit your weaknesses, fears and shortcomings so you can transcend them, and they instead can become some of your greatest strengths. Nothing happens by accident in life, and there is no such thing as a coincidence. The universe is very efficient, balanced and always conforms to your thoughts, feelings, desires, emotions and actions slowly over time. By moving in the direction of your outcomes and disciplining yourself to not become attached to circumstances being a certain way, or certain people being in your life, you'll open yourself up to allowing the right people and circumstances to effortlessly manifest in ways that are even better than you expected." ~ Coach Corey Wayne

This is a bitter and hard pill to swallow for most people, especially people that are in a negative and un-resourceful state. You have to learn to practice infinite patience. That's why, before you take any action, and start moving towards the things that you want in life, and creating the ideal life and lifestyle, is that you've first go to figure out, "What is it that I want?", and number two, "Why do I want that? What is the emotionally compelling reason why I want to have that thing, or experience that thing, or have that kind of a relationship?"

Because, when a plane takes off or a ship pulls out of port, they always know what their destination is going to be. And just like a plane in the air is constantly being blown off course back and forth throughout the whole flight, and constantly making course corrections, a cruise ship also is being moved around by winds, by currents, and it's constantly changing and adapting its approach throughout its journey until it pulls in exactly at the destination, right where it's supposed to be, usually right on time.

LINK: https://understandingrelationships.com/i-thought-she-was-the-one/24413

BEING CAUTIOUS

What Women Want

"Most guys who do not know any better, think that being extra nice, accommodating and attentive to women will cause women to fall for them. This is fine when she is your girlfriend, but not when you just started dating. Men who over-pursue and incessantly call or text women they just met or just started dating, give off the same vibe as a potential serial killer or stalker. This obviously scares women and causes them to run away and lose interest. This is why women will choose the indifferent jerk or asshole over the nice guy. Scarcity creates value. Less really is more when it comes to creating attraction in women towards you. No matter how much you like a woman, unless you allow her to come to you at her own pace, it won't be her idea. If you don't give a woman the space and time to mutually choose you and wonder about you, she will choose someone else. What women say they want and what they really respond to in a man are not the same." ~ Coach Corey Wayne

This is one of the biggest mistakes that I see guys make when I'm doing phone sessions, and I see it in the email, is they just call and a text too much. They try too hard to get a woman's attention and validation, instead of having the attitude that women have, which is, "Is this person good for me? Are we a good match? Do I like this person?" Women have a skeptical, "wait-and-see" kind of attitude when they first start talking to and dating a guy, and men should have the same kind of skeptical attitude towards women. Just because she's hot, and got a beautiful face, and nice boobs, great body doesn't mean she's great girlfriend material or wife material. Most guys get hypnotized by a woman's looks, and then they're too far down the road emotionally to see all the red flags that tend to come out later as time goes by.

LINK: https://understandingrelationships.com/what-women-want/31283

Never Treat Dates Like Girlfriends

"One of the worst mistakes that guys make when they start dating new women, is trying to treat them like they're already their girlfriend. They often start acting dopey, submissive and like a teenager in love for the first time. Women approach dating differently than men. Women go out with the attitude of "let's just see what happens," and are looking to determine if the new guy is a good match for them. When a guy starts acting like they are already in a relationship, she is thinking, "We don't even know each other yet!" This makes the woman feel like she is losing her freedom and she will back away. Predictably, when the woman starts to back away, this usually causes the guy to think he has to do something to get things back to the way they were. He will then start to call excessively, not wait for the woman to call back or return messages, become impatient, have "the talk" with her about where he stands, try to force himself into her life, instead of allowing her to come to him at a pace that feels comfortable to her, etc. This needy and desperate behavior usually leads to being friend-zoned, the woman ignoring him, or her giving him an outright rejection and not wanting to see him anymore. Guys simply need to focus on hanging out on dates, having fun together on their dates and hooking up when the signs are there that she's ready to be kissed and escalate things physically. Men are much better off if they leave the relationship labels and boyfriend/girlfriend talk to women to bring up." ~ Coach Corey Wayne

This is pretty common. Guys try to do too much too soon in the beginning, and they start putting them on a pedestal and treating the women like a celebrity that they're trying to get their attention and validation of, instead of being skeptical and cautious like most women are when they have the attitude of "I'm going to go out and just see what happens," "I'm not sure if he's good for me yet," "Are we a good match?", "Are we good for each other?" These are the kinds of things that women are focused on, but most men have been brainwashed by what they've seen in TV and the movies that they are under the gun, and it's an emergency, it's a five-alarm fire that they have to find out right away where they stand and lock the woman down, otherwise some other guy's going to come along and steal her from them. This makes men come off as needy, insecure, desperate, and un-centered, unlike guys who have their act together, who are cautious, and are taking their time, and are not in a rush. When you look at the older movies, the black and white movies from 40, 50, 60, 70 years ago, this is what you always saw; the women were always chasing the attention and validation of the men and getting the men to become more interested in them.

LINK: https://understandingrelationships.com/never-treat-dates-like-girlfriends/16552

Their Shortcomings Aren't Your Fault

"A healthy relationship is the result of two people sharing their completeness, not completing each other. Get to a blissful place where you love yourself, your life, lifestyle, peer group and enjoy being alone. Then, when you are in a blissful place and grateful for your life, you can effortlessly attract someone who is also in a blissful place. Like attracts like. You will attract people and circumstances into your life that matches and mirrors your current vibe. You must take care of you and your own happiness first, before you'll be in the right place to contribute to the happiness of another." ~ Coach Corey Wayne

A lot of men and women make the mistake of getting involved in relationships with people that have all kinds of flaws, faults, and just things that are really screwed up in their life. They think, "If I could just fix this person, they would be the perfect boyfriend," or, "they would be the perfect girlfriend." The reality is, you're not looking for a fixer upper when it comes to relationships; you're looking for somebody that's a great complement to your already great life. When you're looking to fix somebody or to help somebody, you're falling in love with their potential. Because the reality is, if somebody's out of shape and you want them to get into better shape, you can encourage them and prod them and try to drag them to the gym with you as much as you can, but if they're not willing to participate in their own rescue and you're getting upset about this, you're going to be upset and frustrated a lot, because they're simply not going to match your unreasonable expectations.

The reality is, you either accept people as they are with all their flaws and faults, or you recognize that they don't completely measure up to your standards of what you're looking for. And you have to be strong enough to recognize that they simply aren't in a place where they can be the kind of person that you're looking for. As hard as it is, you have to move on to seek someone better and seek better opportunities, because just like the drug addict or the alcoholic doesn't admit that they have a problem until they do, there's nothing you can do to help them. And people that aren't living up to their full potential, (because the world is full of them), most of them will never make the effort that it takes to move their lives forward, and that's just simply the way it is; that's the harsh truth. So, if somebody isn't already on the same level and they're not willing to take the action that it takes to get your level, it's best to just move on and find somebody else. Because you can't love them for the fantasy of who you want them to be, you can only love them as they are.

LINK: https://understandingrelationships.com/their-shortcomings-arent-your-fault/35667

Men: When Your Game Is Tight...

"Men who are successful with women and who have lots of choices and options with women, tend to treat all women the same. They make all women feel beautiful and special simply because that is their gift to them. They never put any woman on a pedestal, because they know that if they did, they would be treating themselves as if they somehow have lesser value than the woman they're interacting with. They view other women as equals and teammates, not fellow human beings who are any better or any worse than they are. They know that women like men who are curious about them and sincerely interested in who they are as human beings. They also know that women want to be understood and heard and feel like they are the most important person in the world to them. The most likeable people are the kind of people who engage you in conversation, and make you feel like you're the only other person in the world. A wise sage once said that the reason why we have two ears and only one mouth is because we should listen twice as much as we speak. If you want to develop your flirting and charm skills, sincerely become interested in other people by asking questions and being a great listener." ~ Coach Corey Wayne

I always recommend to my clients that they should read Dale Carnegie's *How to Win Friends and Influence People*. Even though this work is over 100 years old at this point, this wisdom is timeless because the whole book and course is geared towards winning friends and influencing people. In other words, it's all about selling yourself and getting other people to like you. Because when people like you, they are more likely to trust you. When people like and trust you, it makes it really hard to say no to them. And so, this is especially true when it comes to women, especially super beautiful women, especially this day and age with all of the beautiful women being on Instagram and literally having access to millions of thirsty single guys hitting on them and telling them how beautiful and how amazing they are. At this point, they've heard that so many times, it means nothing to them. And so, therefore, if you take the time to ask a woman about her hopes, her dreams, her passions, the things she loves to do for fun, to ask her the kinds of questions that she would enjoy answering, you actually set yourself apart from most other shallow human beings that they encounter. And, therefore, as long as they're very outgoing and they haven't been messed up in their childhood—because one thing I have noticed is that women who have a missing father figure in their childhood or who grew up without a father entirely tend to have a hard time opening up and talking to you and telling you about themselves and them being vulnerable.

If you compare talking to women who have a great family or who come from a great family environment, and you asked them a question, they're happy to tell you an answer. Whereas, the more messed up a woman's childhood may have been, the more difficult it is for them to open up and tell you about them because they never got used to that; they never became emotionally anchored to speaking from your heart without fear and being loved and supported. Typically, they have abandonment issues. Now, this doesn't mean 100% of them are this way, but the majority of them are going to be negatively impacted by the lack of a stable masculine father figure in their life. And so, they just never learned what it was like; they don't know it looks like, they don't know what it feels like to open up and share what's in their heart without fear. And this can make it extremely difficult to get to know them, as well as when you're having challenges and issues when you're dating them or in a relationship with them, to get them to open up and actually tell you what's going on inside, so you can work through it together as a team.

LINK: https://understandingrelationships.com/men-when-your-game-is-tight/18242

Betrayed By The Perfect Woman

"Liars and cheaters tend to believe that everyone lies and cheats. They learned in childhood that telling the truth and being honest is too risky. In their eyes, it's better to lie and avoid confrontations at all costs. People can hide who they really are for about ninety days of a relationship. You must look at what people do, not what they say, as a true barometer of who they really are. Dating is like test-driving a used car. You can't know what you've really got until you spend a significant amount of time together. Love cannot exist without trust. Take your time; good relationships are worth the wait and stand the test of time. As the old saying goes, haste really does make waste." ~ Coach Corey Wayne

I see this over and over and over again, is that people who lie and cheat assume everybody else is a liar and cheater. So, if you start dating somebody and they become jealous and insecure of your social media posts, the people you're connected to on social media, the people that you talk to, and they're constantly accusing you of doing something that's inappropriate with those other people, that should be a major red flag to you that something is not on the up and up with them. Cause we all tend a project what's inside of us, and liars and cheaters tend to project their lying and cheating on to other people and blame them and accuse them of lying and cheating when it's actually them that you have to be worried about.

LINK: https://understandingrelationships.com/betrayed-by-the-perfect-woman/38340

Relationships That Will Never Work

"In the beginning of a relationship people can mask who they really are for about the first 90 days until they feel comfortable enough and complacent enough to really be themselves. It is important during the first 90 days of dating to remain objective and not get carried away by your emotions, or you will open yourself up to falling for a toxic person who does nothing but bring drama, heartbreak and inconsistency into your life. Toxic people and relationships will make you unsure of yourself and feel like you don't deserve what you really want. Once your identity and emotions become attached to a toxic person, it can be extremely difficult to do the right thing for you and walk away to find someone else who will cherish and love you unconditionally." ~ Coach Corey Wayne

A lot of guys that I talk to in phone sessions are having problems with one particular woman, and nine times out of ten, they've usually started dating somebody who is toxic and not a good match. Like, to give an example, this morning I was filming a recent YouTube video, and the guy who had emailed me had gotten a divorce after five years of marriage. He ended up knocking up his girlfriend, and then they thought it was a good idea to get married because she got pregnant. Well, after five years of marriage she ended up cheating on him and, obviously, that led to the end of the marriage.

That was two years ago, and he's been following my work for about two years now, and he's got a new girlfriend of about four months and she lives about an hour and a half away from him. And so, the interesting thing about this particular woman, and the way I see that the universe tends to work, is that the same kind of circumstances and people keep showing up over and over until we learn from them, and transcend them, and get the gift. And what was interesting is this particular woman that he is dating and is supposedly his girlfriend has been asking him about moving in together, and on top of that, ever since they met there's a guy that she works with who, as the weeks and months have gone by, she continues to talk more and more fondly about this particular guy. So, he notices his girlfriend texts this guy, he sees the text. The good news is she doesn't hide her phone from him, but the problem is that she's talking about moving in together after only four months of dating, which tells me that she's incredibly insecure. And the fact that she supposedly has a boyfriend that she wants to move in with is not deterring her from hanging out and entertaining and inviting the attention and validation that this other male coworker of hers is giving her. They've spent time together outside of work, and it's obviously not a good situation.

A woman that comes from a good home and a good family is just simply not going to do these things. So, these are major red flags that shows that she lacks integrity and is probably not a loyal person. So, obviously, what's going on is she's sitting on the fence and hedging her bets with her supposed boyfriend, while she also continues to enjoy the flirtation with this other guy at work. So, in essence, she has two guys that want to date her. Even though she supposedly is exclusive with the guy that sent me the email, she's acting like she's a single woman with this other particular guy.

And what was interesting about the email is the guy's saying, "Well, everything else is just great. She's a great girl," but he's a guy that got cheated on with his last wife, and here he is four months into a new relationship with a woman who is talking inappropriately and spending time inappropriately with another guy. He's even tried to set the healthy boundary, but yet, she continues to spend time with this guy and talk to him. And I just told him that this is somebody that's a friend with benefits, a fuck buddy, a sex playmate; this is not somebody you want to make your girlfriend. Because when she feels insecure in the relationship or she's not happy, she's going to be talking to other guys.

LINK: https://understandingrelationships.com/relationships-that-will-never-work/14273

Dating Single Moms

"When a man truly cares for a woman, and deeply loves her, he will love her children from other relationships also. When a man is only into a woman physically and enjoys having a good time with her, but he doesn't deeply care for her, he's not going to want to have anything to do with her children from other relationships. Single women with children should take their time when dating men who don't have kids of their own, to observe a man's actions and make sure he truly cares for them and is not just interested in using them for a booty call or quick hookup. Men should only get involved with women who have children when they truly care for the woman and are open to the possibility of things progressing to the point where he becomes a stepfather to their children. Real men who aren't interested in being a stepfather to someone else's kids, should do the honorable thing, and not date women with children or give women false hope of a relationship, just so they can get laid. Men who know how to seduce women successfully, also need to be responsible with that power and sex appeal that they wield, so they don't break any hearts in the process of fulfilling their carnal desires. Real men who are honorable and who have integrity are also concerned with the welfare and the feelings of other people who could potentially be impacted by seducing the women they desire." ~ Coach Corey Wayne

Sometimes things happen in life. Sometimes women lose their partner through either death or disease or some tragic accident, and the same thing happens with men. This article that I did many years ago on dating single moms, I see some of the nastiest comments from guys in there bashing single moms. What they're really doing is they're revealing their own insecurities and undesirability as a man and as a dating prospect. The reality is, there's lots of single fathers out there and single mothers.

I actually just had a coaching session with a client last night, and they had about a dozen kids between them. They each were married before to other people and had several kids with their previous spouses, and then they got together and also had several kids together. You can imagine, they've got a blended family with lots of kids, and they're pretty tight, and they have a great family type of environment where everybody feels loved and supported. So, you can have a lot of fun with single moms.

The reality is single moms don't have as many dating prospects as women who don't have any other kids, because lots of guys just have the attitude that they don't want to raise somebody else's kids. Which is fine, but the reality is, lots of people get divorces. I mean, our divorce rate is somewhere around 50–60% depending on the stats that you see. And if you're open to it, like, I've had this experience many times over the course of my life, and some of my greatest memories that I have are from some of the women who had children that I got to date and be a part-time dad to. It enriched my life totally in amazing ways and made me the man that I am today. But I love kids, and I love playing with kids, and messing with kids, and teasing them, and having fun with them, and being a good father figure, and watching them grow up, and seeing the influence that you had on them and how it makes them better human beings.

LINK: https://understandingrelationships.com/dating-single-moms/17523

I Dated A Narcissist

"Every man and woman should be aware of, and be able to spot, the toxic traits of lovers who display narcissistic qualities. In stage one of a relationship with a narcissist, called Elevation, the narcissist heaps praise on you, treats you like a king or a queen, puts you on a pedestal and makes you feel like you have finally found "the one." In stage two of a relationship with a narcissist, called De-Elevation, the narcissist starts to find fault with you, criticize and make you feel like you are crazy or that there is something wrong with you. In stage three of a relationship with a narcissist, called Discard, they shut you out, stonewall your attempts to communicate and resolve things, and leave you wondering what the hell went wrong. People who have a low self-esteem or low sense of self-worth are most susceptible to the manipulation and abuse tactics of a narcissist. Therefore, you should become hyper aware, alert and observant when a new lover pursues you too hard, blows too much sunshine up your ass and often makes you feel like things are too good to be true as soon as you meet. Always look at what people do, not what they say. When you spot narcissistic behavior, run like hell and never look back. Narcissists are only interested in themselves, stroking their ego, using others to feel better about themselves and getting what they want." ~ Coach Corey Wayne

I had one experience in my life out of all the women I've had, all the different girlfriends that I've had, I had one who I wouldn't say was a full-blown narcissist, but she sure had a lot of narcissistic behaviors and character traits. I remember when we first started dating, she was full of praise, and flowery language, and how amazing I was—everything I wrote was amazing, my videos were amazing, my Instagram account was amazing, I was amazing, the sex was amazing. And then, as we got a couple of months into the relationship, I noticed that her attitude started to change. Instead of praise, she started heaping slight insults onto me, and putting me down, belittling me, and basically trying to make me feel bad about myself.

What was interesting was after we had broken up, looking back on that behavior, there were times where I really started to question myself. Especially at that phase three—the stonewalling, the being unwilling to communicate. And I remember her even telling me, she was like, "I was married for ten years and I never had these problems." Meanwhile she was married to a dude who neglected their business, was never paying the bills on time, and all he basically did was smoke pot and play video games all day because, obviously, he was tired of her bullshit. And when we broke up it was like, everything was all my fault, she was perfect. I had never had that kind of an experience before or since with any woman. Seeing though, as I do this for a living, I'm glad that it happened, because I learned about these characteristics. It's enabled me to be a better coach and help the people that I work with, because they also sometimes encounter women that are like this.

What's really going on is they have a low self-esteem, and so they bullshit the person, blow their ego up, and once her ego is inflated, and they're infatuated, and they're in love, then they seek to demolish that person, so they feel superior and better about themselves. And then, when you're trying to resolve conflicts or issues, they just stonewall you and say things like, "I don't want to talk about it," and they literally don't want to talk about it. Like, this particular woman, the first time we had a little dustup or a disagreement, she got so mad and upset she just hung up on me right in the middle of our conversation, and I've never had a girlfriend ever treat me like that or do that to me.

It was strange at the time. It was still kind of early in our relationship, and I thought to myself, "That's not good." But because we were already far down the road, I just thought, "Oh, well, maybe she's having a bad day. We'll just talk it out." And she even told me she needed to stew about things for a couple of days, and then once she was over it, she would call me, get in touch, and then she would act like nothing ever happened. The problem was that nothing ever really got resolved. She would get mad, she would get angry, she would go off on her own, give me the silent treatment. And then a few days later I'd hear from her, and she would act like nothing ever happened.

She wouldn't even want to talk about what she got upset with, which was absolutely a first for me. Because all the women that I had ever been with before and since always loved to talk, and loved the fact that a guy wants to know what's going on in her mind, what's going on in her heart, share her feelings, and get to really know her. Most women appreciate that, but a narcissist is really just not that capable of that level of intimacy, hence looking at the supposed ten-year marriage that she had that she supposedly left. I mean, if you're married to a guy and all he does is smoke pot all day long and play video games and check out, there is obviously a big disconnect there; it wasn't a healthy relationship. And the fact that she threw that in my face to try to make me feel bad was just part of that De-Elevation type of stage. So, if you spot those kinds of behaviors, like the quote says, run like hell and never look back.

LINK: https://understandingrelationships.com/i-dated-a-narcissist/19807

Understanding Why I Got Dumped

"Insecure women tend to need validation and attention from many men at the same time. They typically have several male "orbiters" always in the background, even when they are supposedly in committed relationships. These male "friends" are guys who want to date and sleep with them, but just aren't alpha enough or more alpha than their primary lover. When the future of their current relationship looks in doubt, they start spending time with the male orbiters to line up a replacement or to fill the needs that aren't being met by their primary lover. Women who have a healthy self-esteem would never do this. They look forward to being alone and single for a while after a breakup, so they can heal before they start dating again. Women with a healthy self-esteem make much better long-term relationship prospects, because they will hold out for the right guy, and not settle for Mr. Right Now." ~ Coach Corey Wayne

Typically, when you see women who have to have lots of male orbiters and who need constant attention from other men, these, typically, are the hallmarks of women who either grew up without a father figure or a woman who had a bad relationship with her father. What basically happens is these women end up with daddy issues, because they were constantly being disappointed—being emotionally excited and enthusiastic, maybe about seeing their father, who was in and out of their lives, and then being disappointed. They were starved for male, masculine attention from an authority figure when they were younger, and so, therefore, they crave it.

And so, the way they made up for the lack of a stable father or masculine presence in the home is they got that attention and validation from other men. And eventually, once they became adult women, started seeking it from many male suitors who were interested. This doesn't mean that 100% of women who came from broken homes are not good dating prospects. It just means the overwhelming majority of them are not going to be ideally suited for long-term relationship prospects—whether it's boyfriend-girlfriend or potentially being a wife—just because they typically don't value loyalty, monogamy, exclusivity. Because even when they're dating or in a relationship, they still like getting attention from other men, and they're emotionally anchored and conditioned to this. It feels natural to them.

Versus a woman that grows up in a family where she got plenty of hugs and love and positive reinforcement when she was a little girl. She doesn't feel like she's lacking anything in that department, so for her, it would be unnatural to seek attention from lots of different men. She wants to seek attention from special men, and good men. Anything other than that just simply doesn't feel natural to her. So, it's really interesting, when you look at women that grow up in healthy families versus women that grow up in unhealthy families, and how they get emotionally anchored to certain types of behaviors.

Now, it doesn't mean that a woman can't do the work on herself, get therapy, counseling, study self-help, implement it, work on her mindset.

It's just, the reality is, most people, the average human on earth, is just lazy and unwilling to do these things. That's why one of the things I always do when I meet a woman for the first time is I'm going to ask her, "Tell me about your family. Do you have a good relationship with your dad?" or "Are you close with your dad?" and see what they have to say. Because at this point in my life, 50–51 years old, having talked to tens of thousands of women over the course of my life, you see the same pattern over, and over, and over, and over again. And especially what I do for a living, I see the same problems and same issues arise just because of a lack of a good, healthy family.

LINK: https://understandingrelationships.com/understanding-why-i-got-dumped/35867

Impossible & Toxic Relationships

"Men and women who date married members of the opposite sex and put their personal lives on hold in hopes that they will actually leave their spouse are deluding themselves. Most of the time, they never actually leave their spouse and just string their affair partners along with just enough hope and promise of a rosy future to keep them on the hook. The reality is, if you become involved with a cheater, you are usually dealing with a selfish, weak, narcissistic, lying and devious con artist who is incapable of real love, loyalty, commitment and honesty. People who stay hung up on and romantically involved with unavailable, married lovers, really are just living out their limiting belief that they are not worthy of true love and a great relationship. It's how they avoid a real relationship and continually experience wanting love that they never get; this is usually similar to a pattern they became emotionally conditioned to expect and seek out during childhood. You should hit the eject and delete button the moment you find out a potential or new lover is still married." ~ Coach Corey Wayne

What's interesting is that when you see what's in TV and in the movies is this theme where you see two people, they may be involved with other people romantically, maybe they're married, maybe they're in a relationship, but they're not really happy and they're not really doing anything to make their situation better. And what ends up happening is they run into each other, and even though they're both in relationships with other people, they start cheating and having an affair, and of course, in the movies, what's portrayed to us is, "Oh, it was meant to be." And since it was meant to be, the cheating, the lying, the deviousness, it's all okay because they really have something special that they didn't have before. And who cares who they hurt or whose lives they fuck up in the process?

In the movies, it all works out and they live happily ever after. But when you do this in real life, whether you're a guy dating a married woman, or you're a woman dating a married man, nine times out of ten they never leave the person they're with, even though they constantly promise that they will. They're waiting for just the right moment, just need a few more months until this happens or that happens. And the reality is, they're just dangling the carrot and manipulating that person. I've done countless phone sessions over the years with guys that get themselves into these kinds of situations, and sometimes they're several years down the road, and yet the person that they're having the affair with still hasn't left their wife or their husband because it's "not the right time."

When you find out that the person you're dating is still romantically involved with somebody else, their divorce is not finalized, and they're living together, tell them to give you a call once their divorce is finalized. Because if you get involved with them and you think that you're somehow going to be different, and you're more special, and they would never cheat on you, the reality is the way they're treating their current spouse is exactly how they will start treating and cheating on you once they become unhappy or bored in their relationship with you. It's a bad way to go. You want somebody who's single and ready to mingle; somebody who is ready, willing, able, and open to dating.

LINK: https://understandingrelationships.com/impossible-toxic-relationships/21064

She Has A Boyfriend

"The number one most important thing to men in a relationship is loyalty. Women who habitually cheat on their boyfriends or husbands with you are not good relationship material. Commitments, loyalty and being faithful mean nothing to them. When they are unhappy, they simply will look for other men to hook up with instead of working to resolve the problems in their relationship. If you believe a cheater will be different and not cheat on you, then you are simply deluding yourself. They may remain faithful when they are 100% happy, but as soon as they become unhappy, they will start looking outside of your relationship for fulfillment." ~ Coach Corey Wayne

When I look at all the emails coming into my Questions@UnderstandingRelationships.com inbox, just about every day I've got some guy that's emailing me about a married woman that he's involved with. And he goes out of his way to tell me how she's different, and how amazing their connection is, and how beautiful it is, and how meant to be it is, but what a difficult situation she's in. And the reality is, they don't want to admit that they're simply just this chick's side piece. If she really was unhappy in her relationship and she was a good catch that you'd want to have a relationship with, she would leave, take some time to be single, heal, get over it, reconnect with her friends or family, get her life organized and set up to enjoy being single again. And then, when she feels she's ready and she's taken time to heal, then she'll start looking to meet and date new guys.

These are the kind of women that you'd like to date, women that have a healthy self-esteem. Women that are screwballs and messed up, they can't go it alone, and that's why they have no problem cheating when they're married, cheating when they're in a relationship, or having multiple guys they're dating, even though several of the guys that are dating them think that they're being exclusive. They tend to be just selfish and narcissistic and self-centered. These are the kind of women that might be fun to have as a friend with benefits, sex playmate, or an open relationship with, but these are not the kind of women you want to have a family with, that you want to get married to, or that you want to have an exclusive, monogamous kind of relationship with. They simply don't have the ability to have these kinds of relationships, and they simply don't have the experience or the background, let alone the integrity.

LINK: https://understandingrelationships.com/she-has-a-boyfriend/14384

Should I Wait Around?

"Love cannot exist where there is no trust. Even one instance of someone violating your trust will make it impossible for you to ever fully trust him or her again. When it comes to friendships, lovers, business partners and all of your most important relationships, they need to be with people who place the same high value on trust, honesty, communication and loyalty that you do. People don't change who they really are, but they may become a better version of themselves. When people show or tell you who they really are, you should believe them. Never delude yourself into thinking that they will change and become the kind of person you want, when their previous actions have continually shown you their true colors." ~ Coach Corey Wayne

One thing I often say, because I've learned from real world experience, is that people don't change who they are but they may become a better version of themselves. When I look back at my old business partner, one thing that was always interesting about him is that we were often competing. And he was good in a lot of ways as a business partner—because you could count on him, he always worked his ass off, he always took care of the things that he said he was going to take care of (for the most part)—but one thing I didn't like is that if he could find a way to get more cash on his side of the negotiating table, even if he had to bend the rules a little bit, or deceive you a little bit, or out negotiate you because he had a little bit more information than you did, he would do it.

I'll give you an example, we would by HUD foreclosures, which were FHA loans that had gone bad, and I had exclusivity on the FHA foreclosures, meaning I was the only one in our company that could bid on those. That was my exclusive thing, that's what we set up in our partnership agreement with him and my other business partner. And the way he got around that was that he had other guys that also bid on HUD foreclosures, and I was bidding directly against these other guys, and sometimes they would outbid me in price. Well, as soon as they outbid me in price, they would be in my partner's office with the property they had gotten, and they would be flipping it to him.

So, technically my business partner was not bidding against me directly, but he was indirectly bidding against me. And so, instead of these guys coming in to flip their property to me, I'd get outbid and they would bring the property to him. And he, in essence, was still able to buy it, which was incredibly unfair, and I didn't like it, but our other business partner, the one that took care of all of the sales, he looked at it like, "Hey, this is a commission we wouldn't have earned, so I'm totally cool with it."

And so, money tends to cut a lot of ties, and those types of things that went on for over a decade that we worked together and were in business together, that kind of bullshit was what eventually ended our business relationship, because I just got tired of it. There were other things that we all got tired of each other on, and that's why we went our separate ways. I just didn't feel like I was coming to work every day with two guys that had my back. Even though we were business partners, what was happening was I was competing against my business partners. And because they overruled me two to one, I basically had to suck it up until I eventually got sick of it, and then we all went our separate ways.

And one of them has since passed away, and the other one has done well for himself, but he hasn't achieved the level of success by himself that we all had together, and I've since surpassed that. So, in the long run, the way they behaved cost both of them a lot more money than if they'd have been willing to compromise and do what was honorable, just, and fair.

LINK: https://understandingrelationships.com/should-i-wait-around/22316

Rejection, Inner Peace & Confidence

"Most women enjoy respectful romantic interest from men in general, even when they are married or in a relationship. Everyone loves to feel wanted, desired and like they've "still got it." Women who are taken and loyal will be honest and upfront, thank a man for his flattering interest, but politely turn him down when he asks them for a date. Women who are taken, unhappy and not loyal may mislead a man, encourage inappropriate interest, string him along as a backup or male orbiter, or even cheat on her lover when a new man expresses interest. Women who are taken, unhappy but loyal may display interest while mentioning their boyfriend or husband or give out or take contact info in case they decide to end things for good with their lover. A woman's integrity level will determine how far she will take things with another man when she is already in a relationship, but unhappy. For men, it's always best to invite taken women to get in touch if their relationship does not work out and refuse to be involved with them in any way as long as they are taken." ~ Coach Corey Wayne

Part of our culture and what you see in a lot of movies and in TV programs is, you've got an unhappy woman who's in an unhappy relationship—might be a marriage, might be a boyfriend—and then what happens, she meets this guy who she just has this amazing chemistry with, and then kind of starts seeing this new guy on the side while she's deciding whether or not to stick with her current boyfriend, husband, or lover. And that's nice in a fantasy world because the whole idea behind these plots is that the two of them are really meant to be, and it wasn't until this new guy came along that piqued her interest that caused her to make changes in her life, and then of course she runs off with the new guy and they live happily ever after in the movies.

Well, that's great in the movie world, when you've got these geeky people that don't understand women and haven't had any real, sustainable success with women writing about and projecting their fantasies onto their work. The reality is, when you interact with women like this in the real world, when they're married or they are involved in relationships, and they start spending time with you, or are flirting with you, or are talking with you, even though they are supposedly taken, many guys, because they've seen these movies, mistakenly think, "Hey, it's meant to be. This is the universe bringing me the perfect person. There just happens to be a little bit of complication that we've got to get past."

I've done countless phone sessions over the years with guys who have gotten involved with women like this, and the problem is these women are loyal when they're happy, but as soon as they're not happy they start entertaining attention and interest from other men, and they give their current boyfriend or lover the impression that everything is fine while, in reality, they're already looking for the exits and lining up new guys. As a man, you should operate from a place of integrity. And also, it's your job and responsibility to hold women accountable to being integrous in their own interactions. Because whatever you tolerate or enable, you invite more of it into your life. And if you're going around dating or getting involved with women that are already involved with other men, you are sending a signal to the universe to send you more women who lack integrity. The reality is, if she's not happy down the road, she'll cheat on you with some other guy.

LINK: https://understandingrelationships.com/rejection-inner-peace-confidence/21889

Once A Cheater, Always A Cheater!

"Insecure and weak people who lie do so because they have learned to believe that lying is always preferable to telling the truth. They lie and deceive to avoid what they see as inevitable drama that will be the result of telling the truth. They lie to themselves and to others, thereby, creating a prison for themselves. It's very important in any relationship that you only pay attention to what people do, not what they say. When someone learns to lie as a child and they continue lying into adulthood, they are not going to change. They have become emotionally conditioned to the point that they can't live any other way. Lying is a way of life for them. They are no longer capable of recognizing truth either in themselves or in anyone else. Thinking a liar will change and somehow become honest is delusional and unrealistic thinking. When people show and tell you who they are, believe them!" ~ Coach Corey Wayne

I've come to notice that people don't change who they are. They may become a better version of themselves, but at the end of the day, they're still that same person. My friends, my family, the people closest to me, old girlfriends of mine, women that I wrote about in my first book, *How To Be A 3% Man*, the ones that have continued to be in my life, the ones that have continued to stay and remain in my life off and on throughout all the decades, I've gotten to see how they were, and I see the same pattern over and over and over again. We all have flaws, we all have faults, nobody is perfect. But you've got to find the people that are worth suffering for, if you will, in order to have a rich and full life.

Again, people don't change who they are, but they may become a better version of themselves. That's why, if you start dating and being in a relationship with somebody that has a history of lying and cheating and thinking you're going to be different, especially when you see all the red flags that they're a liar and a cheater and they're deceiving you, it's just unrealistic to think that it's going to get any better with that particular person.

I had a phone session with a guy that has been in the military for, I think he was going on 20 years, and his girlfriend that he been with over the last ten years has cheated on him three different times. And he called me because he wanted to get her back, because they had broken up. He actually broke up with her after the third time cheating, and obviously she was trying to get him back. And in the process of her supposedly trying to get him back, she was still dating and sleeping with other guys, even though she was telling him she wasn't. Because they were both in the same cell phone plan, he was able to see her texts and what she was saying to these other guys. And so, once he noticed that and I pointed it out to him, I had to be brutally honest with him in the phone session.

I talked to him a few weeks after that and he was finally able to let this woman go. Because it's tough; he spent a decade with her. But she had cheated on him numerous times, three times at least that he knew of, and there are probably many more. There was just nothing he was going to do that this woman was going to become what he wanted.

LINK: https://understandingrelationships.com/once-a-cheater-always-a-cheater/17119

Facebook Posts & Your Relationship

"When it comes to relationships, actions always speak louder than words. If people who you are dating seem to say all the right things in person, but their actions often don't seem to match their words, you should bottom line their actions to determine how much they really care about you. People will often sugarcoat what they say or exaggerate how much they really care in order to avoid awkward moments or confrontations. When their words don't match their actions, always assume their actions are the most reliable means to decipher their true intentions or feelings." ~ Coach Corey Wayne

A lot of guys I see struggling with this; they believe the flowery language when a girl cancels a date and then goes, "But I really miss you, and I can't wait to see you again," but yet she never seems to find the time to make a date. Or, when a guy's been dating his girl for a while and she needs some space but tells him, "I really love you, and I really care about you, and I miss you. I just need some space," and he insists on trying to convince me of how they have a really great relationship and how much she really loves him. But I just point out, it's like, if she really loved you and missed you and cared about you, she would be with you.

I remember something I heard Doc Love say many, many years ago, "Women vote with their feet. If they're with you, it means they voted for you." This goes for clients, the people you work with, your friends, your family, the women you date; if they say they care about you, their actions are going to match their words. And if their words and their actions are never congruent, you always bottom-line their actions and that will tell you everything you need to know about how much or how little they care about you. And, therefore, once you get that honest feedback through their actions, you act accordingly.

LINK: https://understandingrelationships.com/facebook-posts-your-relationship/13901

MAKING RELATIONSHIPS EASY

The Game Of Love Vs. Manipulation

"Winning at the game of love is about freedom. It is about two people who love as their gift to one another without any attachments to any particular outcome of their giving. The purpose of all relationships is that you go there to give, not to manipulate or to try and either become something you are not, or to force the other person to become something they are not in order that you may feel whole and complete yourself. Love is about two awesomely spectacular human beings coming together to share and relish in each other's divine magnificence and completeness. If you come from a place of sharing your completeness, you'll never feel incomplete or that you lack something. Total self-love and acceptance is an essential prerequisite to being able to love another for their completeness and so that they feel free to be themselves." ~ Coach Corey Wayne

You want to give without attachments. Just like when you extend an invitation to a woman to go out on a date or spend time with you, you put it out there and you're okay with either possibility—she enthusiastically accepts it, or she declines it. The bottom line is you've got to give other people the chance to choose you willingly. If you love yourself, you feel happy, whole, complete, like you don't need anyone or anything else, you feel like you've got life by the balls but you're ready to share your life with somebody else, that's the best place to be in mindset-wise. And that's what you're looking to get to when you're applying the things that are in my first book, *How To Be A 3% Man*.

Having your shit together, having your life together, feeling good about yourself and where you're at but loving to have the potential of having somebody to share that with who also is at the same place in their life. Because if you feel like you lack something and you don't have it all together, more than likely, you're going to attract somebody into your life who also feels like something is missing. When two people are looking towards the other person to fill up what they're missing, they always get disappointed when that other person doesn't live up to their unreasonable expectations.

LINK: https://understandingrelationships.com/the-game-of-love-vs-manipulation/14863

Needing Someone Else To Feel Validated

"The purpose of all relationships is that you go there to give. You are there to help each other grow and become more—two happy, whole and complete people who love their complete lives, but are looking for someone to share their completeness with. If you are single and not totally in love with yourself and your life, do the work necessary to get to the place emotionally, mentally, spiritually and physically, where you are happy, content and peaceful being single. Then and only then will you be in a place where you can give to another unconditionally without needing anything in return to make you feel whole, complete or validated. If you don't, then your happiness will depend upon the love and actions of another. When they don't meet your expectations you will feel slighted, rejected and hurt. If you have an abundance of happiness and love in your life already, it's easy to give to another for the simple joy of giving and seeing another happy because of your unconditional loving and giving." ~ Coach Corey Wayne

You're looking for somebody that is a complement to your life—somebody that can be a net value add. This includes your intimate relationships, as well as your friendships and the people who you spend your time with. If you get to a place and you're happy, you love your life, you enjoy your life, you enjoy your time being alone, and you can have an absolute blast while you're doing nothing but hanging out with yourself, that's the kind of place that you want to be at emotionally and mentally in order to create a good space for a good, healthy woman to come into your life who's basically in the same place—who's thinking and feeling the same thing. Because if you're in a stressed-out state, and you have chaos in your life, and you have lots of drama, you're going to tend to attract women in your life to date who bring drama into your life, as well as having friends and other acquaintances bring drama and chaos into your life.

LINK: https://understandingrelationships.com/needing-someone-else-to-feel-validated/16864

Finding Myself Again

"The purpose of all relationships is that you go there to give. However, focusing on giving does not mean you give up your friends, hobbies, purpose, interests and passions because it's what your woman says she wants you to do, or because it's what you think you should do to make her happy. Men who do this end up losing themselves in their relationships due to their efforts to please their women. Not only do they end up losing themselves, but in the end, they eventually lose their women also, because they stopped being the fun, interesting, complete and charming men they fell in love with. Women want an equal, a teammate and a partner, not men who become little boys who need to be told what to do. Relationships should make you a better version of who you are, not something you are not or something completely different than what you really are." ~ Coach Corey Wayne

Many people who are recently out of long-term relationships oftentimes are looking in the mirror and they don't even recognize themselves or their lives anymore. Just like the quote says, love is about giving, but it doesn't mean you become something else because the other person, or society, or other people tell you that you need to be different. If you're not honoring the core of who you are and you don't have somebody in your life or the people that are in your life are not supportive of this, you need to make new friends, new acquaintances, and find new people to date who love you and celebrate you the way that you are.

People who like the same things tend to like each other. If you're going to be in long-term relationships, it's essential that your goals and your values are aligned and that you have similar interests. It doesn't mean they have to have exactly the same interests, but when you talk about things you're excited and passionate about, they become interested in hearing how your mind works and what you have to say. You want people that celebrate who you are, not people that look at you as like a lump of clay to be molded into what they want.

LINK: https://understandingrelationships.com/finding-myself-again/23790

I Love The Pace We Have

"Love is freedom. It is the celebration of the other person who you love and encourage to be all that they are capable of being. Love is not about imposing your will on another, but encouraging them to be who they really are, without judgment or rules. The divine, innate nature of all human beings is freedom. The best way to love is to allow the other person to come and go as they please, so they can either choose you or find someone else they are more emotionally, mentally, spiritually and physically aligned with. When you love others as they are, without judging or trying to change them, you create the conditions for others to be magically drawn into your life who will love you in the same way." ~ Coach Corey Wayne

If a guy has read my first book, *How To Be A 3% Man*, 10 to 15 times and he has done a lot of practicing, when he starts dating a woman he really likes, he's going to take his time, he's going to be selective, because he knows that most people can hide who they really are for about the first 90 days of a relationship. And so, what he's trying to do is facilitate her getting to a place where she feels safe and comfortable enough to let her guard down and be who she really is with him, so he can make an intelligent and informed decision on whether or not she is a good long-term dating prospect, instead of getting all caught up in the emotions right from the get-go and letting himself get carried away, emotionally. Because once that happens, we human beings, in general, tend to make all of our buying decisions based upon emotions, and then we use logic and reason to justify our purchase.

So, if we allow ourselves to get carried away emotionally with a woman too fast, too soon, too quickly in the beginning of a relationship, we will use logic and reason to justify ignoring all the red flags as they continue to come up in the coming weeks and months as we continue to date them. And then, we get frustrated because we try to change them, and fix them, and get them to be more compliant and act more like we want them to, which just causes more irritation and more frustration. Because the reality is, if we hadn't gotten all carried away, we wouldn't even be in a relationship with these particular women. Take your time; there is no rush. It's like the Rumi quote, "Slow and steady like the river that never grows stale. No hurry, no rush."

LINK: https://understandingrelationships.com/i-love-the-pace-we-have/33129

Am I Fighting A Losing Battle?

"When it comes to lovers, it is not your job to fix someone. You are not responsible for their wounds, shortcomings, flaws, faults, failures or their inability to love openly, freely and communicate like an adult. They were like this before you met them and will continue to be this way when they are no longer in your life. People who are addicted to drama, expect drama, or believe arguments and drama are normal in relationships will tend to attract and stay in relationships with people who are incapable of healthy, loving, effortless relationships. Once you learn to love and accept yourself unconditionally and resolve to communicate lovingly, freely and openly, you will no longer tolerate friends or lovers who constantly ruin your peace and happiness with their never-ending drama, problems, immaturity or hostile argumentative nature. Some people are simply toxic and emotionally conditioned to expect and seek out strife. They are incapable of living any other way because ease, delight, effortlessness, serenity and peace, simply do not feel comfortable, natural or bearable to them." ~ Coach Corey Wayne

If you want to have easy and effortless relationships, you need to have it with high quality women. Ideally, they come from backgrounds where their parents were happy, were together, they had a tight family. They have a good relationship with their father, or at least some strong masculine presence in their family that they learned to trust and know which men are good for them and which men are not. Girls that are raised in toxic environments where there's lots of drama, there's arguing, there is alcohol and drug addiction issues, or there's just dysfunctional behaviors in the family on all sides, this is what they're going to be used to; this is going to be what they're emotionally conditioned to expect. And so, when they blow their top and they start screaming or yelling at you, they're not reacting to you; they're reacting to the way they learned. This is normal to them.

The only thing you can really do in these situations is set healthy boundaries and hold these women accountable to them. It's not your job, just like the quote says, to fix or to save her, or to solve her problems, or pay her bills, or fix whatever kind of issues or drama that's going on in her life. If you date a woman who has lots of drama and lots of problems, that drama and those problems are going to become your life and your reality in short order. If a woman is not doing the things she needs to do to resolve her issues and her problems after gentle prodding and communication, you have two choices: you either put up with it, or you move on and you find somebody better.

LINK: https://understandingrelationships.com/am-i-fighting-a-losing-battle/17109

Problems Are Signs Of Life

"Our problems, challenges and struggles are what shapes us into what we are capable of becoming. Like a good lover can help smooth over our rough edges, our most challenging times and darkest hours can help us to become humble, grateful, teach us patience and understanding, and help us to find the gift in every situation. We often have no control over the things that happen to us in life, but if we look for the hidden gift, lesson, and meaning in every setback, disappointment, challenge, and failure, we can become a little better today than we were yesterday. Small, incremental daily improvements, can teach us how to master ourselves, our lives, and our fates slowly over time." ~ Coach Corey Wayne

Problems are a sign that you've got more work to do. In other words, you haven't evolved completely to reach your potential and all that you are capable of living in this life. A really great woman is a huge complement to a man, and she can really help a guy grow, become more, and reach his full potential together. Because women are going to challenge a guy to grow and to become better, and if you've done a good job at selecting a good woman who becomes your greatest cheerleader and biggest fan, she's going to help you co-create a great life. She'll help you and encourage you in business, she'll help you and encourage you in your career, she'll love you, she'll support you. She'll always have a positive word of encouragement.

But it's really important to make sure that you pick a woman who shares similar goals and similar values to you. Because if you have a woman in your life who doesn't share the same goals and values, and doesn't believe in whatever it is you do for a living, and doesn't support your mission and purpose, you are definitely with the wrong woman and you need to find somebody else. You can't have somebody that close to your inner circle sandbagging your success, because if you put up with it and you tolerate it, you're going to be miserable and you're never going to reach your full potential in life.

LINK: https://understandingrelationships.com/problems-are-signs-of-life/17330

Complacency Ruins Relationships

"Everyone gets complacent and lazy over time in their relationships, which leads to taking their partner for granted. People who place a high value on commitment, loyalty and communication will try to communicate and work things out. If that does not work, they will leave the relationship before starting a new one, because they know it's the right thing to do. People who are weak, selfish, narcissistic, and dishonest usually will focus on getting their needs met elsewhere by cheating or lining up a replacement before leaving their current partner. If marriage, exclusivity, being faithful and loyalty are your core values, then you should only have exclusive relationships with or marry people who have a demonstrable history of being faithful to previous partners. Cheaters tend to always cheat and lie when they are not happy, but loyal people tend to always be loyal, even when they are not happy." ~ Coach Corey Wayne

The reality is, the best candidates, the women who make the best candidates for long-term relationships—whether that's marriage, or a live-in girlfriend, or whatever kind of long-term relationship format you want to hold—women who come from loving families where both parents are together, who nurture each other, who are teammates, where the woman looks at her father as her rock and her mountain, a source of strength, a man she looks up to, admires, and respects, and the same thing with her mother. Ideally, you want a girl who's got a close relationship with her dad and her mom, and her parents are together, and when there's a disagreement, they just simply talk things out. They work things out, because they look at each other as being teammates who want the same thing, so what is the reason to argue and be nasty and hateful towards one another? It's just simply being mean and nasty for the sake of it. But people who come from loving families just simply don't have these problems. So, find a girl that comes from a good family if you want a good, healthy, long-term relationship.

LINK: https://understandingrelationships.com/complacency-ruins-relationships/24379

Healing Our Inner Child

"Most obstacles that get in the way of us having healthy, loving, effortless relationships, are really just barriers to loving ourselves that sometimes have been created in childhood. If our desire to be loved in childhood often was not met, or worse, we were abused verbally and/or physically by those around us, we many times will carry these wounds and fears of unworthiness into our adulthood relationships. This can lead us to pre-suppose that it is only a matter of time before we are disappointed by those we love and want to be loved by. This often will show up as over-pursuing, needy and desperate behavior, irrational fears of being rejected or hurt, and generally doing and saying things because we are driven by fear to the point that we chase those who are trying to love us right out of our lives. We literally will talk those who are pre-disposed to love us right out of what we desire most: being loved. We can start to heal our wounds and dissolve our false limiting beliefs by thinking from the end, not taking ourselves too goddamn seriously, learning to practice infinite patience, and developing an attitude and demeanor where we are unattached to and okay with any outcome. In other words, no matter what happens, we are choosing ahead of time to be happy and grateful. Only by creating new and successful experiences and allowing them to mutually develop slowly over time will we be able to permanently banish our self-built barriers to love that exist in our hearts." ~ Coach Corey Wayne

We really have to think about how our childhood has affected us. If you're new to my first book, *How To Be A 3% Man*, and you've read it once or twice, I'm sure a lot of light bulbs went off in your head that caused you to recognize that there were certain behaviors that you've displayed that are extremely unattractive to women. And also, there were several things in there that were mistakes that I've experienced in my own life that you probably find yourself face palming and recognizing that you've done those same things and women that you've encountered, over the course of your life, have reacted exactly the same way and said the same things.

When a child doesn't get enough love, and hugs, and encouragement, and positive reinforcement, it's going to doubt itself, it's going to fear itself. And especially if it's verbally abused, much like dogs; when a dog does something wrong and you yell at it, and then when it does something good you also yell at it, the dog doesn't really know what the right thing is to do or not do. Because no matter what happens, you're getting pissed off at the dog, and eventually, the dog or the child starts to think that no matter what they do, it's not good enough. And, so this develops a belief within ourselves that we're not good enough—we don't deserve to be loved, we don't deserve to have what we want in our lives.

And then, when we find someone that we want to be with or to date and they like us, deep down we believe we're not worthy, and so we try to force things. We try to force interactions, we call too much, we text too much, we try to touch them too much. We try to advance sex before she's ready, and we don't take the time to warm her up. And then, instead of just taking it as, "We're moving a little too fast, and we simply need to slow down," what happens is we get upset or butthurt and then cause a problem that leads to even more lost attraction and eventual rejection. You've got to really take the time to think about how your environment influenced you growing up, and recognize which fears, insecurities, and doubts you still need to overcome.

LINK: https://understandingrelationships.com/healing-our-inner-child/17199

Breakups As A Weapon

"Ninety five percent of your happiness or your misery is going to come from the person or the people who you choose to spend your life with. The quality of your life is always going to be in direct proportion to the quality of the people who you allow in your life and who you consistently spend your time with. If you want your personal and professional life to be effortless and drama-free, you should only choose to spend your time with people who communicate in a loving, authentic and open manner to positively resolve differences and problems by talking them out. Toxic people, and those who constantly create drama, should be avoided and deleted permanently from your life and social circle. Why? They tend to constantly blow a gasket when upset, ignore you on purpose, leave problems or disagreements unresolved and generally act like a five-year-old throwing a temper tantrum." ~ Coach Corey Wayne

There was a study that I saw several years ago, and it was about what characteristics are involved in couples that spend many decades together and are very happy in their relationships. And some of the characteristics were that they always had mutual admiration for one another. They always tended to talk things out. They admired each other and pushed each other to reach their full potential, they looked at one another as if they were on a team with goals and values that were aligned. When there were disagreements, they simply talked and worked them out.

Conversely, when they looked at relationships that didn't last, when one or both people are constantly threatening to end the relationship as a way to manipulate or to get the other person to conform to their wishes or the behavior that they want to see from them, almost 100% of those relationships never work out. And so, if you find yourself dating somebody and they're constantly threatening to break up with you, or dump you, or stick you in friend zone if you don't comply with their wishes, long-term, that kind of behavior is not going to work.

LINK: https://understandingrelationships.com/breakups-as-a-weapon/19125

Is She Bored, Disinterested Or Turned Off?

"Complacency in relationships is not an overnight thing. Complacency comes when one or both people in a relationship get bored, distracted with other priorities or simply take each other for granted. It's a slow process which is similar to the 'frog and boiling pot of water' analogy. If you drop a frog in a pot of boiling water, it will jump right out. If you put a frog in a pot of warm water and slowly turn up the heat, it will slowly boil to death. When you are dating and not attached, both people tend to be on their best behavior and are paying attention to meeting each other's needs. Determining sexual attraction or lack thereof is pretty easy when you know what to look for. However, in long term relationships, one or both people will slowly stop putting their best foot forward. It's easier to spot problems in casual dating, but much harder once two people have been together for many years. It takes continuous, consistent effort to maintain long term relationships." ~ Coach Corey Wayne

When I do phone sessions with guys that are in long-term relationships and they're struggling, with 95% of them, it's usually due to two problems: the first one being they're not courting and dating their women properly, and the other one is they're simply unaware of or don't know how to communicate and get their women to open up.

I did a phone session recently with a guy who has several kids with his current wife. He has a couple of kids from his first wife, and she has a couple of kids from her first marriage. And they've been together for probably close to fifteen years, and it just slowly happened over time that he became passive, he became too nice, things became too much like a roommate style relationship. And on top of that, he was never really taking the time to open her up and getting her to talk. And the way she made up for it was that she ended up coming across a guy in the course of just family things, and this guy had an interest or was an expert at something that the family needed. And he happened to be single or in the process of becoming single and getting out of a bad relationship himself, and so she went and told this guy that she was in the process of leaving her husband, they were getting a divorce, their relationship was over.

And, of course, my client just started seeing weird things happen—like she was hiding her phone, he would see a message pop up in the window and she turned her phone over, so he couldn't see what was there. She was being kind of secretive, she'd supposedly be out having drinks with her friends. She was neglecting their kids and not really spending time with them like she had been. She wasn't a very attentive mother anymore. And she was out one night, supposedly with her girlfriends, and she told him where she was. They had a babysitter taking care of all of the kids, and he decided he was going to go see where she was and what she was doing. And then he walks into this restaurant, and there she is in a booth with her arm around this dude.

So, that's obviously not the kind of thing, if you're a man who's married and you have several kids with your wife, that you walk in somewhere and she supposedly is with all of her girlfriends, but it turns out she's with this other dude. So, obviously, there was a confrontation—it wasn't pleasant for any of the parties involved. And he ended up having a conversation with this guy, and that's where the guy revealed, he said, "Yeah, she told me your relationship was over, you guys were definitely getting a divorce and you were in the process of it." And, of course, my client, was like, this is the first he'd ever heard of it; he had no idea she was even unhappy.

This is the kind of thing, that it just slowly happened over fifteen years, that they lost that emotional connection, he stopped dating and courting her properly, but most importantly, in that particular relationship, he wasn't opening her up and getting her to talk. And so, that emotional connection and that emotional bond, where he was once her rock and her mountain that she shared everything with, he stopped doing that and he stopped taking the time.

And she had been complaining about for years and years and years, and yet he did nothing, because he was so busy with his business and his career and providing for their very large family. And so, this guy comes along and fills that void of that emotional bond and that emotional connection with his wife. She obviously, naturally starts feeling attraction, because this guy's actually paying attention to her emotional needs. And just like you've probably heard me say many times, if you're familiar with my work, if you don't date your wife or girlfriend, eventually some other dude's going to come along and date her for you; and that was what was happening in this process.

LINK: https://understandingrelationships.com/is-she-bored-disinterested-or-turned-off/14907

Don't Neglect Your Woman

"Usually, when women are upset and complain about their men not making time for them, all they are really asking for is that they date and court them properly by spending time together on a regular and consistent basis. However, the average guy starts to argue and justify why he is no longer dating her properly, instead of simply dating her on a regular basis and making her feel special like he did when they first started dating. This makes women feel like their men don't listen to them. Guys typically dig their heels in and use logic and reason in an attempt to win the argument, as women start to feel like they are not heard, understood or loved. If a man is unable to understand that his woman simply wants to spend more time with him, eventually she will give up and start spending her time with someone else. Guys who can't seem to find the time to spend with their wives always end up finding the time to spend with their divorce attorneys." ~ Coach Corey Wayne

This is a big problem that I help a lot of guys with when I'm doing phone sessions with them, guys that are married or in long-term relationships. It's getting them to recognize the fact that they no longer date and court their women properly. They always have excuses, "Well, we've got the kids. We've got their sports. We've got their hobbies, their activities. You know how it is, Corey." You hear these kinds of excuses all the time. And then the women say, "We never do anything. We never go anywhere." What she's really complaining about is that she would like to be dated and courted like he did back when they were dating. But instead, they've become roommates, and everything is dull, boring, and predictable. And his attitude, often because he is using logic and reason to try to win, was, "Hey, we just went away for a weekend three months ago. That's really expensive. I can't afford to do these kinds of things all the time," and he uses that as an excuse to not change his behavior. And what the woman hears is that he's unwilling to change his behavior, everything is "fine," and he's going to do nothing about it.

Women know that if you love and you care about them, you're going to continue to date and court them, you're going to want to make them feel special. If you've got kids, you're going to take care of getting a babysitter, so you can go out and have a nice dinner together, have a weekend escape together, whatever it happens to be. You're going to continue to do fun things together, so you're teammates and you're partners, and you spend time to work on your relationship between each other. You can't use your career or your kids as an excuse to just keep doing the same thing over and over again.

LINK: https://understandingrelationships.com/dont-neglect-your-woman/22386

You Don't Bring Me Flowers Anymore

"Breakups happen slowly. At some point one or both people who are in relationship with each other stop putting their best foot forward. They may get more caught up in earning a living and providing, than courting each other properly, making each other feel loved and supported. When two people fall in love, they are focused on what they like about each other. Towards the end of the relationship, they are focused on what they don't like or can't stand about each other. People who got into a relationship thinking it would make them happy, tend to withdraw and stop making an effort after the honeymoon period is over and the infatuation has worn off. They are left with the realization that the other person is not the source of their happiness, and they either don't love themselves or their lives. Good, healthy relationships come from two people who love themselves, stand up for themselves, are open to a relationship, want a relationship, are ready for a relationship, who are emotionally and physically comfortable with themselves, and who love their lives and are looking for someone to share their completeness with. Sometimes, when you are not ready, it is better to remain single, so you can figure out who you are and what you want when you are not defined by another person." ~ Coach Corey Wayne

It's so interesting that, when you look at breakups, and I'm sure everybody listening to this has known people who were so lovey-dovey and so complimentary of each other, and all they could do was gush and talk about all of the things they loved about the other person. Then you fast-forward six months, a year, two years, five years, whatever it happens to be, and they're either on the verge of a breakup or they just had a breakup, and all they can do is talk about how much they can't stand and all of the different things they hate about the person that they were with or they're still with. And it's just so interesting; you go from loving and appreciating and giving, based on what you value in the person, and towards the end, you're focused on what you can't stand.

If you're just focused on what you don't like about somebody, whatever you focus your brain on, it's going to expand. And if you're focusing on the things that you don't like, you're going to see more of the things that you don't like. And, just like I talk about in the quote, people that thought the other person or the ideal relationship was going to make them happy, or a woman was going to make them happy, and then once that infatuation wears off and then they recognize that, despite the fact that they have this amazing person in their life, they're still not happy, then there's no motivation to continue to make the effort. Because they're seeking happiness, and yet, despite this person being in their lives, they don't have happiness and fulfillment, because of the associations and the meanings that they're giving to the circumstances of their lives and the people that are in it.

And when it comes to women, if you stop dating and courting women properly, eventually, they're going to feel like you don't love and you don't care about them. And if it continues, eventually, the woman is going to leave him. Because women want to be in a love story. If you love her and you care about her, you're going to continue to date and court her and make her feel special. And if you're struggling and you find out or recognize that you're not happy, despite the fact that you have an amazing woman in your life, you unknowingly will start sabotaging it and not making the effort, because you're trying to figure out what the hell is wrong and why you're not so happy. And what happens is, the guy is not happy, and then on top of that, he creates problems in his relationship, and then that spirals out of control. And then, he has two problems to deal with: the problem of the fact that he's not happy, and the fact that now his relationship has gone in a downward spiral. You always have to date and court your girl properly, and if you don't, eventually, somebody else will.

LINK: https://understandingrelationships.com/you-dont-bring-me-flowers-anymore/16590

Kissing, Touching & Sexual Advances

"Most men are too impatient with women when it comes to kissing, touching and sex. Foreplay, banter, teasing and great conversation build sexual anticipation. Men who understand women know that women will gradually move closer and closer to them the safer, more comfortable and sexually aroused they feel towards them. Women are natural touchers and nurturers. If you simply enjoy the company and conversation of the women you are with, they will start to touch your arm, lean in towards you, sit next to you, let their knee slowly touch yours, bump into you as you casually walk together, bump your hand with theirs, etc., in hopes that you notice their invitation that touching is okay and desired. When it comes to kissing, if you are unsure of when a woman is ready to be kissed, look at her lips while in conversation and in close proximity to her. If she looks at your lips also, she is ready to be kissed. Go for it! Kissing leads to heavy petting. Then, after some passionate kissing and heavy petting, you can say, "Would you care to join me for a glass of champagne, (or tea or coffee if you're not a drinker), back at my place?" If she says "yes," then kissing and heavy petting back at your place leads to SLOWLY wandering hands, and clothes starting to come off. Safe (hopefully) sex usually follows shortly thereafter. Men should lead the interaction to a successful conclusion in the bedroom, but only after women extend the physical invitation and their receptivity first, before escalating things sexually to prevent rejection." ~ Coach Corey Wayne

The idea when it comes to sex and seduction is to go slightly slower than the woman is going. Because when you move a little slower than she's going, she starts to get frustrated, and when she gets frustrated, she starts to make more of an effort to get noticed, to touch you, to be closer to you. The same thing when you're kissing and making out and foreplay before you penetrate her, physically; lots of tension gets built over time. And then, when you finally penetrate her, she's wound up so much, because the sexual anticipation had grown so much that she has been waiting for you to do it.

Again, the idea is to go slightly slower than she does. But most guys just simply do not understand it. The first time they try to kiss and move things forward, they start feeling her up, and they get a little bit of resistance, they'll say something along the lines of, "What's wrong? Did I do something wrong?" And they create a weird, awkward moment, instead of just recognizing that they're going a little too fast, they need to slow down, back off, continue to talk more, and then maybe in 10 or 15 minutes take another run at it. And you slowly wear down her resistance. This makes it easy and effortless to seduce the women that you're into and who are into you without any kind of fear of rejection at all.

LINK: https://understandingrelationships.com/kissing-touching-sexual-advances/17087

I Wasn't Behaving Like A Man

"Masculine energy is about purpose, drive, mission, succeeding, accomplishing, achieving goals, breaking through barriers, etc. Feminine energy is about opening up to receive love, bonding, connection, etc. In order to maintain the sexual polarity in relationships, men need to focus on the things that make a man a man, so his woman will feel safe and comfortable enough to stay in her feminine and let him lead the relationship. However, if he fails to be the leader, it forces her to move into her masculine to make up for his weakness. She will resent this and become bitchy and distant. This destroys sexual polarity and creates unnecessary drama." ~ Coach Corey Wayne

Many guys start out doing most things right when it comes to dating and courting their women. And, over time, what happens is they slowly abdicate their responsibility in the courtship to women. Especially if they start having kids or they have a family together, they have a household to run, oftentimes the guy just starts abdicating to the woman. This is the kind of thing that happens slowly, over many months and years, until they've been together five, six, seven, eight years, whatever it happens to be. And now the man has become the woman in the relationship, and the woman has become the man, and she resents it. And because she doesn't feel safe and comfortable in the relationship, she doesn't really feel comfortable in her feminine energy because she's so used to being in her masculine energy.

What's interesting about this is, physically, she'll start to take on a more masculine presence and demeanor. She'll typically cut her hair really short, wear a boyish style haircut, instead of long and sexy like it was. She stops wearing makeup, she stops going to the gym, she stops taking care of her body, and as she starts to put on weight, she starts to wear baggy clothes. And the same thing happens to him; you see both of them are kind of dressed alike, and there's no sexual polarity. They're both overweight, and wherever they go together, the woman is always a foot or two in front of the guy and he's just kind of following her lead. And she's bitchy and resentful, and then you sit and watch them at the table together when they're having meals, and they're just completely ignoring each other, or they're sitting there flipping through things on their phones and just not even paying attention.

LINK: https://understandingrelationships.com/i-wasnt-behaving-like-a-man/13974

Pushing For A Commitment

"The purpose of all relationships is that we go there to give—not to possess or control the other person out of our own feelings of inadequacy, neediness or insecurity. We must allow the other person the time and space to feel free to love us and be loved by us. If the person we love feels like we are trying to make them commit to something they are not ready for, they will quickly leave the relationship. Allow love to happen, instead of trying to make it happen."
~ Coach Corey Wayne

As Thich Nhat Hanh said, "You must love in such a way that the person you love feels free." Guys that don't know any better, out of their own neediness and insecurity and doubts and fears about themselves, push for a relationship commitment before the woman is emotionally ready. A woman has to engage her emotions slowly over time in order to fall in love with the guy. And this is a process that you have to go through. That's why I teach guys the Three H's: hang out, have fun and hook up. It's a simple formula.

As a man, when you see a really attractive woman that you like, if you're honest with yourself, you're thinking about putting your dick inside of her. That's the first thought—"I'd really like to fuck her"—that's what you're thinking. And all the relationship stuff tends to come afterwards, but what got your attention, what caused you to notice her, was her attractiveness, her sex appeal, her femininity, her beautiful body and curves, and her luscious lips, and her beautiful, kind eyes, and her sweet demeanor; that's what attracted you in the first place.

As the saying goes, "Men, all they care about is sex." Well, it's true, from that perspective. And if guys want sex and romance in a relationship, they really should just simply focus on hanging out, having fun, and hooking up. This causes them to live in the present moment and to focus on having fun together. Because when a woman feels heard and understood and like the guy cares, the legs open and then he can easily have his way with her effortlessly. But if she doesn't feel heard and understood, the legs close, and the guy is going to be getting a bad case of blue balls.

LINK: https://understandingrelationships.com/pushing-for-a-commitment/13839

NON-ATTACHMENT

Move Forward Together Or Walk Away?

"The object of romance is not a relationship. The object of romance is to have fun together. Having fun together leads to good feelings and an increase in sexual attraction. Increasing sexual attraction leads to a sharing of each other's bodies and souls. Then separation and exploring freedom happens again until a mutual desire draws them together once more. A relationship happens as a natural byproduct of continuous and perpetual hanging out, having fun and hooking up. The masculine one provides the logistics, leadership, planning and execution of dates, while the feminine one opens up to receive love and is preoccupied with bonding, connecting, commitments and relationship labels that lead to a sense of security and comfort." ~ Coach Corey Wayne

A lot of guys, when they start dating, are too focused on a relationship and locking a woman down to a commitment—either to soothe their own neediness and insecurity, or because they've seen too many TV shows and movies that say you've got to hurry up and rush and get the girl, to propose to her and get her to agree to be your wife or your girlfriend. Otherwise, some other dude is going to come along and steal her from you. When you act this way and behave this way, you're putting out the vibe that's subtle but that communicates you don't think you're worthy and you're "not deserving." And, therefore, you're not courageous, and you're not brave enough, and you're not strong enough to act like you deserve to be with her. A woman wants a true teammate and an equal—a man who leads from the front, not the rear.

LINK: https://understandingrelationships.com/move-forward-together-or-walk-away/32254

Crazy Needy Jealous Love

"One of the biggest turnoffs in relationships is when the person who you are dating, in relationship with, or married to is constantly getting insecure, paranoid and butt-hurt about someone else stealing you away from them or causing you to fall out of love with them and in love with someone else. Jealousy is an insecure, weak feeling of not being worthy or good enough to have someone else love you of their own free will. It is a feeling that you are somehow inadequate, inferior and that you fear losing your lover to someone better. The proper and healthy attitude to have is to see yourself as a catch and as a gift who has no equal. If your lover chooses someone else over you, then it's their loss and you should really feel that way. All you can do is put your best foot forward with the knowledge that it still might not be enough. The right person will stick around if you love them without fear or attachment, but everyone one will eventually leave you or cheat on you if you constantly act like a needy insecure jackass." ~ Coach Corey Wayne

For people that are jealous and insecure, it's counterintuitive for them to create the conditions where their partner may cheat on them and be disloyal to them. If you're thinking about a long-term commitment, whether you want to live together and start a family, or you plan on getting married, it's good to see how the other person behaves when they get really comfortable in the relationship. When a guy is dating a girl and he's unsure of whether or not she's a good long-term prospect––because I do a lot of phone sessions with guys that are in these situations, where these women have male orbiters, and there's other guys in the background, in the picture that they talk to, and he's "just a friend, somebody that you don't have to worry about,"—what happens is they try to control things by getting jealous, and telling her that she shouldn't or can't hang out with the other guy, or talk to that other guy. But what you're really looking for is, what happens when she is super comfortable, and she thinks that you're totally committed to her and she has you?

Women that come from a background where there was lying, there was cheating, and there was deviousness, or where they grew up without a father often times were missing that masculine validation that they normally get from a father figure. And so, when they become adults, they love the attention they get from other men. And even though they may be in a relationship, oftentimes, these types of women will encourage and invite other men to flirt with them, hit on them, even give out their phone number, because they like the attention and the validation.

And so, if you're trying to determine whether or not your woman is a good, loyal, long-term, monogamous dating or relationship prospect, you want to see how she behaves after the infatuation and honeymoon period has worn off, and this usually happens about 6–12 months in most cases. So, when she's super comfortable, if she's constantly telling you about other guys that she's talking to, guys she's going to lunch with that she works with, and she's talking about these other men in glowing terms, even revealing sometimes that these guys are hitting on her or liking her, it's just not appropriate for a woman who's in a relationship to invite and accept the attention of other men. Because a good, loyal, faithful woman is going to say, "I'm sorry, I can't. I have a boyfriend." And that's what you want to hear. You want to hear your girl telling you about this guy that hit on her, but she shot him down because she thinks you're the shit. That's what you want.

When a woman invites his attention and says it's totally innocent and you shouldn't really be getting upset about that, and then on top of that, she gets jealous of you talking to other women, those are some major red flags. So, instead of being jealous, give her enough space and freedom to see what she does after the infatuation and honeymoon period has passed, so you can make an intelligent, informed decision on whether or not she's actually a good match and will be loyal long-term. Because women that are not, they will give themselves away if you give them the opportunity.

LINK: https://understandingrelationships.com/crazy-needy-jealous-love/14658

Masculine Men Keep Women Feminine

"Women are like cats and tend to roam free and come and go as they please. Men who don't understand this try to force, manipulate and use logic and reason to influence women to behave more like they want them to. This has the opposite effect on women and drives them away, much like trying to pick up a cat that no longer wants to be petted. The more you try to force, manipulate and control women to do what you want, the more they will be repulsed, rebel and flee from your presence. Therefore, be grateful when they are affectionate and want to be with you, and indifferent when they don't. Accept them as they are and let them come and go as they please, while you always focus on your mission and purpose in life. Your interest in women has no effect on their attraction towards you. How you make them feel about you is the only thing that matters to influence their attraction to you. The right ones will stay, and the wrong ones will stray." ~ Coach Corey Wayne

This is such a helpful analogy for men to understand how women are. Men are usually confused by women who are really excited to be with them and spend time with them but notice that the more time they spend with them, the less interested they seem to become, almost as if they're bored. And when you understand that women are kind of like cats, and when they get bored, they tend to take off and go roam the neighborhood, you've just got to let them be and understand that, eventually, they will make their way back home.

If you've ever had a cat, you notice how cats are—they come into the room, they look at you, they look around. They walk around to other people, they maybe walk by your leg, touch your leg with their tail standing up in the air, and then they go off. And then, a few minutes later, they come back in, maybe they go in between your legs. And the next thing you know, they jump up in your lap and sit down and start purring. And then you start petting them for a while and the cat seems to enjoy the petting, and then at some point, the cat has had enough petting, and then it hops up and then just takes off. And then you don't see it for a while.

The worst thing you want to do when the cat's gotten bored is to run after it. Just let it be. When the cat starts to miss you, it eventually comes back. Because us guys tend to be more like dogs. Dogs are very loyal, they never leave your side. And, obviously, if a dog leaves your side you think, "Hey, there's something wrong." But when a cat leaves your side, (i.e., when a woman leaves your side), and goes off and does other things, you should just look at it as, "Cats are going to do what cats are going to do," and be okay with it.

LINK: https://understandingrelationships.com/masculine-men-keep-women-feminine/38142

Dating: Texting, Calling & Messaging

"It's a scientific fact that women are more attracted to men whose feelings are unclear. Women like guys who are mysterious, interesting and more difficult to figure out, and tend to lose interest in guys who are always available 24/7 to chit chat, message and talk on the phone. Men should be busy with their mission and purpose in life, not sitting around waiting to spring into action to be a woman's therapist or digital pen pal when she gets bored. Women need time and space away from a man to understand, contemplate and grow their feelings of attraction for him. Men should only use the phone, texting or messaging to set dates, not give out information or to get to know someone. When they violate this principle, they predictably get friend-zoned. Act like her fun, charming and mysterious lover, not her friend or buddy, when your interest is romantic." ~ Coach Corey Wayne

When a guy is available 24/7 to chit-chat, what happens over the days and weeks of their early interactions is that... women are kind of unpredictable. They might text you or message you three or four days in a row, and then all of a sudden, you don't hear from her for a day or two. Now, when this happens to the average guy, he thinks, "Oh shit, something's wrong. She doesn't like me. Maybe I screwed up. Maybe I need to call her and apologize to her." And so, then they go into what I like to call "The illusion of action," and they think they have to do something to get her to like them. Sometimes, she's just busy, and what you have to understand about women is that their emotions are kind of like Mother Nature. One day, they're really, extremely attracted to you. Then you spend a weekend together, because she reaches out and calls you, but then when she leaves your house on Monday morning, it almost seems like she really doesn't care that much, she's not as excited as she was when you first spoke to her on Friday night when she came over. And then you start thinking, "There's something wrong."

You can't take these things personally. You've just got to let it be. And if a woman senses that you're weak, or that you're insecure, or maybe she's just unsure of her feelings and needs some time to figure things out, you've got to just let her be. Because if she demonstrated a clear history of reaching out to you first on most occasions, then all of a sudden, she stops moving forward after a couple of days, just let it be. Wait to hear from her. Because if you start messaging and texting her because you're afraid you're going to lose her, she can sense this and pick up on this. And what happens is, she'll back away and call and text you even less. And typically, what guys do, is they tend to pursue more in those instances. So, you've got to practice infinite patience. You've got to get past that barrier of fear.

And what typically happens as you're learning this, you might back off too much and be too much of a cold fish and she'll lose interest, and you might text too much which, obviously, causes her to lose interest. But you have to practice this. And this is why it's essential, when you're learning the things in my first book, *3% Man*, that you have multiple women you can practice this with. Especially if you have three or four different women that you're dating—some of them you may be sleeping with, some of them are new women that you're meeting—because this helps keep you in a non-hungry state. Whereas, if you just have one good prospect, so it doesn't send you into emotional turmoil if you've only got one prospect every time that she doesn't do something you expect.

That's the beauty of women; they're totally unpredictable. And you don't know when they're going to call, when they're going to text. All of a sudden, they're into you for a week in a row, and then you don't hear from them for three days. You just can't take it personally. You've just got to let them be. They are like cats; they'll come back eventually, as long as they're sincerely, authentically interested in you.

LINK: https://understandingrelationships.com/dating-texting-calling-messaging/21791

The Promise Of More Later

"Like attracts like. You can only attract a relationship when you are ready, willing, able and open to one manifesting by creating a space in your life for a romantic lover to fill. It is not healthy, and it creates unnecessary obstacles to your personal life goals to date, get romantically hung up on, or attached to married, unavailable, uninterested, messed up, or toxic lovers. When you create a space for someone to fill and look forward to its inevitable manifestation, without any attachments to time frames for it to happen in, meeting them simply becomes a matter of time. In the meantime, enjoy your life, focus daily on becoming a better version of yourself, take care of your body, work towards creating your dream life, spend your time with like-minded people and attracting the right person will become a synchronistic, unexpected, magical, memorable, life changing, and certain future event." ~ Coach Corey Wayne

When I look back on my life, when it comes to my personal life, getting to date and experience what it was like to be in a relationship with a woman I considered my dream woman and who was also head over heels in love with me, it wasn't until I was 31, 32. And yet, I had been yearning for that moment and dreaming of that moment from the time I was a kid and became interested in women, all the way back to when I was in middle school. So, if I look at this, when I was 31, 32, that would have been 2001, 2002. When I think back to when I was in middle school and had crushes on girls and wanted to date, even though

I had friends that were dating and having girlfriends back then, this was like 1982, 1983, 1984. So, I had that dream, I had that desire to experience what it would be like to feel those kinds of intense emotions. It was a two-decade journey to get from that place to where I eventually got to experience what it was like to be with somebody—the kind of woman where I walked down the street, and I felt like I was with the hottest girl on the planet. And people were checking her out, and looking at me, and then looking at her, and looking back at me, and going, "What the hell is she doing with that dude? He's just an average looking guy. What has he got?"

It was great for my ego, and how I felt about myself, and my self-esteem, but that was a 20-year journey. And if you had told me back when I was in sixth, seventh, eighth grade that it's going to be another 20 years before you really get to experience what you dream about, that was longer than I've been alive at that point in my life. How would that have affected me? What would that have done? Would I have ever really done the work on myself and done the experiencing if I knew it was going to take two decades to get there? Maybe, maybe not, I don't really know. But it's a metaphor for everything in life; everything takes a really super long time.

When I look back when I was 18 years old and deciding what I wanted to do with my life career-wise, it was about 15 years from the time I started college until I reached the pinnacle of my success in the real estate, construction, and mortgage industry. And when I look back on the time that I got out of that industry and became a full-time life coach, right now I'm in year 14, 15 of that new experience of being a life coach, and I feel like I'm just now starting to hit my stride after all of these years.

I mean, I'm obviously, right now, in the process of recording my third book, which is a book of quotes. And this particular recording is actually for the fourth book, because right now I think I'm going to end up with probably five or six volumes of quote books. But the point being is that success takes a long time. The successes, the wins, the victories are long in coming, and most people don't see all the years or decades that it takes to get from where their starting point is to where they feel like they've made it.

LINK: https://understandingrelationships.com/the-promise-of-more-later/21861

Trying To Force Things

"When we fear that someone who we want won't love us, we tend to try and force things. We call too much, show up at their place of work, send excessive emails and texts, etc., all in an effort to avoid the rejection we fear happening. When we try to force things, all we do is come off as needy, unworthy, and inadequate to the other person. When we try to force things, we're unconsciously inviting them to take advantage of us, take us for granted or mistreat us. The self-loving thing to do that communicates confidence and value is to bottom line their actions, notice their level of effort, and allow them to choose us of their own free will. If they really want you, and you act worthy, you will allow them to come to you at their own pace. That is the only way you can be content that they chose you for you and not because you forced things, manipulated them or cajoled them into being with you. You deserve someone who loves you for you. Allow love to happen. Don't try and force it. You'll only demean yourself and end up broken hearted." ~ Coach Corey Wayne

The worst thing you can do with women is try to force them to spend time with you, try to force them to like you. A lot of guys make the mistake of trying to tell a woman how much they love and care about them, and how important they are, and what their emotions and what their feelings are. The reality is women don't care how you feel about them; they care about how they feel about you. And your interactions with them should be all about causing them to feel good feelings towards you. Because if a woman feels good when she's with you, she starts to associate good feelings with being with you.

LINK: https://understandingrelationships.com/trying-to-force-things/14812

My Girlfriend Might Move Away

"You don't have any control over what other people choose to do or how they choose to show up in your life. The only thing you have control over is what you do and how you show up in yours. In order to cause people to want to stay in your life long-term, you must be their best option by focusing on being your best self. The purpose of all relationships is that you go there to give. The reality is your best self may not be enough to cause someone else to want to stick around and be in your life and choose you above all others. Therefore, you must love and give unconditionally but give other people the freedom and choice to stay in your life or leave you forever. By giving other people the choice to stick around, you will ensure that the right people who are meant to be in your life will stay in your life. However, if you try to force, manipulate, or control other people into staying in your life, you will lose them forever." ~ Coach Corey Wayne

One of the most powerful quotes that I've ever heard when it comes to relationships and human interactions is the quote by Thich Nhat Hanh, the Vietnamese monk, who said, "You must love in such a way that the person you love feels free." Because the reality is our divine nature is freedom. Love is freedom, God is freedom—having the freedom to come and go as you please. And when somebody gives you the freedom to honor and be who you are, you're naturally going to appreciate and value that. But the more you're around somebody who tries to control, manipulate you, shame you, force you to act a certain way, the more you're going to resent it and the less you're going to want to spend time with them.

This is especially true when it comes to dating and relationships, because when a guy doesn't give a woman the freedom and space to come and go as she pleases, she feels that he is not masculine enough and strong enough and has his shit together enough to be worthy of being her man. He's acting like a needy, insecure little boy, and needy, insecure little boys don't have confidence. And one of the things that is an aphrodisiac to women is a man who has confidence and takes risks to go for what he wants. Men who are confident, and who are certain of themselves, and sure of themselves go for what they want, and they expect to get the results they want, and if they don't, they don't care; they just simply move on to the next prospect, the next person, the next employer, the next business opportunity, whatever it happens to be, until they find the right circumstances and the right people that are willing to give them what they want.

The only thing you have control over is what you do and how you show up. And if you've taken care of yourself, and you're doing all the right actions, and you give other people the time and space to miss you and to make a mutual effort, this is the best way to live. It keeps you in a non-attached, non-hungry state of being, and it makes things easy and effortless for the right people to willingly come into and fill that space in your lives that you created for them.

LINK: https://understandingrelationships.com/my-girlfriend-might-move-away/18326

Love Is Giving, Not Holding Back

"The purpose of all relationships is that you go there to give. You're there to help each other grow, become more and to meet each other's needs. Loving, therefore, is about giving, not holding back. Fear and hurt imprison the heart. The love that you withhold is the pain that you carry. When we fail to authentically compliment what we like in another, we hold back our love out of fear or for manipulation to get what we want, we experience pain, suffering and regret. Once you give the gift of your heart without attachment, no matter the outcome, you'll be able to walk away at peace within yourself and feeling content that you gave it your best. Just showing up in life is half the battle." ~ Coach Corey Wayne

Just like the quote says, "Fear and hurt imprison the heart." And in our relationships, when we are afraid of getting hurt, we hold back. We don't do the things that we know we should do, and we don't express the things that we know we should express. If you can give from your heart without any expectations and do it because you simply want to bring a smile to somebody else's face, that is the essence of pure giving and pure love. And when you love yourself and you value yourself, you give the gift without attachment; you're okay with nothing coming back in return.

And if you've done the work ahead of time prequalifying and pre-sorting the people that you allow into your inner circle, you should have mostly people in your inner circle that are also givers. Because, when you give to a giver, the giver is going to give back. If you give to a selfish person, people that are narcissistic, or people that are not givers, they're simply going to take, and take, and take, and not reciprocate, just because that's who they are. Always notice what you're getting in return in your relationships, and make sure you spend more time with people who give to you freely and make you feel like they want you there.

LINK: https://understandingrelationships.com/love-is-giving-not-holding-back/14764

Never Chase After Being Dumped

"It takes two people who have mutual interest, respect, desire and empathy for one another, in order to make a relationship happen or to rekindle a romance. If someone no longer wants to make the effort to keep you in their life, it is demeaning, unloving and disrespectful to yourself to continue chasing, begging and pleading with them to change their mind about you. The strongest negotiating position is being able to walk away and mean it. The self-loving thing to do if you have been dumped is to seek out a new lover who will appreciate you, not staying stuck in the past wishing things will change. Not accepting the reality of what is, only leads to suffering. You were not put on this earth to suffer, but to create magnificent things and a magnificent life for yourself. Therefore, the only option is to keep moving, keep searching and keep taking action to make your dreams, goals and desires a reality." ~ Coach Corey Wayne

Rejection breeds obsession. And so, typically when a guy gets dumped (because women, typically, 70–80% of the time are the ones ending a relationship and doing the dumping), oftentimes, what I see when I'm doing phone sessions with guys is that they got dumped, really, because at some point in the past they stopped putting their best foot forward. On some level, they recognized that the person they were with or the relationship they were in wasn't really meeting their needs but thinking about being single again and getting back out in the dating world was something, like most people, was just simply not appealing to them.

What happens is, as time goes by, they continue to take the other person for granted because, deep down, they really don't want to be with them anymore. They don't value that other person enough to make that same level of effort that they once did in the past. And with women, they sense this, they can feel this. They'll tell you, they'll complain, about certain things over and over and over, and keep bringing the same things up over and over and over again. And, eventually, they end up leaving. And then the guy tells himself that, "Oh, this is the one. I've lost the love of my life. I have to get her back." And the reality is, because they got rejected, they weren't the ones that ended the relationship, now their interest has shot through the roof, because they really weren't ready to be single yet, and hadn't made any plans for that, and don't want that.

The reality is you never want to try to keep somebody in your life who doesn't want to keep you. And the more you do that, all you're doing is reinforcing a belief that you don't deserve to have what you want. Because if you keep chasing somebody who is unwilling to give you what you want, then you're communicating to the universe that this is your reality, that this is what you're okay with, instead of just recognizing that it wasn't ideal, wishing them the best, loving them and hoping that they find somebody that's better suited for them. Bless them, wish them well, because if you love somebody, you want them to be happy—even if it's not with you.

But if you've been doing things where you've screwed up, and you've ruined attraction, and you turned her off, and she's asking you for space and pushing you away, the worst thing you can do is keep calling, keep texting, and keep trying to get her to spend more time with you and to come back. You state what you want, and then you let it be. And if there's any kind of attraction left in her towards you after a few days or few weeks, she'll be back in touch, she'll come up with a reason to contact you. And if there's not, then you'll never hear from her again, and that tells you everything that you need to know. You want somebody who will mutually choose you.

And the reality is, most people simply aren't going to do that. You have to be okay with that. Otherwise, you end up in a relationship where you're more into the other person than they are into you, and you're always going to feel that. You're always going to have some level of fear, and worry, and doubt about yourself and your relationship if you're doing too much of the pursuing and the chasing, like I talk about in my book *3% Man*.

LINK: https://understandingrelationships.com/never-chase-after-being-dumped/16850

I Made A Mistake, I Want You Back

"If you want an ex-lover back who dumped you, due to mistakes you made that turned them off, the best way to re-attract them is to walk away and never look back. Never call or contact them again. Move on with your life as if they are part of your past and you will never see or speak to them again. Start dating again and resolve to find someone better, no matter how much you don't feel like doing it. If they start contacting you again, don't focus on a relationship or getting back together. Do not agree to be friends in any way, shape or form. Be clear and direct that you are only interested in them romantically, not platonically. Invite them to come to you to have dinner at your place, or you are not interested, for the first 2-3 dates. Treat them like first dates. Hang out, have fun and hookup. They dumped you. Therefore, it must be their idea to rekindle things. Wait for them to bring up getting back together or being exclusive again. Let them do 100% of the calling, texting, and pursuing. Make dates when they reach out, no unnecessary chit chat. They blew you off like you were nothing, therefore, they must treat you like you are important and necessary to their lives. They must earn you back." ~ Coach Corey Wayne

I discuss this at length and in detail in the article and video I did, called "7 Principles To Get An Ex Back." The whole philosophy is, even though you may have been the one to do a lot of unattractive things that caused the other person to lose interest and not want to date you anymore, it's up to them to fix it. Because they unilaterally ended the relationship on their terms, therefore, they have to fix it. They have to seek out your attention and validation. They have to give off the vibe that shows they're seeking your attention and validation to getting another chance. They ended it; therefore, they must fix it.

Like the old saying goes, "If you break it, you buy it." So, if they're the ones that broke it off, they've got to show to you, through their actions and their words matching their actions, that you are a priority in their life. That's why you let them do 100% of the calling, texting, and pursuing, and making the effort to spend time together, and then all you have to do is make dates. And like I discuss in "7 Principles To Get An Ex Back," you want them to come to your house at least three dates in a row. And if you hang out, have fun, and hook up all three dates in a row successfully, then you can start meeting them out, and picking them up, and going out on dates.

But they still have to do 100% of the calling, texting, and pursuing from that point forward, because if you start focusing on a relationship and a commitment again, you're the one trying to seek their attention and validation. If it's their idea, you don't have to worry about getting rejected or being pushed away. Guys that don't do this end up stuck in friend zone perpetually. Because the strongest negotiating position is being able to walk away and mean it.

LINK: https://understandingrelationships.com/i-made-a-mistake-i-want-you-back/17165

She Wants To Be Friends First

"We tend to project our desires, dreams, ideals and hopes onto people who either don't measure up or who will let us down. We often only see what we want and ignore the fact that what we want does not feel the same way about us. We often bullshit ourselves into believing that things in life are either better than they actually are or worse than they actually are, but very rarely do we tend to see things as they actually are. Most people will do more to avoid pain and disappointment than they will risk to potentially experience pleasure and reward." ~ Coach Corey Wayne

I see this a lot in my phone sessions, especially when guys are struggling with a particular woman. They're projecting their fantasy of what they want the situation to be, and they ignore the reality of all the red flags, or the toxicity that this woman brings the table, or the fact that her communication skills suck, or that she's creating unnecessary drama. Or, in other instances, they're doing and saying things that make them appear weak and needy, so they justify calling too much and over pursuing too much.

I had a recent phone session with a guy who dated this particular woman for about a year and a half, two years, I think it was, and most of the time they were together he was doing 70% of the pursuing. And, eventually, she dumped him, and within a couple of months of breaking up with him, she was in a relationship with another guy. And then a year, year and a half went by, and she came back in the picture because she supposedly broke up with this other guy, and then, he kind of went right back to over pursuing and calling and texting too much, instead of letting her do all the calling, texting, and pursuing since she was the one that ended the relationship and blew it up, basically. And this particular guy had read my book and listened to it, like, dozens of times, (at least he claimed that). I was pointing out to him, "Dude, you're doing the opposite of what my book teaches and you're getting negative, undesired results that are exactly detailed in the book." He just had a really hard time accepting it, because he was seeing reality as he wanted it to be and not as it was.

By the end of the phone session, I was able to get him to recognize and realize it was actually his behavior, (instead of the rationalizations and justifications that he was coming up with), that was actually turning her off. You've got to see things as they are, not better than they are or worse than they are, but you've got to see reality as it is. Because, if you delude yourself and you take actions based upon your delusions, you're going to take yourself further and further away from the outcomes that you want to achieve.

LINK: https://understandingrelationships.com/she-wants-to-be-friends-first/13714

The Clueless Creepy Stalker

"In order to attract a woman and maintain that attraction, you must continually make her feel safe and comfortable. If you are a man who has lots of choices with women, you are going to be focused on making sure you pick the right one. That means the best one for you who fulfills all of your needs, wants and desires. You'll see yourself as a catch. If you are a man who feels he has no choice with women, you will be focused on trying to force, control and manipulate women into wanting you and being with you. That is a scarcity mindset. The reality is that there are about 7 billion people on the planet, and about half of them are women. It is physically impossible to date all of the women who would go out with you when you act like a man who has abundance and choice. However, if you believe and act in ways that are consistent with not being worthy of any woman, you will scare away and repulse every woman you encounter." ~ Coach Corey Wayne

So, this article is a doozy, and you should definitely check it out—"The Clueless Creepy Stalker." I mean, this guy, he'd been following this girl around, and it turns out she was really young, and he was, I think, probably her parents age. It was to the point where he was showing up and putting things into their family mailbox, and just talking himself into it like, "Hey, we've got something there. There's synchronicity playing out." I mean, you've got to check it out, because it'll definitely make you laugh. And this particular guy had no idea that the way he was behaving was inappropriate. But the reality is he just got attached to a girl and projected his fantasy of what he wanted onto her, and ignored the fact that, not only was she not reciprocating, but it was just totally inappropriate, his behavior.

He saw this girl out in public one time and then just became fixated on her, started talking to her, and then just continually showed up at places over and over where her and her mother would go hang out, and shop, and eat, and then just accidentally bump into them. When you behave this way and you interact with women this way—because you've seen this over and over in movies and in TV shows that this is the kind of strategy that is how you get your dream girl—in reality, it freaks people out and it scares them, to the point where they ended up contacting the police to get him to kind of go away. And he had a hard time accepting that. I just let him know, I had to lower the boom on him, because his behavior is just inappropriate.

The idea is a man extends his invitation of what he wants to the woman, and it's up to the woman to decide "Yes" or "No" or politely decline. Because, again, you want somebody who's enthusiastic about being with you and spending time with you. And, as rare as it is, the right woman will want to spend time with you. That's why you continually have to get better, you've got to improve your skills, because when and where you meet a girl that you really click with, you just never know when it's going to happen. And it usually happens when you least expect it, when it's not even on your mind. You'll turn around in the grocery store, and then there'll be an angel standing behind you with a smile on her face, and she'll engage you in conversation, and make it easy and effortless to talk to her.

Maybe you're at a friend's house, maybe you're at a wedding, maybe you're attending a barbecue on the weekend with some coworkers and there's a girl there you start talking to, and it just feels like you've known her forever. You have to continually circulate and keep an open mind. Extend your invitation but be okay with it not getting accepted. As a matter fact, you have to get okay with, almost all of them, getting rejected. But when you do find somebody that accepts it and expresses enthusiasm, your dates are going to be much more effortless and a lot of fun to be on.

LINK: https://understandingrelationships.com/the-clueless-creepy-stalker/17341

Dating Your Employee

"When we become emotionally invested in or attached to someone, something or some outcome we want in life, we tend to see what we want to see while ignoring all kinds of red flags and warning signs that things are not as we believe them to be. One of life's greatest challenges is to see reality as it is so we can make good decisions, instead of making bad decisions based upon either seeing reality as better than it is, or worse than it is. You can ignore reality, but not the consequences of ignoring reality." ~ Coach Corey Wayne

I think it was Master Yoda that I first heard this from—it was one of the Star Wars movies, and I don't remember which one it was—but he said something to the effect of, "Attachment leads to suffering." It may have been something that even the Buddha said at one time in the past, but it is such a true thing, especially when it comes to relationships. You get attached to a certain woman because you're projecting your fantasy onto her, and she looks like you wanted her to look, and she's as much fun as you wanted to have fun with a girl. You love the sound of her voice, you have lots of things in common. You start spending a few weeks together, you're hooking up, you're having a blast. She's having fun, she's putting her best foot forward, you're putting your best foot forward. But, little by little, you start to see these little red flags peeking out, but because things are so good with so many other aspects of your interactions, you're like, "Oh, it's fine. That'll be fine. This is fine," and you'll talk yourself into it.

And then, six months, a year down the road, two years down the road, when the infatuation has worn off and the honeymoon period is over, then you're faced with the fact that you ignored those red flags and things that violated your value system, and your principles, and the things that she just simply didn't share the same goals, but you proceeded anyway. And now, you're having to go through a painful breakup. Then you've got to tell all your friends and family why you didn't stay together, and it's just never a fun process. That's why you've really got to keep your eyes open.

I know, as hard it is, because I've never been perfect at it myself, I've made lots of mistakes. If you read my book *3% Man*, you'll see them all laid out in there. And it's hard, man. It's hard when your emotions get involved in things that you want, and you get attached to people or events or circumstances. But the way I look at it, this is how the universe exposes us to our blind spots, and our weaknesses, and things that we need to work on to become better human beings.

Because, when we overcome those flaws, those faults, those rough edges of ours and we improve ourselves, we actually become better for better quality people. And, therefore, by holding a space open for a better-quality person to fill, as you become better, you're going to easily and more effortlessly align with that better quality person. Whereas, just a few months before, if you interacted with them without learning and overcoming those weaknesses and flaws, you would've turned them off. But now, since you've overcome them, it's easy and effortless, and you kind of fit like a glove in each other's life.

LINK: https://understandingrelationships.com/dating-your-employee/13806

Attachments Create Suffering

"Attachments to things you want, people you want to loved by and time-frames that you want things to happen in create suffering and prevent you from being happy in the present moment. Jobs, careers, businesses, relationships, lovers, friends, etc., that no longer serve you will dissolve and disappear from your life. Let them. The reason they dissolve is that they have served their purpose in helping you become the person you are right now. In order for you to fulfill your destiny, new people and better circumstances need a space in your life so they can fill it. Without that space, they cannot manifest. Therefore, you must allow people and circumstances to effortlessly choose you and to choose to be in your life, instead of trying to hold on to the past and force what does not belong to stay. If you focus on allowing what you want to come into your life instead of trying to force things, your life will be much easier, stress free, effortless, efficient, and you'll be a much happier, healthier and content person." ~ Coach Corey Wayne

This is something that I really struggled with when I was younger and I transitioned through the different seasons of my life, is that when you're young and you make friendships, you think that those people are always going to be with you throughout your whole life. The reality is, as I got into my 20s, I had a large group of people that I thought were friends, but they were really just kind of acquaintances. And as I really started going for the things that I wanted in life, they really weren't of the same mindset and didn't have the same hunger for success that I did.

And as the years rolled by, a lot of those people were just kind of screwing around and not really taking their life seriously in what they wanted and were joking about the fact that things were not going well in their life, or they were working a shitty job, but they just weren't willing to do anything to help themselves. It's kind of like hanging out with the stupid kids in class; they're not really focused on doing well in school, and when they get a bad grade on a test, they tell all of their other friends how poorly they did, and they laugh about it.

I remember this was the case when I was in my first year of high school. I went to a public high school that ended up closing at the end of the year, and then, I went from that environment where it was cool to do lousy on a test to a college preparatory private school. If you didn't do well on a test, you were an idiot. And so, as I transitioned through my 20s and into my 30s, those friends that I had, who were cool people but just didn't have any real goals or ambitions, they just kind of fell by the wayside. Especially as I started doing better, and becoming more successful, and advancing in my career, and making way more money than they were, it many times became a problem for them. Because then, they started making fun of me, teasing me, putting me down, kind of being jerks about it, and I just slowly gravitated away from them.

And then, I saw the same thing when I was making a transition out of the real estate, mortgage, and construction industry, because so many of the people that were in my life were built around that business, were built around that lifestyle and just how I lived my life. A lot of them were not very supportive when I transitioned into becoming a full-time life coach, and the same kind of thing happened. A lot of those relationships, and life circumstances, where I lived, the homes I owned, the cars I drove, the business that I had, the office building that I had with my partners, all that stuff went through a bunch of transitions, and I just transitioned out of the old life and made a lot of new friends, and a new group of people came into my life.

And that's what you notice, is that there's just people that are going to come and go in your life. There are circumstances that come and go, there's jobs that come and go, careers that come and go, companies that come and go. If you're an entrepreneur, like me, there's businesses that come and go. A great business today might not be viable 10, 15, 20 years from now, because of changes in technology or what have you. So, you've got to become okay with letting go of your attachments to the way things were, because that's what enables us to go from where we were, to eventually where we want to be.

LINK: https://understandingrelationships.com/attachments-create-suffering/16038

I've Finally Started Living Again

"One of the most empowering, enlightening, amazing and successful mindsets that a man who wants to be more successful in life and with women can adopt, is one of being indifferent, carefree, happy, bold, courageous, charming and unattached to any outcome or desire. Most men would love to be more successful with women, in their career and in life, but they are not because they have consciously or unconsciously adopted an inferior, scarcity mindset. A scarcity mindset is rooted in fear and causes them to chase, to try and force things, and to act unworthy of their desires and dreams. Successful men who adopt an abundance mentality already have too many choices and options and are forced to be selective with whom they allow into their lives and spend their time with. This causes them to appear to other people who are looking for what they have as being highly valuable, scarce and also causes them to make an extra effort to get their attention and time." ~ Coach Corey Wayne

It's kind of like the analogy you've probably heard once or twice in your life, "Don't try to force people to stay in your life; the right people will come and stay willingly." It turns out to be really true. And the more you can be indifferent, carefree, humorous, unattached to any outcome—because somebody who is abundant and has abundance in their lives has lots of choices and lots of options, their cup already runneth over, so to speak—they don't need any more women; they don't really need any more money or business opportunities, because they've already got more than they can handle. They already are working at a job or career that they love, even though they're constantly being courted and recruited to work for other companies because they're such a superstar employee. As far as friends go, they always have lots of great friends and people who want to hang out with them and, therefore, they're never in a rush, they never try to force things. They spend their time with people who really love, value, and want them around.

If your life is not like this yet, think about it, imagine it, visualize. Contemplate yourself, as Wayne Dyer would say, as being surrounded by the type of conditions that you would like to create. What's your body language? What's your physiology? What's your self-talk like? What's the tone of your voice like? What kinds of things and thoughts would you be experiencing in your body, would you be saying to yourself? How would you interact with other people if you had an abundance of really great choices? Well, you certainly would not be in a big rush to make anything happen. You're going to entertain any and all offers, and then you're going to take the best offer, and then slowly respond to that best offer in time. It's a great way to visualize yourself and imagine what your life would be like if you were in an abundance mentality and abundance was just simply a way of life for you.

LINK: https://understandingrelationships.com/ive-finally-started-living-again/19121

BEING INDEPENDENT

Wounds Become Your Strengths

"Our difficulties, challenges, wounds and shortcomings are gifts from the Creator for us to transcend and overcome. It is in the process of overcoming our past and our burdens that we can learn how to do it, so we can help others who may not be as far along in their own journey of self-actualization. The events of our lives do not define us. We are defined by the meanings we give to the events and circumstances of our lives. Ask quality questions, and you will force your brain to come up with quality answers. Look for the good, utility and benefit in every experience. The quality of your life is proportional to the quality of the questions you ask yourself on a continual basis." ~ Coach Corey Wayne

It's really powerful and helpful to recognize that life is happening for you, not to you, because if you perceive that life is happening for you, that means that every person you meet, every circumstance of your life is something that can be a teachable moment for you to help you become better. If you look at life as something that just happens to you, then you're a victim of circumstance; you really don't have any control to shape and change your destiny, you're just at the circumstances of luck and whatever happens to show up in your life. It's the difference between being self-reliant and dependent upon someone/something outside of ourselves, such as somebody in the government, our favorite politician that makes all these BS promises, or waiting on our employer to give us a raise instead of going and asking for it. And then, if they won't give us a raise or the promotion we want, then taking the time to go find a different employer who will give us that next opportunity instead of waiting for things to happen to us.

Self-reliant, self-actualizing people must be what they can be. They have to go for the things that they want, and they don't let their current circumstances get in the way of achieving their goals and their dreams. If things are not working for them, they're looking for a way to get around, over, or under that particular obstacle.

LINK: https://understandingrelationships.com/wounds-become-your-strengths/31714

People Who Change Our Lives

"The universe works in magical and mysterious ways. When we become stuck in relationships, jobs, careers, businesses, friendships, patterns of living and belief systems that no longer serve us, synchronistic events and people seem to magically show up and completely change the way we look at things. These people and events facilitate the destruction of our old lives so we can create something new and more harmonious that is aligned with and enables us to take the next step to reach our full potential. Nothing happens by accident. Everyone and everything that comes into your life is there to give you exactly what you need to nudge you in the right direction. The more you ignore your heart, feelings and intuition, the more uncomfortable it will become to stay stuck in ways of thinking and living that are holding you back. Life is change. Growth is optional. The more comfortable and adaptable you are to change, and the more open you are to taking advantage of new opportunities when they arise, the more effortless, easy and synchronistic life will become for you. When your life matches and mirrors the dreams of your heart, you will see how efficient, divine, loving and magical the universe is as it conforms to your wishes and desires." ~ Coach Corey Wayne

Something I've learned in my study of network chiropractic care and how our body and nervous system works is that human beings that deal with unpleasant things over and over again, and it doesn't feel safe to experience those emotions or whatever's going on in our environment, (usually, obviously, trauma in our childhood), is that when our nervous system is overwhelmed and there's nothing we can do to avoid it, what happens is, this gets stored as muscle tension in our nervous system. And what happens, as the years and the decades roll by, whenever certain things that trigger us emotionally in the same way that we were triggered in childhood happen, our vertebrate subluxate and they twist and pinch the nerves that come out of it. And what's interesting is that every vertebra is associated with a different part of our personality. It's like, our naval area tends to be associated with willpower; the area where our rib cage comes together, you know, an inch or two underneath our nipples, that usually is associated with our emotions; and then the breastbone area, the part that's two or three inches above our nipples that have, like, those two bony protrusions, that area deals with accessing the heart. And what's interesting, based upon whatever the trauma is that we've experienced in childhood, it will determine where those subluxations are and, therefore, the spine will correspond to that in the back with what's called armoring, where you literally become like a turtle.

So, for me, personally, the area that I had a lot of problems with was the emotional area. I had a bit of a hunchback in that part of my body. And through lots of network chiropractic care—because this accumulated over many decades of my life, and I didn't get into network chiropractic care until I was in my mid-30s—and by focusing on that area and causing the neck to unwind and lose the twist that it had in it, that area of my emotional body started to loosen up, and I no longer had that same negative charge on things anymore that I once had. It completely transformed all of the relationships in my life.

What was interesting is, people that were toxic and negative in my life that I put up with and they really didn't bother me before, a few months after I got into network care, I no longer wanted to hang out with those people. And so, I started moving away from those people and more towards people that were more balanced and brought more ease and delight in my life, and it completely transformed everything. When you get to a place where you've kind of healed this part of your body and your spine elongates—you lose the twist in your neck and in your lower back—you just feel more chilled out, you feel more relaxed. And, for me, I set about the task of trying to incorporate more peace, more ease, and delight in my life and moved away from a very unbalanced life and two business partners that brought a lot of stress, and toxicity, and chaos into my life. I even had people working for me that were also toxic, and constantly bringing drama into my life and constantly causing problems.

And now, when I look at my life and the way things are set up, everything facilitates me being in a peaceful and relaxed state; I simply don't tolerate BS. And even when I do my videos or my articles that I have with people, I make it known that I like working with people who are easy-going, easy to get along with, who aren't disrespectful. I speak my truth, I speak what's on my mind, and if people get butthurt and offended about that—which, there's plenty of people every day, (there's probably somebody right now on one of my social media platforms that are sending me an email to bitch about something they don't like about me)—these people never become my clients, because I don't tolerate it. And when I answer enough emails and do enough videos talking about where I come from, people that don't resonate with that, almost 100% of them, never book a phone session with me. I just simply don't have to deal with those kinds of people, because I've made it very clear about the kind of people that I want to work with and what I enjoy when it comes to coaching people.

I've built my whole business and my whole life, presenting to the world, "This is my truth. This is how I live. If you want to play in my playground, you're welcome to come in and play, but it's a privilege to be here; it's not a right. And if you're an asshole, if you're calling me names, and you're being harsh to other people in the community, you get blocked, and you get muted, and then you're gone forever." It's a beautiful thing setting your life up in a way that brings you more peace, more ease, more delight.

LINK: https://understandingrelationships.com/people-who-change-our-lives/16993

Mindsets, Monogamy, Marriage & MGTOW

"Life requires your participation in order to create the life and lifestyle you've always wanted. The moment you start blaming others for your current circumstances, you give up your ability to do anything to shape your destiny. Success is a process. In order to feel successful and happy, you must feel like you are making incremental progress towards creating your dream life. Successful people take action, and they take full responsibility for everyone and everything that shows up in their lives. Unsuccessful people make excuses and blame others to absolve themselves from any personal responsibility for making their lives the way they want them to be. You either believe you are in control and responsible for your life and making it the way you want, or you are abdicating control and hoping that someone else does it for you." ~ Coach Corey Wayne

You have to take control for everything that happens in your life and every person that is in your life that you somehow, someway attracted to you—either with your thoughts, your words, or your deeds—into your life. You have to participate in your own rescue. If you are not happy with where you are or with the way your life is right now, it's up to you to do something about it. You've got to participate your own rescue. Nobody is coming to save you; you have to do that yourself. If you depend on other people, circumstances, and things outside of yourself to come along and fix your life for you, nothing is ever going to change, and you are completely powerless to shape and change your destiny.

LINK: https://understandingrelationships.com/mindsets-monogamy-marriage-mgtow/27376

What A Jerk I Was!

"Life might not always be what you want or expect, but when you are able to, years later, look back upon past events, it's pretty easy to see how everything that happened helped you to become the person you are today. If you have weaknesses or rough edges that need smoothing out, challenges and hardships will arise to humble, strengthen and help you become better. If you have trouble making decisions, life circumstances will manifest that force you to make decisions quickly, as being indecisive will cause you emotional, mental, financial or even physical pain. If your heart is closed, someone will come into your life to help it flower and open fully. In every moment of every day, we either choose to get better, or stay the same." ~ Coach Corey Wayne

Everything in life happens for a reason. Life tends to happen for you, not to you. Every day, you're faced with a set of choices and circumstances. And if you know who you are, what you want, and why you want it, then you'll be able to look at the things that you have to do on a daily basis and do them, even if they are things that aren't pleasant or don't bring you a lot of joy, because they are simply essential to getting things done. Like, for me, personally, I personally don't enjoy lifting weights. I do it because I like the way it makes me look, it makes me feel good, and it helps keep me mentally sharp. And so, when I think about the fact that I don't feel like working out, and I'm associating pain with working out, I think of it from a different perspective. I think about how good I'm going to feel after the workout is completed. I think about how good it's going to make me look. I think about how it's going to put extra lead in my pencil, (which, obviously, the ladies definitely appreciate that).

You've got to take care of your body. And whether it's work that you're doing, whether it's physical activity, maybe it's having unpleasant meetings and having those unpleasant conversations that you've been avoiding, you have to do it. Because in order to get from where you are to where you want to be, it's not always going to be all sunshine and roses. There are always unpleasant things that have to be done that are essential to you being productive, and not just being busy. Don't get caught up in doing things that feel good, that keep you busy if they're not the kinds of things that are productive or that are going to move your life and you closer to the things that you want.

LINK: https://understandingrelationships.com/what-a-jerk-i-was/22787

He Got His Man Card Back

"It's liberating to take your power and life back after you have given it away to please others, bent yourself into a pretzel to make a lover happy, or have simply been focused on every else's needs but your own. To have truly great relationships with yourself and others, you must first focus on making yourself happy and meeting your needs first. Only when you know who you are, what you want, what's important to you and you love and accept yourself, will you be strong and centered enough to love another without losing yourself in the process. The healthiest and strongest relationships are relationships between two happy, whole and complete people who have come together to share their completeness." ~ Coach Corey Wayne

It was really liberating for me back in 2005, 2006, and 2007 when I was in the process of disengaging from my old business partners from the real estate, construction, and mortgage industry. We had been in business together and worked together for over a decade at that point, and quite frankly, all three of us were pretty much sick of each other and had other things, and interests, and new directions that we all wanted to go into in our individual lives. And I remember, after it was finally done, I felt really free; freer than I had ever been. Because being in a business partnership with two other guys, not only are you in partnership with them, but you also have to deal with the consequences of their relationships with their significant others, because they're going to have a significant influence on their husband's lives and indirectly your life. And it was really nice, really freeing to be out of that type of restrictive environment, and for the first time in my life, have complete, total control of my time, without having to worry about what other people wanted for it.

LINK: https://understandingrelationships.com/he-got-his-man-card-back/17354

Work Affairs

"When it comes to your personal life, your professional life or the kind of life and lifestyle you want to create for yourself, you need to become crystal clear about what your outcome is first. You must also learn to see things as they are, not better than they are or worse than they are, so you can be realistic and make choices based upon the reality of the value people and circumstances can bring into your life. Some people are great sex playmates, but terrible relationship partners. Some people are great lovers and very loyal to be in a relationship with, but their lack of communication skills makes a healthy and loving relationship with them impossible. There are also people whose lives are so full of drama, dysfunction, challenges, strife, and calamity, that they're simply too toxic to allow into your life in any way, shape, or form, because of their destructive nature. If you can discipline yourself and maintain your emotional self-control, you'll only allow lovers into your life who are aligned with your relationship goals, instead of deluding yourself into falling in love with someone's potential and inviting them to make your life a living hell." ~ Coach Corey Wayne

This is where it's important, when it comes to your personal life, that you know what your important relationship goals and values are. In other words, what kind of a goal do you want, or set of goals do you want, to create and achieve with your partner? And what kind of a value system is important to you as far as the way you guys look at money, the way you look at loyalty, integrity, communication, the values that you have centered around family and close friends, and just how you want to conduct yourself from an integrity point of view? Because, once you have that list and as you're dating, you're going to match up that person that you're dating—as you spend time with them, and you get to know them, and you get to see what their qualities are really like—to see how well they match up against your list.

When you find somebody that has a lot of the qualities, and you really like her, and she's really starting to like you, and then you start to see these little things where the value system doesn't really match up to yours, it's really hard—especially if it's been a while since you've met somebody that you really jive with—to admit that, to admit that they don't really mesh with you. And it's better just to move on, as hard as it is to move on, to keep circulating, and find somebody new.

Because, when you settle, and you think, "I can work with this," and it's something that's really important to you personally, as far as your value system or the goals that you want, a simple thing like, if you want to have kids but she doesn't want to have kids, you think, maybe down the road she'll change her mind once she really gets to know you, because everything else is so great. And then, you're six months, a year or two down the road, and you really want to have kids, and she's still adamant that she doesn't. Now, you're faced with a situation of one of your major goals, you're not going to be able achieve it with this particular person. But because you've spent a year or two in a relationship hoping that, eventually, they'll changed their mind, now your identity is associated with being in a relationship with this person.

And then, just to up and leave when everything else is so great, so you can find somebody who actually does want to have kids, it's really hard.

For a lot of people, these kinds of emotional anchors are what keep them in a relationship many months, years, or even decades longer than they should have. And true maturity means having the strength to say to yourself, "You know what, as awesome as she is, she's not exactly what I want. And these goals, these values are too important to me to settle. I don't want to get to the end of my life and not have a family, because I chose to be a relationship with somebody that didn't want to have a family."

So, often, that's how life is. You will get faced with things, whether it's you want a promotion but it's not the promotion that you want, and you want an increase in your salary. You get one, but it's not the increase that you really wanted. And then you just stay, hoping it's going to get better, instead of saying, "You know what? I really want more responsibility. I really wanted that kind of position. I really want this kind of money, this kind of compensation. I have the experience. I know other people in the industry that have the same level experience, or even less experience than me, and they're earning that kind of income, they have that kind of responsibility," and recognizing that you don't have it, and that you've got to seek to go and create it.

Anything you want in life, you really have to go after it to make it happen. But, oftentimes, there might be a relationship that needs an end, or a job that you need to look to moving on from, or a friendship with people that are just simply holding you back, and getting in the way, and starting to sandbag your goals, your hopes, your dreams because they really don't have the strength to do it themselves, and so they are sandbagging your success, trying to simply validate how they operate in the world. Sometimes these might be people you grew up with and you've spent a lot of years with, but by the time you get in your early 20s, they're just kind of toxic, and they never really have anything positive to say, and they're not really helping you move in the right direction. It's hard to let go of people that you love and care about, but deep down, you know that they're not right for you.

LINK: https://understandingrelationships.com/work-affairs/18251

I Have Tremendous Anxiety

"Self-acceptance is an art. Not a science. Success and inner peace come from learning to embrace all that you are without judgement or condemnation. That means embracing your fears, worries, anxieties, anger, shame, guilt and sadness, in order to feel it and be fully present with it. When you accept, embrace, experience and feel the unpleasant feelings and emotions as they bubble up inside you, you are feeling them so you can heal and move past them. When you judge them, try to avoid them, or numb them with drugs or alcohol, you are simply avoiding and resisting them. What you resist persists. What you look at disappears. Failure to embrace, accept and love all that you are, including your icky feelings and emotions, is the root cause of suffering. Life isn't all sunshine and roses. Sometimes life just sucks and feels like crap. It's all part of being human. Ignoring or avoiding your bad feelings and emotions is just like a parent who neglects their child, causing it to misbehave. Surrendering to what you feel will free you from it. Avoiding it will keep you chained to it." ~ Coach Corey Wayne

This is such a helpful tool to take time, be present with your feelings, especially the icky ones, the ones where you suffer, where life feels hopeless, just spending time alone, whether it's in your bedroom, or in your car if you're on a lunch break, and just saying out loud what you're thinking and feeling, and being authentically present with your emotions, not trying to judge them, not trying to wish them away, not trying to numb them with anything—any kind of substances or food—just allowing yourself to feel whatever it is, to allow those feelings to wash over you to where you get immersed into it. Because when you immerse yourself in your feelings, you have to get into it before you can get out of it. When you embrace the "suck," so to speak, when you say to yourself, "I feel like shit," "I feel sad," "I feel depressed," "I feel lonely," "I feel like nothing works," "I feel it never gets any better," "I feel I have to do everything on my own," "I feel like life is hopeless sometimes," whatever it is, when you say those feelings and you feel what it is and you verbalize it, you are giving your nervous system what it needs to move that stuck energy through it—express itself just like a child expresses their emotions, without trying to put a time limit on it—and it just moves through you and dissolves. And before you know it, ten minutes later you're daydreaming about something completely unrelated to how crappy you were feeling.

It's a tremendous gift to live that way. Try it, it's a great exercise. Anytime you feel like shit and you've got something you're avoiding, talk about it, verbalize it to yourself, put a pillow over your face and scream into it. Whatever you're thinking, whatever you're feeling, just let it wash all over you. Because when you do that, it'll dissolve and go, just as quickly as it came. And the more you do it, the quicker you're able to move through those icky parts of your life and your day.

LINK: https://understandingrelationships.com/i-have-tremendous-anxiety/16918

Success, Ambition & Attraction

"Masculine energy embodies success, ambition, goals, mission and purpose in life. Women are much more attracted to men who know what they want, why they want it and are taking action to achieve it, than men who don't know what their purpose in life is or who have unexpectedly seen their success, business or wealth disappear. A woman will support a man going through a hard time for a while, but if he only complains about his situation and does not do much or do enough in her eyes to help himself or turn things around, eventually she will lose attraction and respect for him to the point that she dumps him. A man must not let challenges, setbacks, job loss, business failure, financial hardship, etc., diminish him to the point that he gives up or stops trying to turn things around in his life. If he does, she will no longer trust his masculine core and it won't be long before he finds himself being unexpectedly dumped by his woman." ~ Coach Corey Wayne

This is the embodiment of masculine energy, because life is going to throw us curveballs. We might lose our job unexpectedly, and obviously, in the current environment, that is something that's happened for millions of people; because of the coronavirus and the lockdowns, a lot of people found themselves out of work or saw their businesses get destroyed, because they were forced to close and simply didn't have enough cash flow or capital to sustain them through the lean times. When these kinds of unexpected challenges happen, especially because of the boom-and-bust cycle of the central banking system, the older you get, the more you go through these cycles and you kind of see the ups and downs of life, you plan accordingly. But, when you're younger and you don't know any better, these things can be incredibly challenging. And the most important thing to remember as a man is that despite whatever life throws at you, you've always got to focus on your mission, your purpose, your passion in life, and continually be going for what you want and the things that you want in life, and not get discouraged by all of the things going on around you.

I don't remember who it was, but there is an old quote that I learned many years ago and it said, "Obstacles are the scary things you see when you take your eyes off of your goals." That's why it's so important for men in general to have a mission and a purpose in life that they are relentlessly pursuing and seeking to make a reality or maintain in their reality, no matter what is going on in your life. As a man, you can never lose sight of your purpose and mission. If you do, the woman or women in your life are going to lose attraction and respect for you, and that just creates a negative downward spiral.

LINK: https://understandingrelationships.com/success-ambition-attraction/16739

How To Live & Be A Man

"Masculine energy is about purpose, drive, mission, succeeding, breaking through barriers, overcoming challenges, courage, accomplishing and striving to reach your full potential. Women are naturally more attracted to men who take risks, go for what they want and who have a mission and purpose that energizes them and that they are relentlessly pursuing to achieve, despite any obstacle. Any man who embodies these traits and vibe will be infinitely more attractive and desirable to women than a man who is simply dabbling his way through life without focusing on or trying to master anything in particular." ~ Coach Corey Wayne

When a guy displays these masculine strength characteristics of having his life in order, his mission and purpose in order, he takes care of his body, he looks good, he wears tight fitting or firmly fitting clothes that show off his nice, in-shape physique—and I'm not talking about skinny jeans, I'm just talking about wearing firmly fitting clothes that show off the fact that you're in really great shape—men who do this love themselves, and take care of themselves, and appreciate life. They tend to have higher energy, they tend to be high achievers, they tend to be risktakers. That's why by developing yourself and, especially, taking good care of your body, you're stacking the deck in your favor. You're making it easier for women to find you attractive, versus some guy that wears dumpy, baggy-looking clothes, is overweight, and has a big gut that hangs over his belt. Men who value and respect themselves are going to take care of their bodies, and they're going to take care of their lives. If you're responsible enough and driven enough to do these things, you're going to display all the masculine strength characteristics that women find attractive.

LINK: https://understandingrelationships.com/how-to-live-be-a-man/31788

How To Meet More High Quality Women

"It's infinitely easier to grow your confidence, happiness and success when you have emotionally compelling reasons and choices. It's way easier to seduce, charm and display charisma around a woman who knocks your socks off, than a woman who you think is average. It's almost impossible to reach your full potential in your career if you don't like what you are doing for a living or the people you are working with. An average looking man who is surrounded by beautiful women where he works and plays is going to be way more attractive and confident around women, because he has more great choices and options, than a good-looking guy who lives in a town with only one traffic light. Live and work in a place that gives you unlimited entertainment, career and social life options. Scarcity makes you fear loss and makes you less attractive. Abundance makes you more attractive, confident, cocky, charming, and willing to walk away from mediocre friends, lovers and jobs to find better ones." ~ Coach Corey Wayne

This is such an important part of people's lives that, usually, they don't give a lot of attention to. If you're single and you're trying to meet great female dating prospects, you've got to be in an area where lots of beautiful, single women are going to hang out. Just because, simply, that process is a numbers game. And what's interesting about women is, the more women there are in environment and the fewer guys there are in an environment, the more that particular guy is going to be seen as attractive by all of the women that are in that environment, because the man is now a scarce resource. So, set your life up in a way where there's lots of really great, high-quality people in the area that you want to live, work, and play in, because you'll meet a lot more people that you can become friends with, you'll meet a lot more women that you can date, because you'll be living and working in a place where you like to play, you like to have fun, you like to hang out.

And if you live in a cool area that's a fun place to live, all the friends that you're going to have are also going to want to come hang out with you in that area because it's so much more fun. This is an essential part of it. If you don't like where you live, or if you're living out in the middle of nowhere, or you're living in a place where it just doesn't offer a lot of great social options, then you've got to go move to a place, even if it means getting a studio apartment somewhere in the city or some area where there's lots of people that congregate doing the kind of activities and fun that you like doing. This will help your social life immensely, as well as help you emotionally and mentally, just make you feel better and more confident. Because what guy does not love to be surrounded by beautiful women wherever he goes?

LINK: https://understandingrelationships.com/how-to-meet-more-high-quality-women/36005

Attracting The Right Woman

"In order to accomplish great things in life, you must have the courage and conviction to take consistent action towards making your grandest goals and dreams a reality, despite the potential for failure. You don't have to be great to start out, but you must make the required effort to learn, grow and become better slowly over time, in order to become great and exceptional. Until you succeed and finally manifest your dreams, a lot of time is going to pass, and you will have to get used to wondering if your efforts will eventually pay off, despite experiencing long periods of failure, setbacks and doubt. A burning desire and passion for your goals and dreams is the necessary fuel you'll need to stay motivated and persevere when the future is in doubt. This is the essence of masculine energy. Taking risks, overcoming challenges, breaking through barriers and having a purpose and mission that is emotionally compelling to you. Your actions are evidence of your conviction about yourself and your capabilities. Taking action makes you feel more confident and hopeful. Inaction makes you shrink from challenges and fear the future. As you make progress and see positive results, this builds your confidence and makes you more attractive to women because of your bravery, despite future success being in doubt. Attracting the right woman is the result of becoming the kind of person you want to attract. This happens when you feel great about yourself and your life, even when you have a long way to go to reach your dreams." ~ Coach Corey Wayne

Women love men who are confident, who have a vision for their lives, who are going for the things that they want. Because if a guy is able to make himself happy, if he's self-reliant and able to create the life and lifestyle that he wants on his own terms, of his own choosing, then he typically will know how to treat her, how to be a great father, a great husband, a great boyfriend, a great teammate, and a great person to share and spend your life with. People who believe in themselves and who expect to be successful, they're taking action to move towards the things that they want in life. It doesn't matter whether or not they just started on this journey, but they have something that's emotionally compelling that drives them, something internally that lights them up on the inside that they're going for.

This is what optimistic, high-achieving people do; they move towards the things that they want, and they don't let obstacles, or failures, or setbacks hold them back. Whereas, a guy who has given up on himself and is looking to a woman to make him happy and be the source of his happiness, if he's not able to be self-reliant and make things happen for himself, how could he possibly be able to consistently give to her in a way that makes her feel loved and appreciated? Because you can't give away what you don't feel for yourself. If you don't love yourself, you don't value yourself, you don't value your life, and your lifestyle, and the people in it, it's going to be pretty hard to convince a woman to get excited about it.

LINK: https://understandingrelationships.com/attracting-the-right-woman/37818

She's Slowly Ceasing Contact

"Men who are not 100% focused on their purpose and mission in life tend to think a woman is the solution to their happiness, boredom and the fact they are not really that excited about their own lives. This often causes them to try too hard to the point they smother, over-pursue and come off as needy and clingy. They also mistakenly try to substitute controlling their women for their lack of personal self-control and the fact they feel totally out of control in their own lives, because they are not doing anything to shape, change and control their own destiny. Men must get their professional lives in order first, before they can reach their full potential in their personal lives. Having an unbalanced and unfocused professional life leads to turmoil and inconsistent success in your personal life." ~ Coach Corey Wayne

If a guy doesn't have his personal and professional life in order, if he's not taking care of his body, if he's not moving towards something he loves and enjoys, if he doesn't know what he wants or why he wants it, what's going to happen is he's going to be extremely unbalanced. And so, when he's having a good day, he's going to tend to do the right things with women in his life and pull them in closer to him. When he's having a bad day or he's struggling for several days in a row, most guys tend to want to naturally withdraw, ponder, contemplate, think about what they can or can't do in the future. But what happens is, when they get stuck in their own minds and are worried about how they're going to pay their bills or what may or may not happen in the future, this gets in the way of them displaying confidence and certainty with the women that they're either in a relationship with, or that they're trying to date and eventually get into a relationship with. What's happening is they're giving off a different vibe, because their lives aren't really stable.

The reality is, women are more attracted to men who are stable, who have their life together. It doesn't mean they've achieved all their goals and dreams, but they know what they want, they know why they want it, and they're making a path in their life, they're on the journey to making these things happen.

LINK: https://understandingrelationships.com/shes-slowly-ceasing-contact/34651

Self-Improvement & Sexual Attraction

"Men who are successful at getting what they want in life have a vibe of abundance and success. They have high standards and do not settle for any kind of mediocrity in their lives. They easily brush off criticism from weaker people who seek to impose their beliefs, opinions and worldview by using shame or guilt as a tool of manipulation and control. Once you decide what you want in life, you must resolve to pay the price to get it and tune out the countless people you will encounter along your journey who think they know better and have the right to dictate and determine what you should and should not be. When someone tries to impose their limitations onto you, they are telling you their story, not yours." ~ Coach Corey Wayne

It's hard for all of us to really go for the things that we want in life and strive to reach our full potential, because we're surrounded by people that are doing the exact opposite of that. And so, as you start striving and moving towards the things you want in life and taking action, and then you start making progress, what you're going to start to find out really quick is who's really on your team, and supportive, and wants to see you succeed, and who's going to be working against you, and trying to discourage you and sandbag your success. Because the more you go for the things you want in life and start to achieve them, the greater the sense of discomfort you're going to see and sense in other people who are not doing the same things in their own lives.

And the reality is, most people do not like to be reminded of or woken up to the fact that they are living lives that are way less than they are capable of living. So, you have to become good at enduring criticism and distancing yourself from people who are not helping you reach your full potential and move towards people who are. It's super important to surround yourself with like-minded people who are just as excited and enthusiastic about your success and potential successes in the future as you are about theirs.

LINK: https://understandingrelationships.com/self-improvement-sexual-attraction/30539

Haters Gonna Hate

"The world is full of people who think they have a right to bully, intimidate, shame and force you to live and think like they expect you to. People in general feel better about themselves and their choices if they can influence others to make the same choices. They literally seek validation for their own behavior and beliefs by trying to make other people more like them. Successful people tend to be optimistic and look for the value in every situation or life experience, regardless of whether or not things unfold as they want or expect. We all have to deal with haters. Haters don't really hate you. They hate themselves, want to be you or simply are jealous and envious of what you have or who you are. Never take their insults personally, because they are simply projecting what's inside of them. You are never responsible for what other people think of you. It's simply none of your business." ~ Coach Corey Wayne

This is a great philosophy to have towards dealing with other people, because the more successful you become, what you're going to notice is people that are closer to you—maybe even people in your peer group or acquaintances of yours—who are deep down jealous and envious of your success are going to start to basically be jackasses towards you and have negative things to say. Because if they can belittle you, and label you, and diminish you in their own eyes, then they don't feel so bad or guilty about the fact that they're mediocre and they are living lives that are way less than what they are capable of living.

You can't take ownership for other people's self-hatred and self-loathing; it really has nothing to do with you. The best way to respond is to just let it be, because they're telling you their story, not yours. People project what's inside of them. No one will ever do or say anything to you that isn't a direct reflection of how they feel about themselves in a moment.

LINK: https://understandingrelationships.com/haters-gonna-hate/26139

Never Feel Sorry For Yourself

"One of the smartest decisions you can make in life to help yourself become more successful in every area of your life that is important to you and attract the kind of people and circumstances that your heart desires is to love and accept yourself as you are right now in this present moment. As Einstein once said, all of us have one fundamental decision to make in life: Do I live in a friendly or a hostile universe? The way you perceive yourself is exactly how you will cause others to perceive you. In order to get where you want to be in life, you must focus on what is great about you and your life right now, instead of doing what most unsuccessful people do, which is to focus on their shortcomings and what they are lacking. What you focus on will expand. By focusing on what is already great in your life right now and seeking to make it better, you will move yourself and your life closer to where you really want to be." ~ Coach Corey Wayne

Your self-perceptions and your self-talk and how you perceive yourself has a huge impact on your life, and what you notice, and what you're able to attract into it. If you believe that everybody's out to get you, or everybody's out to screw you over, or that most women aren't going to like you, or no women like you, you're already going to be predisposed to looking for something negative. And whatever you focus on, whatever you tell your brain to focus on, whatever kinds of questions you ask your brain, (because most people don't ask very empowering questions), is going to cause your brain to continually come up with negative answers. And if you're predisposed to something negative, just like the Einstein quote said, "Do I live in a friendly or hostile universe?", that's going to be your perception; that's going to be your reality.

Whereas, if you believe everybody is a potential friend, ally, and good-natured person, you're going to come from a completely different place. And because you're in a happy place, you're bringing a higher vibrational energy to every situation and every interaction with other people. Whereas, if you come to interactions with other people and you're angry, and you're pissed off, and you assume the worst, people are going to match and mirror that. And those same people, if you bring happiness, joy, positivity, it's a more efficient vibration and they will naturally entrain with you and look for reasons to be relaxed, to be peaceful, and to have joy. You attract how you act. It's that simple.

LINK: https://understandingrelationships.com/never-feel-sorry-for-yourself/19265

STAYING HEALTHY & HAPPY

She Discarded Me Like Trash!

"Other people's opinion of you is none of your business. The only person's opinion of you that should matter is the opinion you hold of yourself. Why? Trying to live your life according to the unreasonable expectations of another will always leave you frustrated and disappointed. Try as you may, you will never be able to please everyone and when your happiness depends upon the fickle approval of another, you will have no control over your own ability to make yourself happy, because your happiness will never feel like it depends upon you or your actions. Sometimes people are unloving, unkind, cold, heartless, selfish, rude and self-absorbed to the point that they really could care less about your feelings, needs, wants and desires. If you have smartly not made your happiness or contentment dependent upon the actions or approval of another, you will be free to find ways to make yourself happy on a consistent basis. Happiness begins and ends with you and the associations and meanings that you give the circumstances of your life." ~ Coach Corey Wayne

I don't remember who said it, but a wise person once said, "There is no way to happiness; happiness is the way." But what does that actually mean? Well, at the end of the day, we are the ones who decide whether or not we're happy. We decide what things and circumstances in our lives mean to us. In other words, we give the meaning to all of our thoughts, actions, and circumstances of our lives. We decide if something is good or bad, if something makes us happy, or something is upsetting to us.

One of the greatest gifts you can give yourself towards achieving your greatest goals and dreams is to adopt a positive and empowering mindset that trains your brain to give you and to look for reasons to be happy and to be grateful. Whatever your brain focuses on, it's going to look for more of that. That's why it's so important to manage your own thoughts and what's going on in your mind and what you're focusing on. And when you catch yourself trying to be negative or be pessimistic about the future, ask yourself a simple question: "What can I be grateful for right now in my life?" It can be something as simple as "I can be grateful for my health," "I can be grateful for my youth," "I can be grateful for my friends," "I can be grateful for my family," "I can be grateful for the fact that I'm optimistic," "That I'm quick to change my approach, but slow to change my mind on the things that I want," "I'm grateful that I'm more determined than most other average people are," "I'm grateful that I know what I want, I know why I want it, and I'm making the effort to make it happen," whatever it happens to be. If you give yourself good-quality questions, it's like what Tony Robbins said, "The quality of your life is in direct proportion to the quality of the questions that you consistently ask yourself." And a great gift you can give yourself is to continually focus on asking yourself good, high-quality questions.

LINK: https://understandingrelationships.com/she-discarded-me-like-trash/16595

Do You Miss Me?

"Most exclusive relationships start off as casual affairs. Over time, and as both people start to become more and more interested in each another, other people they may be dating slowly fade away. Women find men who have many options with other women to be more attractive than guys who have no other options. However, in order to maintain a woman's growing attraction for a man, he must make her feel more special than any other woman he may be dating. If he makes her feel like just another notch in his bedpost, or as if he is only using her for sex, she will lose interest and back away. Therefore, as a woman's attraction grows, she will start inquiring how much or if you miss her, ask about other women you are dating, and where you think things are going. Why? The more a woman likes you, the more attention of yours she will seek. Make her feel special, but never mislead her about your true intentions." ~ Coach Corey Wayne

Most people are extremely impatient, especially in our society of instant gratification. They want everything now. They want the job promotion now, even though they might not have the time and the experience to warrant it. They want to be exclusive and married with kids, even though they haven't even gone on their first date yet. They want everything to happen instantly. And when you watch TV and movies, it constantly reinforces and validates that this is how the world works.

The reality is all great things take time. I often use the analogy of, how often do you meet somebody that becomes a really close friend? These are things that very rarely happen and are very special, and most of us don't pay attention to the fact that great friends hardly ever come along; it's just not something that happens every day. And the same thing happens to great loves.

I'm almost 51 now, and when I look back over the course of my life and the people that are still in it, (that have been in it for many decades), and the difference that makes the difference is that they always stay in touch. Myself, or them, we always make the effort. Even though some of my really close friends, as the years have gone by, when I look back over the last 30–40 years, some of them, we've gone months or even a year or two without talking when life has gotten in the way, or you got too busy, we were living in other cities or other states. But, at the end of the day, we always found a way to reconnect and make the effort. And that's what you're going to see when it comes to your romantic life, as well. There's going to be very few women that are going to really make the effort and deserve your time and your interest. Great things take time, so practice infinite patience.

LINK: https://understandingrelationships.com/do-you-miss-me/21630

The Right Headspace

"Life is full of people and circumstances that will test your ability to remain at peace internally. Remaining at peace and taking your time to respond on your terms after careful consideration and thought is a conscious choice. Surround yourself with people who make it easy to stay in a peaceful and relaxed state, because that is also where they live emotionally. The events and circumstances of your life only have the meanings that you give them. You will always do your best work when you are in a peaceful and relaxed state. You can either choose to remain calm and at choice to make the best of all situations, or you can choose to lose your shit and make everything worse by becoming run by irrational emotions." ~ Coach Corey Wayne

As I sit here reading this particular quote, it really brings home something I've been dealing with. I've got a bunch of big projects that I've been working on with my web developers, and they're just not getting things done in a timely manner. Like, before I started recording this morning, what happened was, literally right before my sound engineer showed up, I was having a problem with the website. And there is a main link for my coaching scheduling that when you click it, it takes you right back to the last page that you were on. And it's incredibly frustrating, because we did some major updates to the site over the weekend, and then something didn't work like it was supposed to, so my web developers removed this plug-in, but they didn't bother going back and double check everything to make sure all the links worked. And so, as soon as I go on to check something on my website and click some of these new links, I find out that one of them, the coaching one, is not working at all, and people can't even get to the page where they can purchase coaching.

So, obviously, I was pretty irritated and frustrated because my engineer is literally here waiting to start a recording session, and I want to reach through the computer and Skype and choke my web developer for not double checking the website when they've made changes. And so, I've got errors on my live site, and he has no clue to do this. And the guy does beautiful work, but he frustrates the fuck out of me. And being the impatient person that I am, naturally, I want to just go, "You're fucking fired, dude. You're outta here. Fuck off!" But when I think about the reality that it would take me several weeks to find somebody else, and then probably another few weeks to get them familiar with the website, it's just much easier to bite my lip, and be patient, and give them the short period of time that it takes the fix this particular issue.

So, if I was impatient, I could do something that would really cause a lot of problems in my business for several weeks, or I can deal with the fact that I'm raging on the inside, and I want this guy to fix my website now and give them the time that's required to do it.

These are the kinds of things that you get faced with, and you get stressed. It's just like Wayne Dyer says, "When you squeeze an orange, what comes out? Orange juice. Why? Because it's an orange." Well, when life squeezes you like I got squeezed this morning, what comes out? Obviously, I was pretty frustrated and pissed off about something that I shouldn't even have to be dealing with, but other than that, that's just what happens. My life is mostly pretty easy-going, but sometimes I have unexpected things happen, just like what happened this morning. And you've just got to find a way to put your head down, be patient, bite your lip, and don't do anything rash that you might regret later because you're impatient and you want everything to happen now.

LINK: https://understandingrelationships.com/the-right-headspace/30289

Time, Space & Love

"In music, it is the spaces in-between the notes that creates the sounds of music. Otherwise, music would just be constant noise. In friendship, love, and relationships, you must give others the time and space to miss you and realize what you mean to them. This gives them the space to still be themselves and enjoy their freedom to be and express who they are, but also appreciate the gift and blessing you are to them in their lives. If you act neurotic and come unglued when you are away from them or don't hear from them in the time you expect, you will create noise in the music of your relationship, and they will simply change the channel on you and find someone else who they make better music with. That's something to think about." ~ Coach Corey Wayne

When you're balanced, you're happy, you love yourself, you love your life, you have a great social life, and you love what you do for a living, you're going to tend to be in more of a peaceful and relaxed state, feeling contentment for your life. There will be times where you'll experience pressure, because you're always going to be faced with challenges and obstacles, but if where you live emotionally contributes to your life to create a greater sense of peace, of ease and delight, emotionally, most of your time is going to be spent in a peaceful and relaxed state—even though you may experience a lot of friction, hardship, and difficulty when you're doing things that aren't pleasant or you're stretching outside of your comfort zone.

That's something really important understand, is to set your life up in a way that you only have to deal with difficulty, and challenges, and chaos, and drama, or hardship, or failure when you're doing things to stretch outside your comfort zone. But you've got to give yourself plenty of time to rest. That means getting a good night's rest. That means having leisure time where you can do the things you want and spend it with people who contribute to peace, and ease, and delight.

LINK: https://understandingrelationships.com/time-space-love/14505

Gaining Clarity & Closure

"Network Chiropractic Care, which is also known as NSA, (Network Spinal Analysis), is the most life changing and life enhancing healing modality I have ever experienced. What is so amazing about it is, by making light contacts on your spine and neck, a Network Chiropractic Doctor facilitates your brain, re-connecting to all of your body's organs, systems and structure to release all muscle tension, vertebrae misalignment and nerve pressure. This basically puts your body into a peaceful and relaxed state that supports optimum health, flexibility, proper frame and structure alignment, and organ and brain function. When human beings are in a peaceful and relaxed state, we naturally and instinctively make healthier food choices, exercise habits, relationship choices, career, business, financial and life choices." ~ Coach Corey Wayne

I've been a huge advocate for Network Spinal Analysis/NSA/Network Chiropractic Care for about the past 16, 17 years now, because it's completely changed my physiology and the way I feel in my body. I used to have kind of a big hunchback in the middle of my back, which lines up where your emotional center is, because your willpower center is where your navel is, where your rib cage comes together in that little 'V' at the bottom, that's your emotional center. And the breastbone area that's a few inches above your nipples in the center of your chest, that's the area that is associated with your heart. And wherever you're disconnected from, wherever you have subluxations in your spine, is typically what you're going to struggle with.

So, if somebody has lower back issues around the navel area, they typically will have a problem maintaining and doing things that they know they need to do; in other words, they'll be disconnected from their willpower. If somebody has, like in the area where the rib cage comes together, in that 'V' area, if they're disconnected there, like I was, they get a lot of armoring and that causes them to have difficulty emotionally in relationships experiencing and feeling emotions. And then, if you're disconnected in the area that's associated with heart, typically what you'll see is people that have heart problems will have subluxations in that area, and it will impact in a negative way their ability to be loving, open, and free in their relationships with other people.

It's great for aligning your structure, because, think about from this perspective: if you're all hunched over and your pelvis is out of alignment, as you go through life, just walking and moving your different body parts, what happens is all your joints are misaligned. And what happens is, over time, that can wear out the cartilage in your joints, and then, eventually, you get bone-on-bone, and then you run into problems when you're older having to get hips replaced, shoulders fixed, knees fixed. And often, that's why you see a lot of athletes that continually reinjure the same part of their body—whether it's their legs, their lower body, their knee, their shoulders—and they seem to keep getting the same injury over and over and over again until they've had so many, they can no longer play.

LINK: https://understandingrelationships.com/gaining-clarity-closure/20800

How To Make Corey's Green Juice

"The human body is alkaline by design and acidic by function. Your body needs alkaline minerals, enzymes, and vitamins to neutralize the metabolic acids produced by the cells of your body. The ideal diet to be free from dis-ease and illness symptoms is 80% alkaline and 20% acid. The average human diet consists of 95% acid forming foods and only 5% alkaline forming foods. By giving your body the proper nutrients it needs, you enable your body to build healthy blood. Red blood cells are the building blocks of every kind of tissue and bone in your body." ~ Coach Corey Wayne

This is an article and video that's on my website—it's actually two different articles, the second one being, "Rediscovered: The Fountain Of Youth"—and in the video and the article with the recipe, I go through a green juice recipe that I've been basically drinking and perfecting for almost two decades now. I went from having hay fever, sinus problems, clogged up nostrils, getting the flu several times a year, getting a colds several times a year, having headaches, having skin problems, having constipation problems—I basically had all kinds of health problems—and once I learned how your body actually works and functions, I was able to modify my diet to incorporate this green juice.

I usually drink two to three glasses a day of this green juice, in addition to the alkaline smoothies, which I've talked about in the article and video, "How To Make Corey's Green Alkaline Smoothies." So, my diet, what it typically consists of now, is I almost never eat any kind of sugar or junk food—maybe once a month—because I've had skin cancer twice now, in my life. I only eat, garbage or junk—pizza, pasta—I eat that kind of stuff maybe once a month on a cheat day. But my normal day-to-day food intake is chicken, fish, turkey, and every once in a while, if I'm at a good steakhouse that has a really good, nice, tender filet, I might, occasionally, a few times a year have a nice filet mignon with some béarnaise sauce or some hollandaise sauce. But other than that, those are the proteins I eat.

As far as carbohydrates, I typically will eat some kind of rice or some kind of red potatoes, and very rarely do I eat pasta or anything like that. And then, obviously, I have the greens, the juices, the green smoothies. I get a healthy mixture of nuts, which I go into detail on these in my second book, *Mastering Yourself*, and which ones I eat on a daily basis. I usually eat one to two apples a day as well. And I feel amazing, I look amazing for my age, (I mean, that's what everybody keeps telling me). I feel healthy, I don't get colds, I don't get the flu, I don't get sick, and my energy levels are high, my mental clarity is high. And for me, personally, I have to eat this way, because if I eat junk and the typical American diet, it literally will kill me. I enjoy living, and I want to live as long as possible. And I want to be as healthy as I can possibly be.

LINK: https://understandingrelationships.com/how-to-make-coreys-green-juice/14439

Staying Centered, Peaceful & Certain

"No matter what is going on in your life, you should not lose your feeling of inner peace and optimism about your future. When we allow the circumstances of our lives to uncenter us or diminish us in any way, by assigning negative meanings to the circumstances of our lives, this will negatively impact our happiness, finances, business, relationships, friendships and our overall quality of life. The only thing we have control over in life is the meanings that we give to the events and circumstances of our lives. If we allow ourselves to become uncentered and fearful, many things we hold dear in our lives will unravel quickly and create even greater chaos and fear." ~ Coach Corey Wayne

It's great to be optimistic about your future, but you shouldn't be delusional about your present reality. In other words, you want to see things as they are—not worse than they are or better than they are, but as they are. When I was younger and I would take risks to, whether it was starting a new business, or moving to a new city, or an advertising campaign, part of being young and inexperienced was I was very impatient. And when I look back on what I wrote about in my second book, *Mastering Yourself*—about how I quit my job at Centex-Rooney, borrowed $50,000 on my credit cards, and believed that in a matter of months, I could fix up a couple houses, get them ready to market, get them on the market, find a buyer, get them sold and closed before I ran out of money—when I went through the process, even though looking back on it all these decades later, it worked out, if I had to do that all over again, I probably would've kept working some kind of job or some kind of part-time job, so I could keep cash flow coming in.

Because I left my job in October of 1996, when I was working for Centex-Rooney, and by late February, early March, I was working for a real estate investment company that I was actually getting all of my properties from, in order to have enough cash flow to pay my bills, earn commissions, and learn the other side of the business. And so, what I realized after about 90 days, that $50,000, it didn't really go that far when you're putting $15,000–$20,000 into fixing up each property. And so, by early January, I was starting to get really stressed financially, because I was looking at the bills I was going to have to pay in a matter of weeks. And even though I had a contract on my first house to close after only being on the market for a few weeks, it was still going to take a month for the buyer's loan to get approved and a closing to happen.

So, I was very stressed out and worried because of the financial stress that I was under at the time. But if I'd have had cash to put into these properties and enough cash flow to pay my bills, I would've felt a lot better about the path that I had taken. And even when I left and started my new life coaching business, I had enough capital to last me for several years, but even looking back on it now, I spent way too much money on different experiment—advertising experiments, marketing experiments, different permutations of my website—trying to figure out how I was going to get my business model to work. So, I became impatient, because I was so worried about the future, and so I tended to waste a lot of money. It's easy to look back on it now, because hindsight's always 20/20, but I spent a lot of money unnecessarily on things, and excessive amounts of money on things, where I could've spread that money out probably for another year or two, because I was still looking for the next thing I tried to be the thing that made everything finally work.

But, you know, looking back on it now, what it was, what ultimately make things work was a process—the process, in my case, of creating content for my website, videos for my YouTube channel, and teaching aids on my website to slowly build an audience. And it's a great metaphor for life; great things take time. Like, in my case, especially this day and age, where everything is all digital online, if you're going to sell some kind of product or service to an audience, you're going to have to create useful content that they can learn from, because this free content that they're able to read, watch, and engage with teaches them what they need to know, in order to become convinced to buy your product or service.

LINK: https://understandingrelationships.com/staying-centered-peaceful-certain/16760

Sometimes It's Not Meant To Be

"Instead of focusing on the amount of time your relationships last, as a barometer of how "successful" they are, you should focus on being the best quality partner you can be and having high quality experiences together. The purpose of life is to enjoy it and to create great memories. Most people try to hold on to relationships that need to end or should have ended a long time ago. They stay too long, simply because they fear the unknown and worry about finding someone of equal or better quality, or they worry the next person will be worse. The only way the next relationship partner will be worse is if you settle. If you have high standards, then you understand the universal truth that it is simply a matter of time before the next great love of your life comes along, provided you don't settle by giving up or becoming impatient." ~ Coach Corey Wayne

This is hard for a lot of people to grasp and to endure. Most of us don't like to be alone or to be single, and a lot of our identity is wrapped up and associated with our intimate relationships. And when that intimate relationship dissolves, then we're desperate to find somebody new to replace them, so we can get back to a place of certainty in our life. And the reality is, when I look at my own life—I see the same pattern in my own life that I see my clients and I've seen through friends and family over the years—is that the average person is only going to meet one, two, maybe three really great members of the opposite sex that they really jive and click with, to where the conversation is easy and effortless, you have similar goals, similar values. You're completing each other's sentences, you never run out of things to talk about, and it just feels like, from the moment you met, you've always known each other. So, you've got to be patient, and you've got to hold out.

But again, just remember, in the last ten years of your life, how many people have you met that became really great, close friends? It's something that hardly ever happens. And so, if we look at how often we meet somebody that becomes a really close friend in our lives, we shouldn't be surprised or disappointed in the fact that really great women don't come along very often. But if you're impatient and you're desperate, what's going to happen is you're going to end up settling. And then, at some point when you're in that relationship with somebody that you settled for, you'll meet somebody that knocks your socks off, and then you're unavailable. Or worse, you start dating that other person or talking to them, and then you end up cheating on the person that you're with, so you can have an experience. It's just a bad way to go. Have the guts to hold out for somebody really great. Just don't agree to be in a committed relationship with somebody that it doesn't feel right in your heart to do.

LINK: https://understandingrelationships.com/sometimes-its-not-meant-to-be/24179

Coaching Services

If you know of anyone that you think may be interested in this book or could benefit from what you have read here, please send them to my website, UnderstandingRelationships.com. If you have read this book and you really need some help integrating these concepts or need some help to turn things around in your life fast, I also do one-on-one phone and Skype coaching on a first come first serve basis as my schedule permits. You will find the information on phone and Skype coaching on my website at UnderstandingRelationships.com/Products. I am happy to help you and help any others to find the power in their lives that I have found in mine. I salute you for having the courage to take your power back and become the person you were meant to be.

Closing Credits

This has been Quotes, Ruminations & Contemplations, Volume II.

Written and narrated by Corey Wayne

© 2022 by Corey Wayne

THE END

Printed in Great Britain
by Amazon